**WALES**

Atlas Ffyrdd

CW00369136

CONTENTS cynnwys

Key to Map Pages............2-3
allwedd i dudalennau'r map
Road Maps........................4-67
mapiau ffyrdd

Index to Towns and Villages......68-81
mynegai i drefi a phentrefi
Index to Places of Interest.........82-96
mynegai i lefydd i ddiddordeb

REFERENCE *cyfeirnod*

MOTORWAY	**M4**
Under Construction	
Proposed	
MOTORWAY JUNCTIONS WITH NUMBERS	
Unlimited interchange **4** Limited interchange **5**	
MOTORWAY SERVICE AREA	**MAGOR** Ⓢ
with access from one carriageway only	Ⓢ
MAJOR ROAD SERVICE AREAS	**ROSS SPUR** Ⓢ **GRASBY** Ⓢ
with 24 hour Facilities	
PRIMARY ROUTE	**A55**
PRIMARY ROUTE DESTINATION	**NEATH**
DUAL CARRIAGEWAY (A & B Roads)	
CLASS A ROAD	**A48**
CLASS B ROAD	**B4246**
MAJOR ROAD UNDER CONSTRUCTION	
MAJOR ROAD PROPOSED	
GRADIENT 1:5(20%) & STEEPER	«
(Ascent in direction of arrow)	
TOLL	TOLL
MILEAGE BETWEEN MARKERS	8
RAILWAY AND STATION	
LEVEL CROSSING AND TUNNEL	
RIVER OR CANAL	
COUNTY OR UNITARY AUTHORITY BOUNDARY	
NATIONAL BOUNDARY	+ + +
BUILT UP AREA	
VILLAGE OR HAMLET	○
WOODED AREA	
SPOT HEIGHT IN FEET	• 813
HEIGHT ABOVE SEA LEVEL	
400' - 1,000' 122m - 305m	
1,000' - 1,400' 305m - 427m	
1,400' - 2,000' 427m - 610m	
2,000' + 610m +	
NATIONAL GRID REFERENCE (Kilometres)	100

TOURIST INFORMATION *gwybodaeth i dwristiaid*

AIRPORT	✈
AIRFIELD	
HELIPORT	
BATTLE SITE AND DATE	✕ 1066
CASTLE (Open to Public)	
CASTLE WITH GARDEN (Open to Public)	
CATHEDRAL, ABBEY, CHURCH, FRIARY, PRIORY	✝
COUNTRY PARK	
FERRY (Vehicular)	
(Foot only)	
GARDEN (Open to Public)	
GOLF COURSE 9 HOLE 18 HOLE	
HISTORIC BUILDING (Open to Public)	
HISTORIC BUILDING WITH GARDEN (Open to Public)	
HORSE RACECOURSE	
INFORMATION CENTRE	🅸
LIGHTHOUSE	
MOTOR RACING CIRCUIT	
MUSEUM, ART GALLERY	
NATIONAL PARK OR FOREST PARK	
NATIONAL TRUST PROPERTY (Open)	*NT*
(Restricted Opening)	*NT*
(National Trust of Scotland)	*NTS* *NTS*
NATURE RESERVE OR BIRD SANCTUARY	
NATURE TRAIL OR FOREST WALK	
PLACE OF INTEREST	*Monument* •
PICNIC SITE	
RAILWAY, STEAM OR NARROW GAUGE	
THEME PARK	
VIEWPOINT	
WILDLIFE PARK	
WINDMILL	
ZOO OR SAFARI PARK	

SCALE graddfa

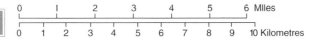

0 1 2 3 4 5 6 Miles

0 1 2 3 4 5 6 7 8 9 10 Kilometres

1:158,400
2.5 Miles to 1 Inch
2.5 milltir i l fodfedd

Geographers' A-Z Map Company Ltd

Head Office *(prif swyddfa)*: Fairfield Road,
Borough Green, Sevenoaks, Kent TN15 8PP
Telephone *(ffon)*: 01732 781000

Showrooms *(ystafelloedd arddangos)*:
44 Gray's Inn Road, London, WC1X 8HX
Telephone *(ffon)*: 020 7440 9500

Edition *(rhifyn)* 4 2001

INDEX TO SELECTED PLACES OF INTEREST
Mynegai i Lefydd Dethol o Ddiddordeb

Abbey / Friary / Priory
Abaty / Mynachlog / Priordy 82

Aquarium
Acwariwm 82

Arboretum
Arboretum 82

Aviary / Bird Garden
Adarfa / Gardd Adar 83

Botanical Garden
Gardd fotanegol 83

Butterfly Farm
Fferm Gloynod Byw 83

Castle & Garden
Castell a Gardd 83

Castle
Castell 83

Cathedral
Eglwys Gadeiriol 84

Cave / Mine
Ogof / Safle Mwyngloddio 84

Country Park
Parc Gwledig 84

Farm Park / Working Farm
Parc Fferm / Fferm Weithio 85

Forest Park
Parc Coedwig 85

Forest Enterprise Information Centre
Canolfan gwybodaeth Menter
Coedwigaeth 85

Fortress
Caer 85

Garden
Gardd 85

Hill Fort
Caer ar Fryn 86

Historic Building & Garden
Adeilad hanesyddol gyda gardd 86

Historic Building
Adeilad hanesyddol 86

Horse Racecourse
Maes rasio ceffylau 87

Industrial Monument
Heneb Ddiwydiannol 87

Motor Racing Circuit
Trac rasio ceir 87

Museum & Art Gallery
Amgueddfa a Oriel Gelf 87

National Park
Parc Cenedlaethol 90

National Park Information Centre
Canolfan Wybodaeth y Parc
Cenedlaethol 90

Natural Attraction
Atyniad Naturiol 90

Nature Reserve / Bird Sanctuary
Gwarchodfa natur / Warchodfa Adar 91

Place of Interest
man diddorol 91

Prehistoric Monument
Heneb Cyn-hanes 93

Railway
rheilffordd 94

Roman Remains
Olion Rhufeinig 94

Theme Park
Parc Thema 94

Tourist Information Centre
Canolfan Groeso 94

Vineyard
Gwinllan 96

Wildlife Park
Parc Bywyd Gwyllt 96

Windmill
Melin wynt 96

Zoo / Safari Park
Sw / Parc Saffari 96

KEY TO MAP PAGES
allwedd i dudalennau'r map

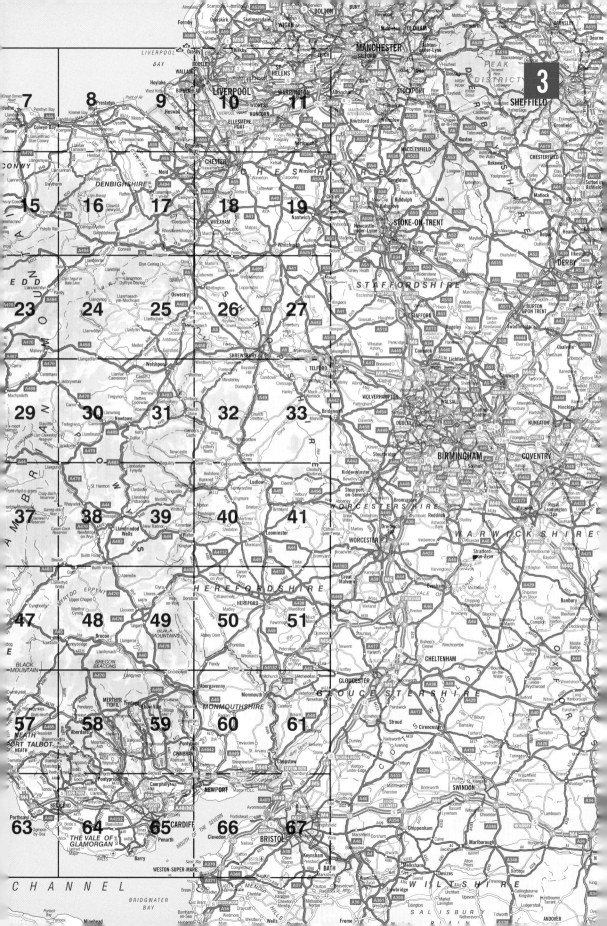

A   **B**

I R I S H

S E A

The Skerries
(Ynysoedd y Moelrhoniaid)

Carmel Head
(Trwyn y Gader)

Church Ba
(Porth Swta

1

Holyhead to:
Dublin 3hrs. 15mins.
Dublin 1hr. 50mins.
(Fast Ferry)
Dun Laoghaire 1hr. 40mins.
(Fast Ferry)

HOLYHEAD   Lf

BAY

2

Breakwater

Porth-y-felin

Salt Island

Gogarth
Bay

Caer y Twr
Hill Fort

Arch

HOLYHEAD

(Caergybi)

South Stack
Cliffs

Mountain

Hut
Group

Penrhos

Llaingoch

Stryd

Penrhos

Penrhos

Ellin's Tower

Penrhos Feilw
Standing
Stones

Kingsland

Hut
Circles

Ty-Mawr
Standing
Stone

Burial
Chamber

Trearddur

(YNYS

B4545

Four Mile
Bridge

Llyn Din

3

Rhoscolyn

St. Gwenfaen's
Well

GYBI)

Cymy

Bay

A   **12**   **B**

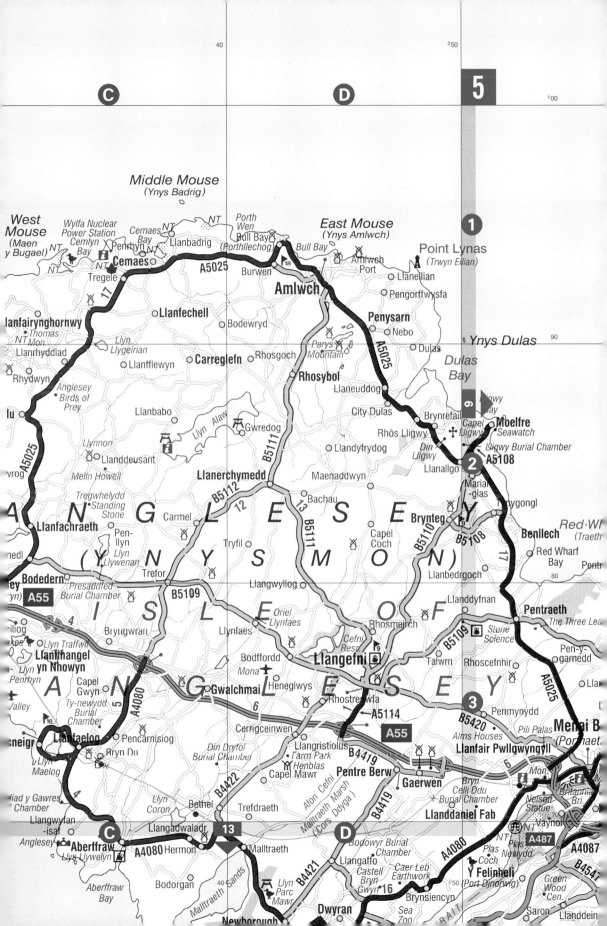

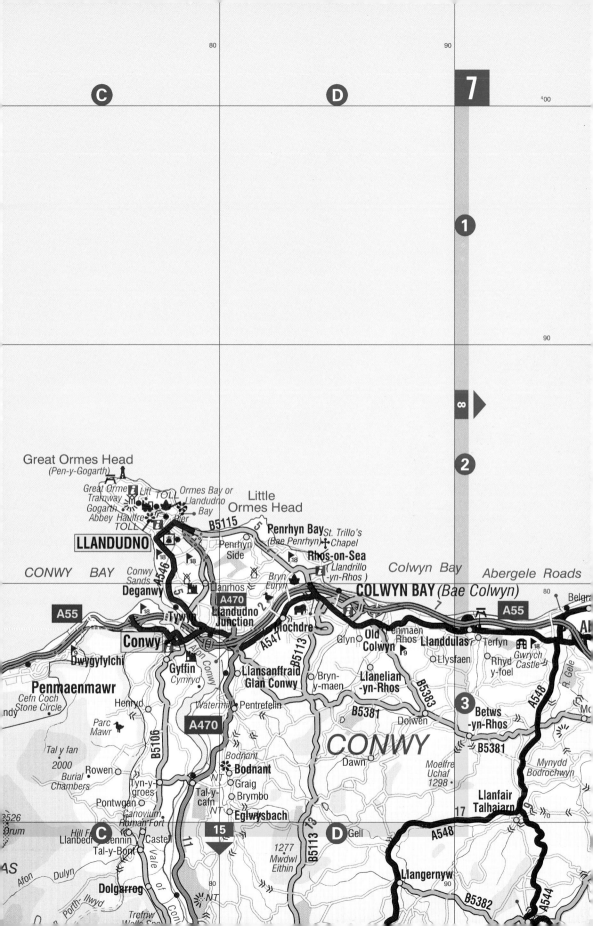

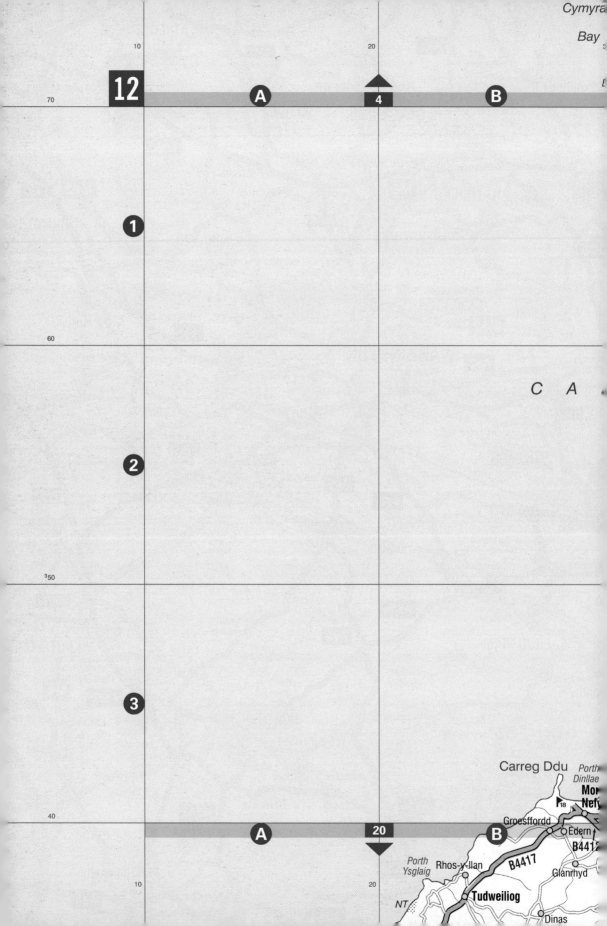

Cymyra

Bay

10

20

70

A

4

B

1

60

C A

2

3 50

2

3

Carreg Ddu *Porth*
Dinllae

Mor
Nef

18

40

Groesffordd

A

20

Edern

B

B441

*Porth
Ysglaig* Rhos-y-llan

B4417

Glanrhyd

NT

Tudweiliog

Dinas

10

20

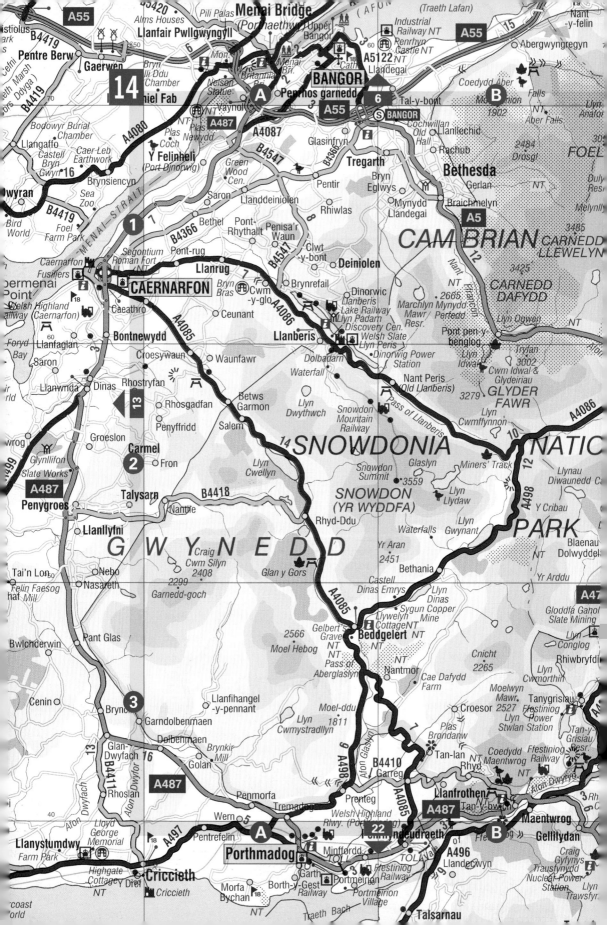

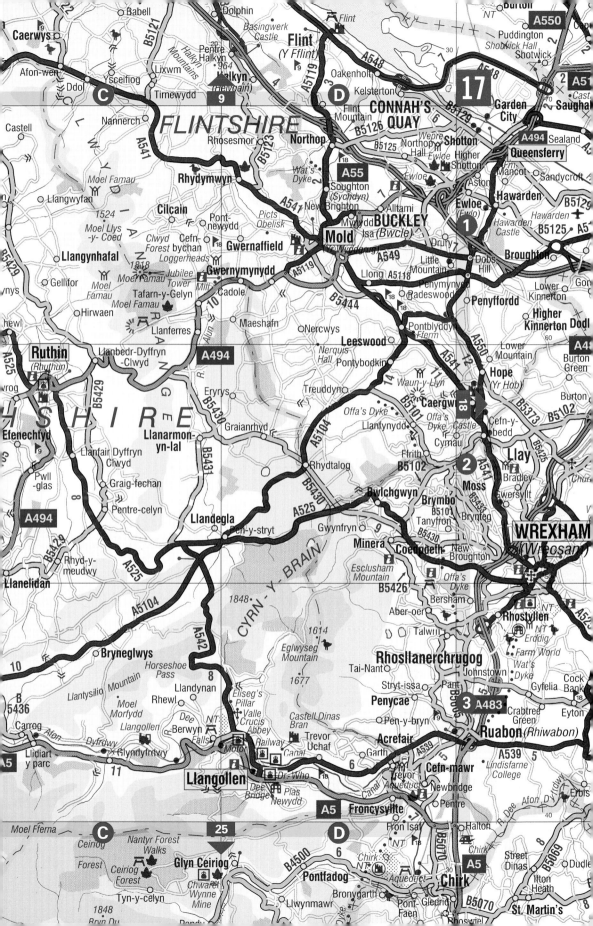

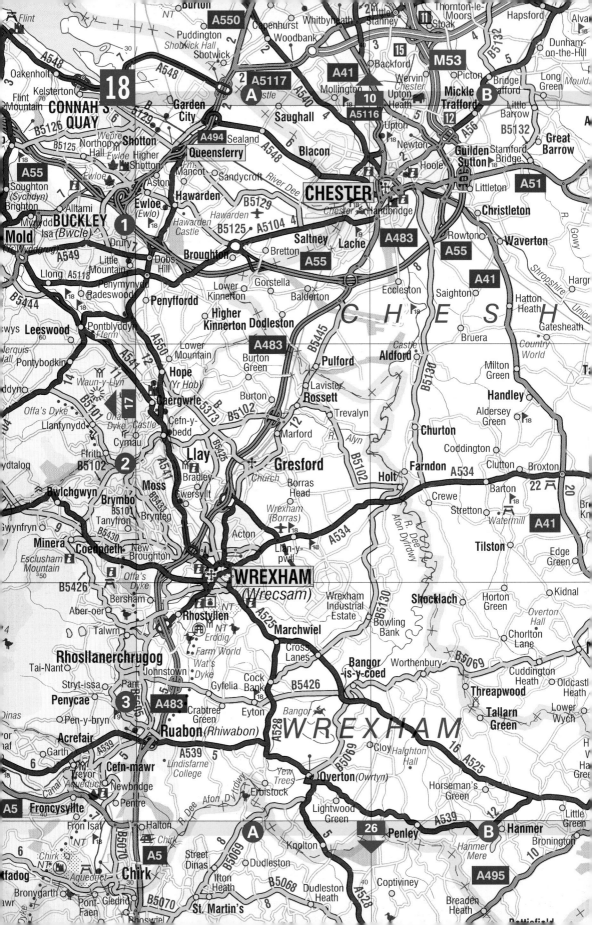

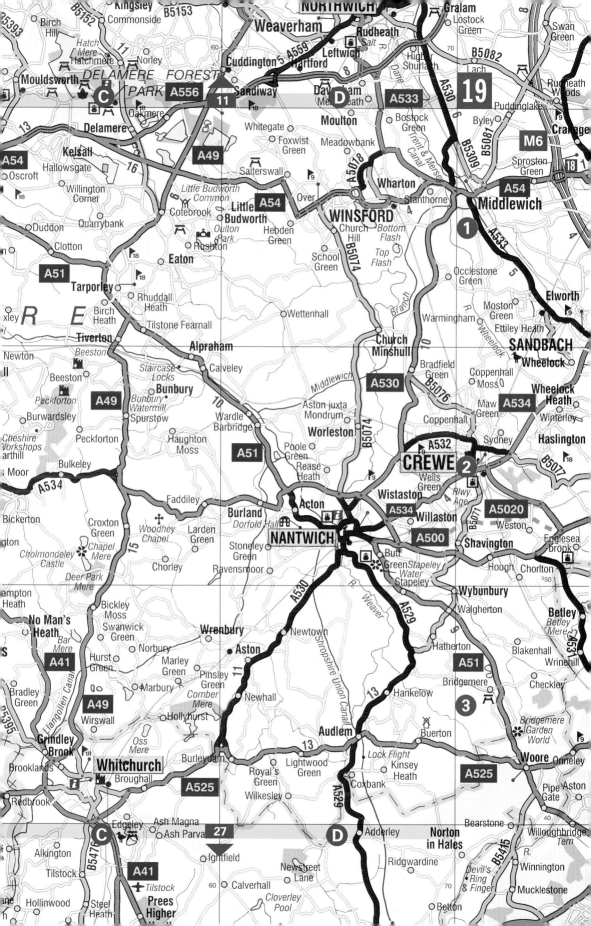

210   20

340

Carreg Ddu *Porth Dinllaen* Mor▸ Nefy

▸18

Groesffordd Edern B4412

Glanrhyd

Porth Ysglaig Rhos-y-llan

Tudweiliog

NT Dinas

Porth Colmon Rhos-ddu • *Fort* Garn-fadryn

Penllech Llaniestyn

Llangwnnadl Bryn-mawr

Pen-y-graig

Penrhyn Mawr Sarn Meyllteyrn

Bryncroes **Botwnnog**

Porth Oer Rhydllos 16

❶

30

NT Rhoshirwaun NT

NT Llawr Dref

Braich Anelog Penycaerau Rhiw

Anelog Plas-yn-Rhiw Llanengan

NT B4413 NT *Porth Neigwl or Hell's Mouth* Bwlc

Aberdaron Llanfaelrhys NT

Braich y Pwll NT NT NT

Uwchmynydd NT Trwy Cila

❷ *Aberdaron Bay* **Ynys Gwylan-fawr**

BARDSEY SOUND *(SWNT ENLLI)* Pen y Cil

St. Mary's Abbey

Bardsey Island (Ynys Enlli) C

20

(B

❸

10

210   20

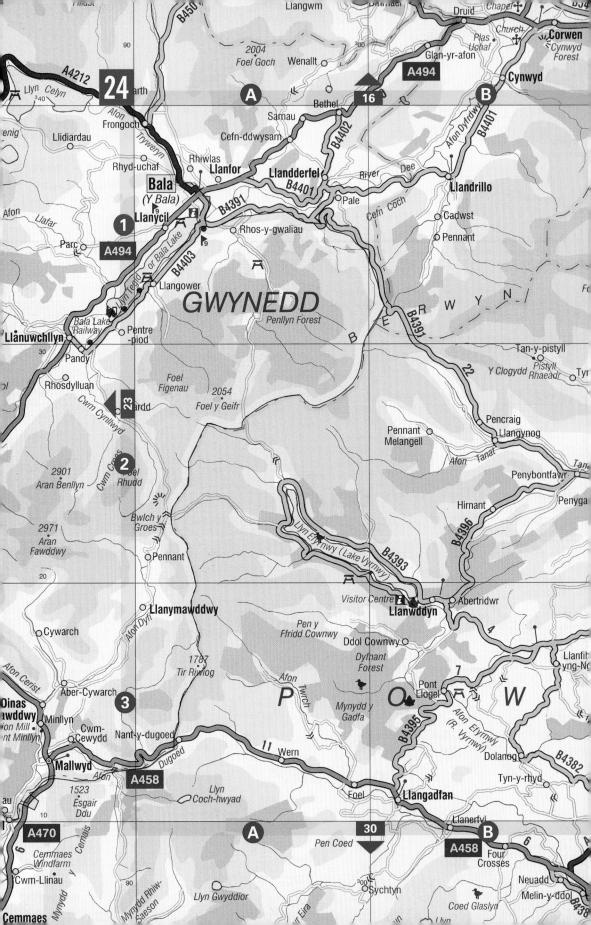

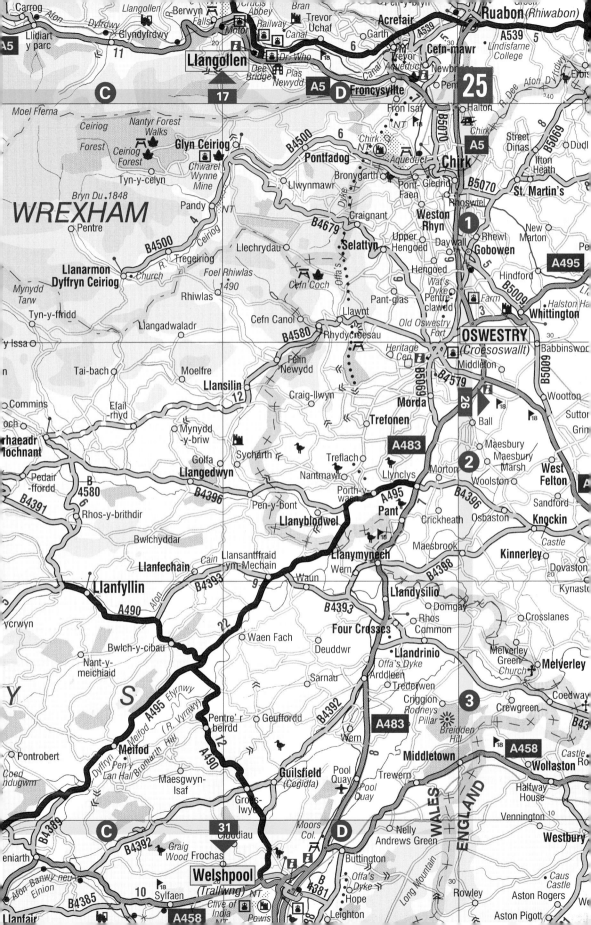

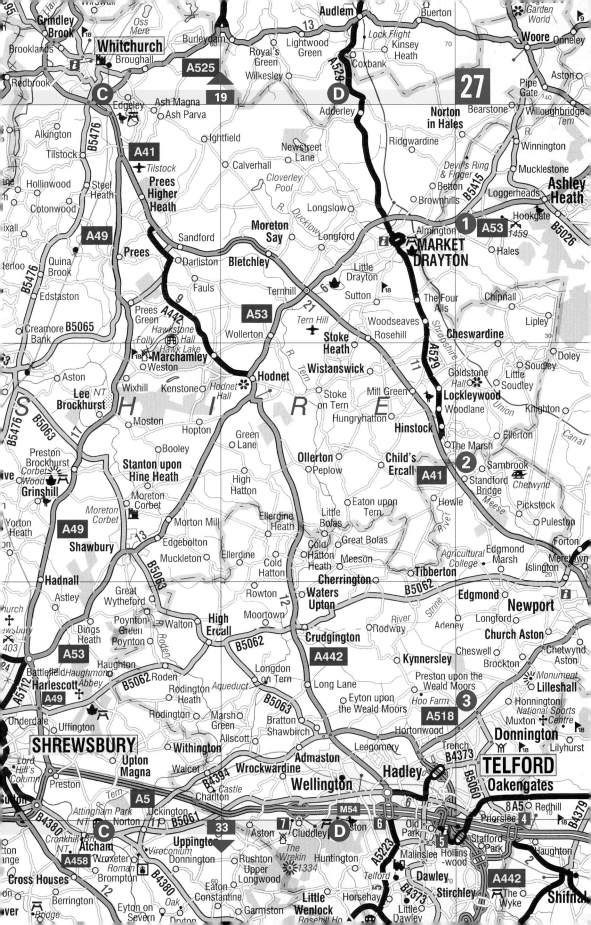

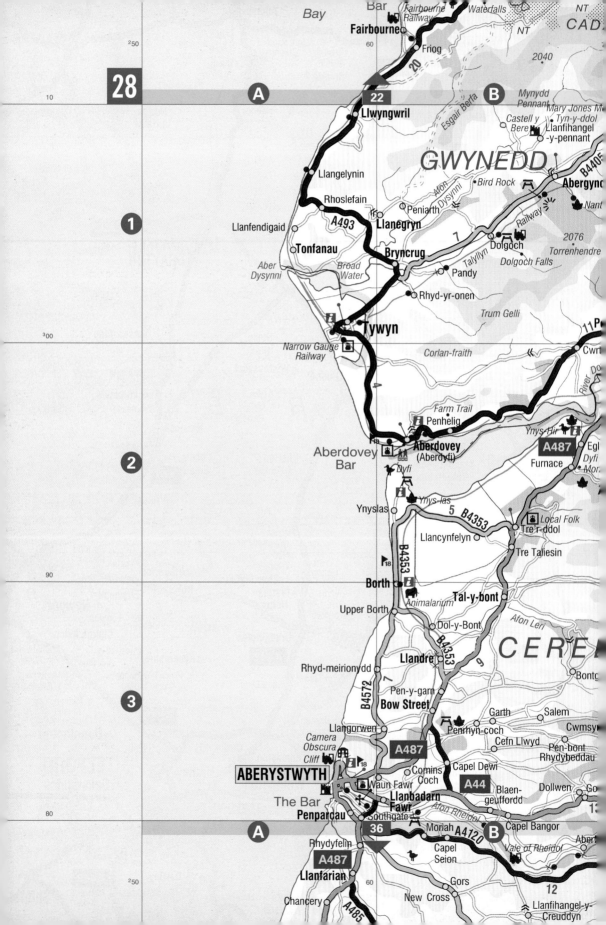

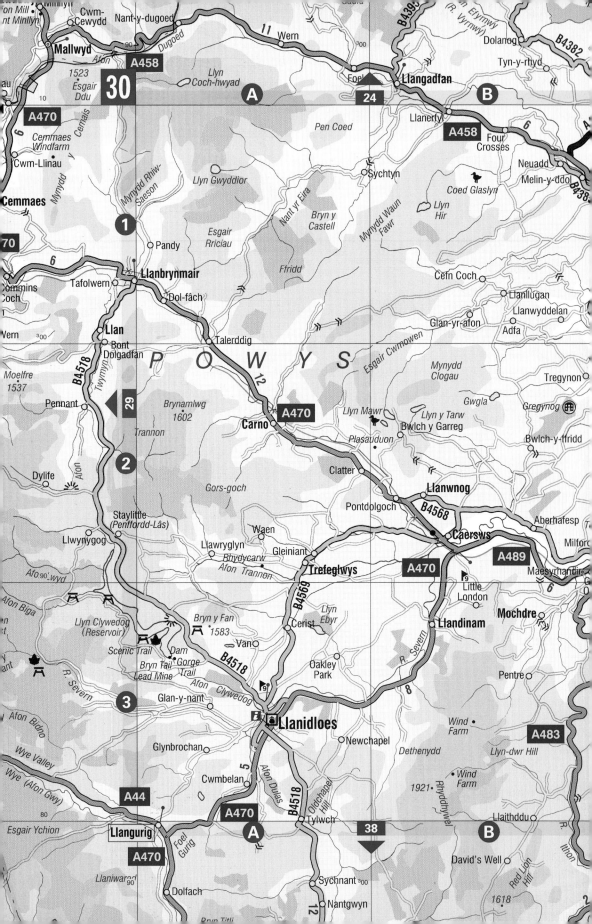

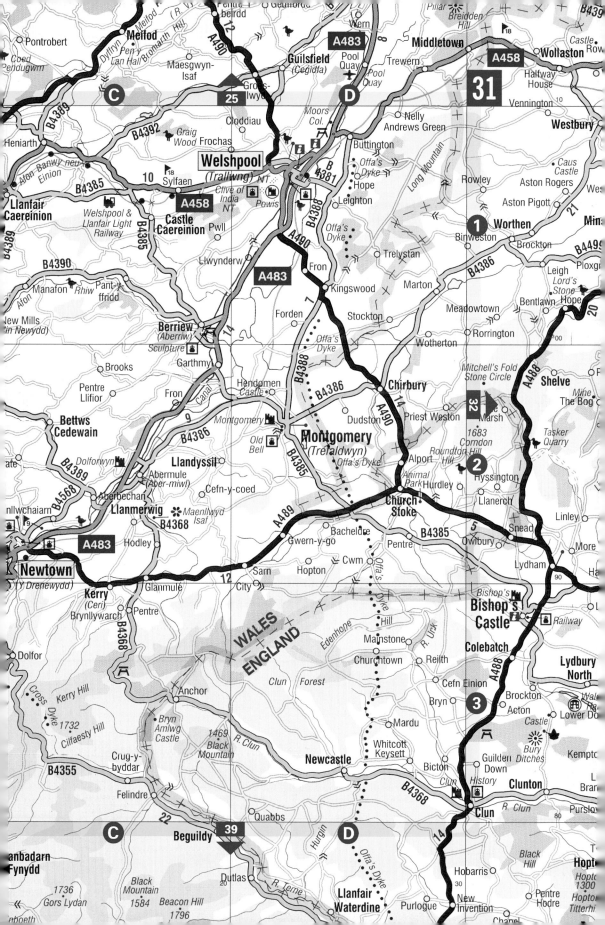

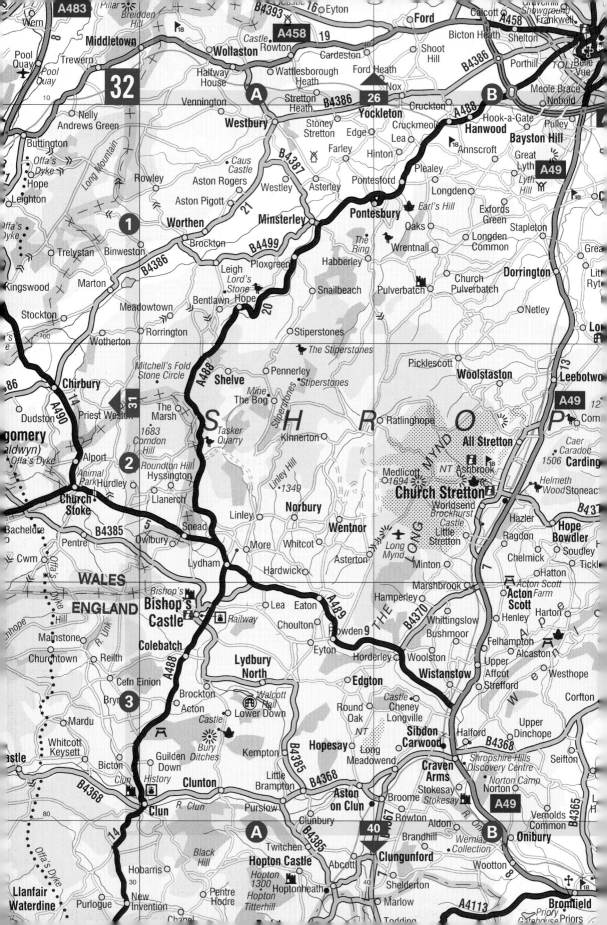

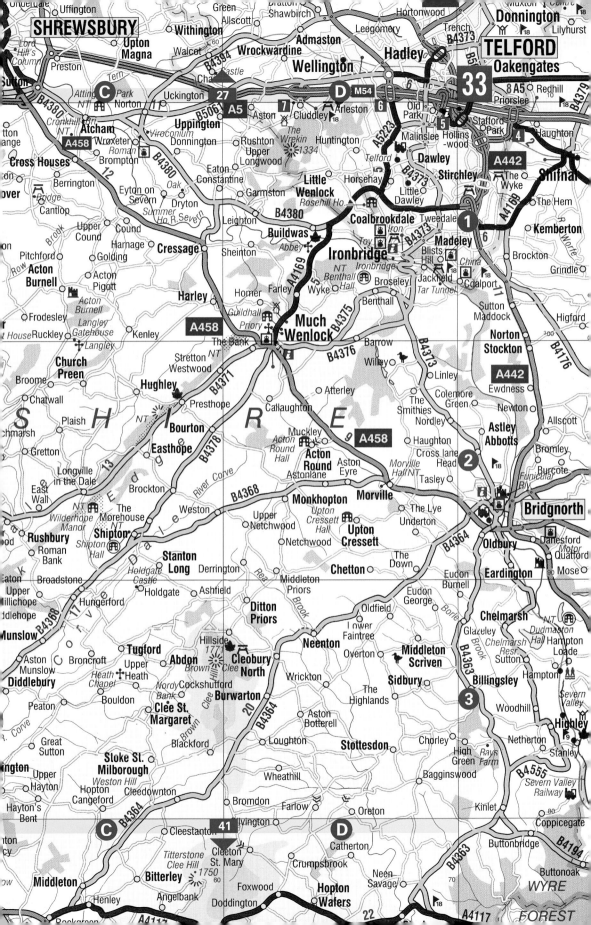

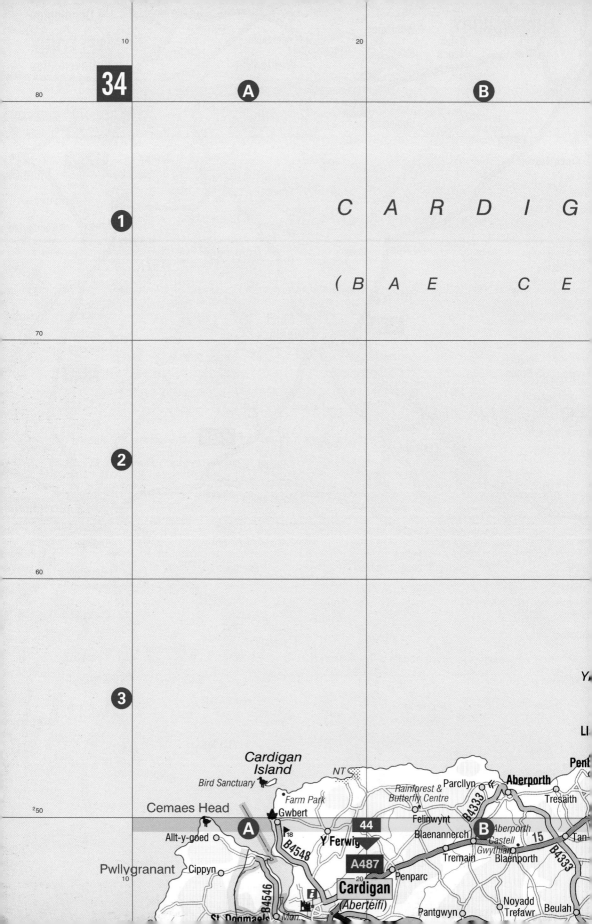

10 20

80

Ⓐ Ⓑ

1

C A R D I G

(B A E   E   C E

70

2

60

3

Cardigan
Island
Bird Sanctuary 🐦
NT
Rainforest & Parcllyn **Aberporth**
Butterfly Centre
Cemaes Head • *Farm Park* Felinwynt Tresaith
50 Gwbert
Ⓐ **44** Blaenannerch Ⓑ *Aberporth*
Allt-y-goed ○ ⊨18 *Castell* **15**
B4548 Y Ferwig *Gwythian* Blaenporth Tan-
Pwllygranant Cippyn ○ **A487** Tremain
10 Penparc
Cardigan Noyadd Beulah
(Aberteifi) Pantgwyn Trefawr

Y
Ll
Pent
B4333
B4333
B4546
Mon.

40 250

1

AN BAY

E D I G I O N)

Carreg Ti-pw 70

Llanrhystud 18

36 LLlansantffraed

Llan-non
A487

7

B4337

2

Rhos
Haminiog

Neb

B4577 Aberarth **Pennant**

Cross
Inn

*Sea
Aquarium*

Aberaeron

*Honey
Bee*

Monachty

11

60 Cilcennin

Vineyard
Aberaeron

Ffos-y-ffin

A482

Llanaeron

Llanerchaeron
NT

New Quay
(Ceinewydd)

Llwyncelyn

Newbridge

Ciliau
Aeron

Afon Aeron

Gilfachreda

A486

8

B4342

Llanarth

*Oakford
(Derwen Gam)*

B4339

8

Trefilan

Llu
fa

*Bird &
Wildlife
Hospital*

Maen-y-
groes

Cwmtudu NT

Cross Inn

Nanternis

Caerwedros

4

*Honey
Farm*

Pen-cae

B4342

Geneva

Dihewyd

Ystrad
Aeron

Talsarn

Lochtyn
NT

Llwyndafydd

Blaen Celyn

Mydroilyn

B4342

Felinfach

3

B4337

Pontgarreg

B4327

A487

Synod Inn or
Post-mawr

CEREDIGION

Temple Bar

Ffynnon-
oer

nog

B4334

Plwmp

A486

*Noah's Ark
Farm Park*

Pentregat

Brynhoffnant

B4338

Cribyn

250

au

*Countryside
Collection*

B4334

C

45

Bwlch-y-fadfa

Talgarreg

B4459

D

Gorsgoch

B4337

8

Maestir

Capel
Cynon

Ffostrasol

40

*Castell
Howell*

Aber

Cwrtnewydd

Lan
(Llanbe
Stef

ynarthen

Brithdir
Hawen

Rhydlewis

Llanwnnen

A475

Felin
Wnda

Penrhiw-pal

11

Pont-sian

12

Cwmsychpant

B4338

250

Pentre-b
Felin yr Abe

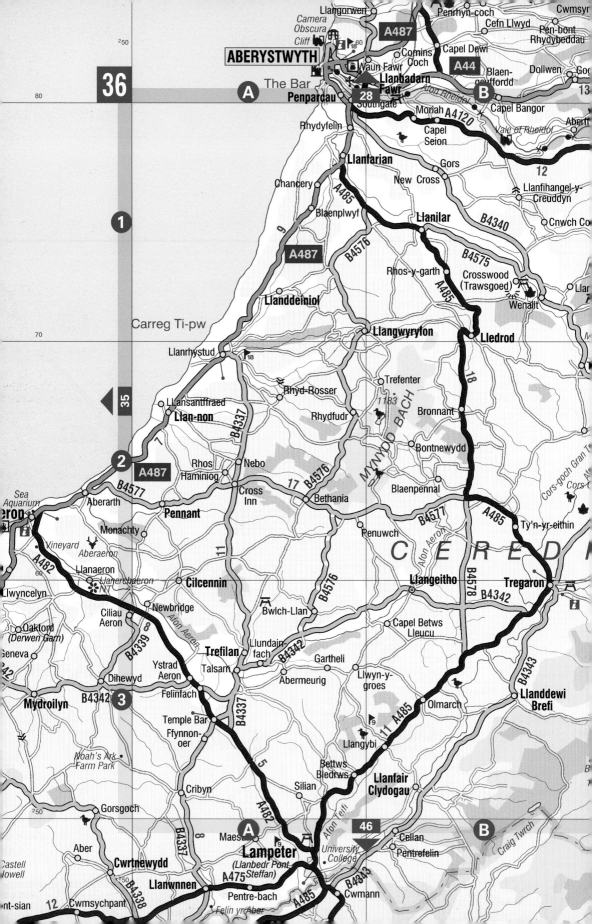

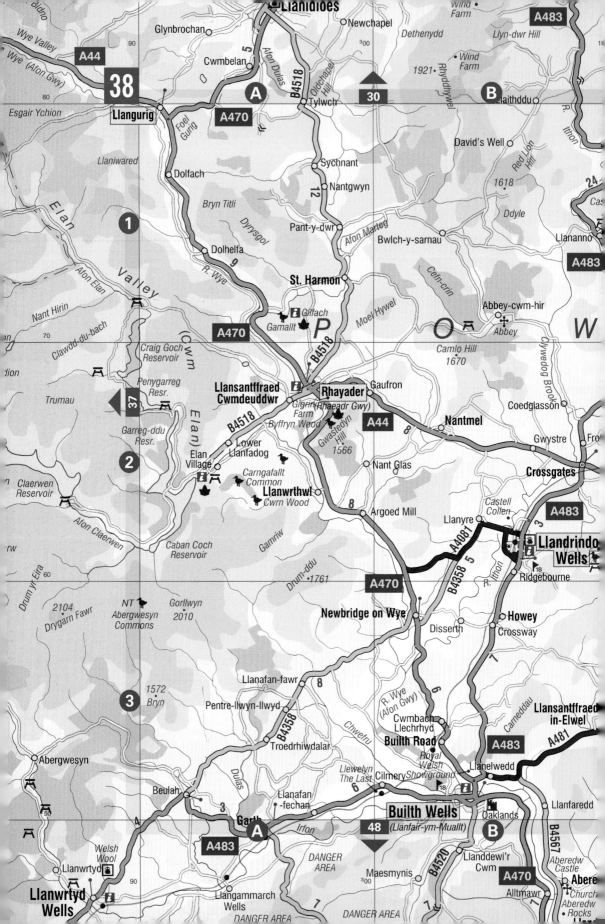

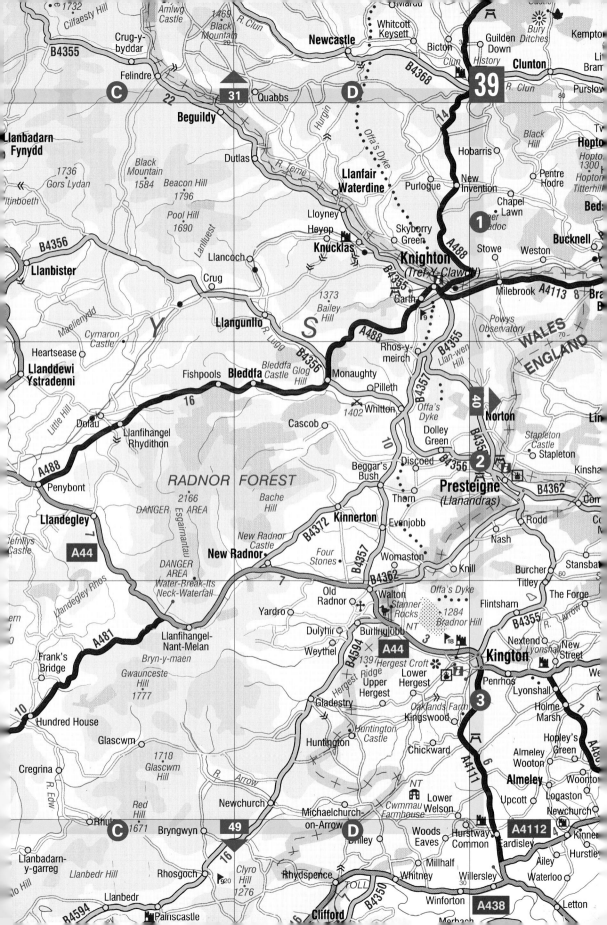

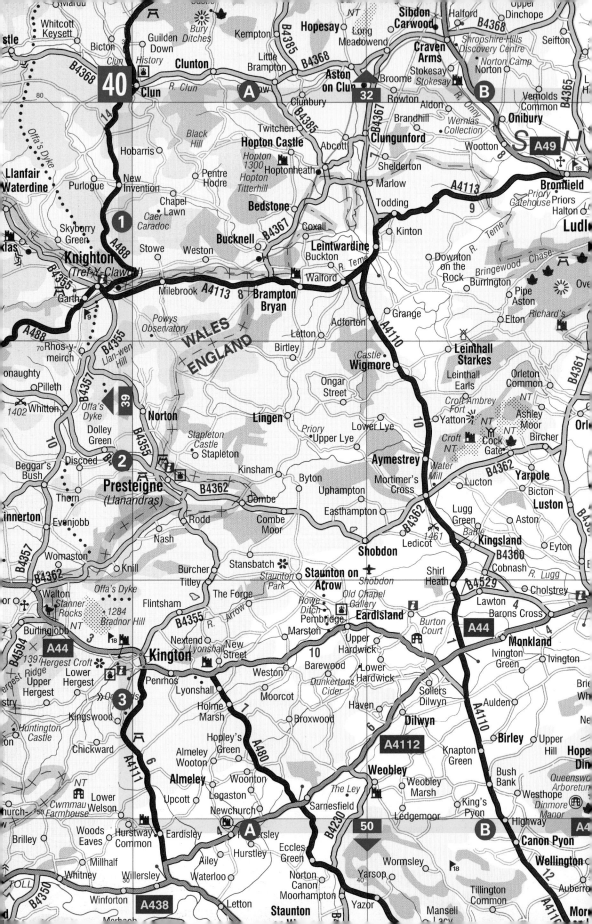

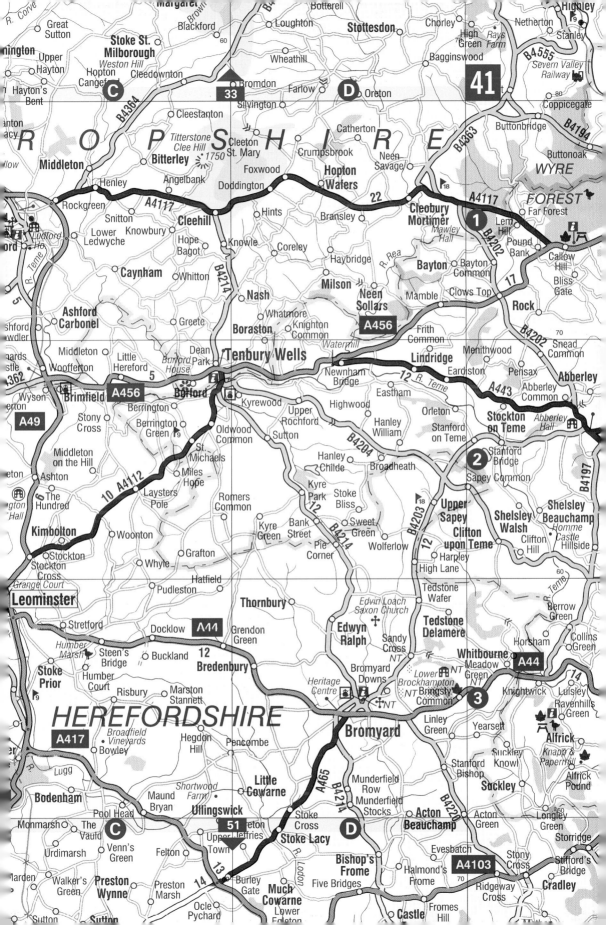

70

80

9

²50

Ⓐ

Ⓑ

❶

40

❷

STRUMBLE HEAD

Pen Brush

Trefasser

Penbwchdy

Abercastle

Penclegyr

Porthgain

Trefin

Mathry 10

*Blue
Lagoon*

Carreg-gwylan-
fach

Abereiddy

Llanrian

Castlem

B4330

Croes-Goch

30

Penclegyr

Penllechwen

NT

Tretio

Treffynnon

PE

ST.
DAVID'S
HEAD

NT

Treleddyd-
fawr

Rhodiad
-Y-Brenin

Carnhedryn

6

R. Solva

*Whitesand Bay
or Porth-mawr*

B4583

9

Farm

A487

Caerfarchell

Llandeloy

R. Alun

Farm

*St.
David's*

Woollen Mill

Hayscastle

Rhosson

St. David's
(Tyddewi)

Whitchurch

Brawdy

❸

*Ramsey
Island*

Cathedral &
Bishop's
Palace

NT

Solva

A487

Gignog

Chapel

NT

Penycwm

Ynys Bery

Green Scar

Newgale

Wood 16

Roch

Castle

Ramsey Sound

Simps
Cros

20

Ⓐ

52

Ⓑ

Rickets
Head

Simpson

Nolton

S T.   B R I D E S

Nolton
Haven

Moto

70

80

La

B A Y

Druidston

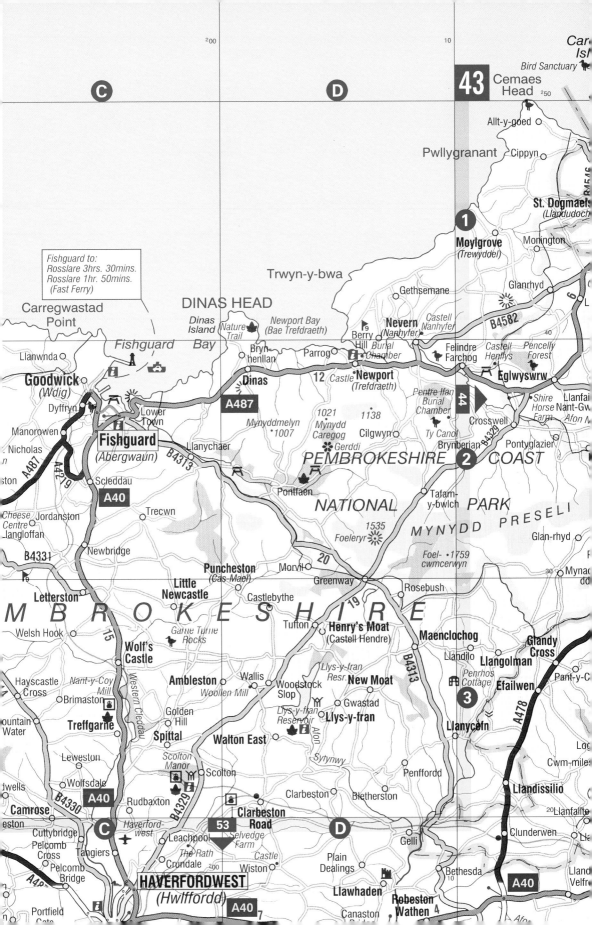

Car Isl

Bird Sanctuary

Allt-y-goed   Cippyn

Pwllygranant

St. Dogmaels
(Llandudoch)

1 Moylgrove
(Trewyddel)

Monington

B4582   6   L

Trwyn-y-bwa

Glanrhyd

Gethsemane

Fishguard to:
Rosslare 3hrs. 30mins.
Rosslare 1hr. 50mins.
(Fast Ferry)

Carregwastad
Point

DINAS HEAD

Dinas
Island   Nature
Trail   Newport Bay
(Bae Trefdraeth)

Berry
Hill   9   Nevern
(Nanhyfer)   Castell
Nanhyfer

Felindre
Farchog   Castell
Henllys   Pencelly
Forest

Eglwyswrw   Llanfai
Nant-Gw

Llanwnda

Fishguard   Bay

Brynhenllan

Parrog   Burial
Chamber

12 Castle   Newport
(Trefdraeth)   Pentre Ifan
Burial
Chamber   44   Shire
Horse
Farm   Afon

Goodwick
(Wdig)

Dyffryn   Lower
Town   Dinas   A487

Crosswell   B4329   Pontyglazier

. Nicholas   Manorowen   Fishguard
(Abergwaun)   Llanychaer   B4313   1021
Mynyddmelyn
•1007   1138
Mynydd
Caregog   Cilgwyn   Ty Canol   Brynberian   2   COAST

n

Scleddau   A40   Trecwn   Gerddi   PEMBROKESHIRE   NATIONAL   Tafarn-
y-bwlch   PARK   Glan-rhyd

Cheese
Centre
Llangloffan   Jordanston   Pontfaen   1535
Foeleryr   MYNYDD PRESELI

Newbridge   20   Foel- •1759
cwmcerwyn   Mynad
dd

B4331

Puncheston
(Cas Mael)   Morvil   Greenway   Rosebush

Letterston   Little
Newcastle   Castlebythe   19   B4313

Welsh Hook   Game Turne
Rocks   Tufton   Henry's Moat
(Castell Hendre)   Maenclochog   Glandy
Cross

M B R O K E S H I R E

Hayscastle
Cross   Wolf's
Castle   Wallis   Llandilo   Llangolman   Pant-y-C

Ambleston   Woodstock
Slop   Llys-y-fran
Resr   New Moat   Penrhos
Cottage   Efailwen

Brimaston   Nant-y-Coy
Mill   Woollen Mill   Gwastad   3   A478

Treffgarne   Golden
Hill   Llys-y-fran
Reservoir   Llys-y-fran   Llanycefn

ountain
Water   Spittal   Walton East   Afon
Sytynwy   Penffordd   Llo

Leweston   Scolton
Manor   Scolton   Llandissilio

dwells   Wolfsdale   B4330   A40   Rudbaxton   Clarbeston   Bletherston   Llanfalte

Camrose   C   Haverfordwest   Haverfordwest   Clarbeston
Road   D   Gelli   Clunderwen   Lla

ston   Cuttybridge
Pelcomb
Cross   Leachpool   53   Selvedge
Farm   Bethesda   A40   Lland
Velfr

Tangiers   The Rath
Crundale   Wiston   Castle   Plain
Dealings   Llawhaden

Pelcomb
Bridge   200

Portfield
Gate   HAVERFORDWEST
(Hwlfford)   A40   7   Canaston   Robeston
Wathen   4   Afon

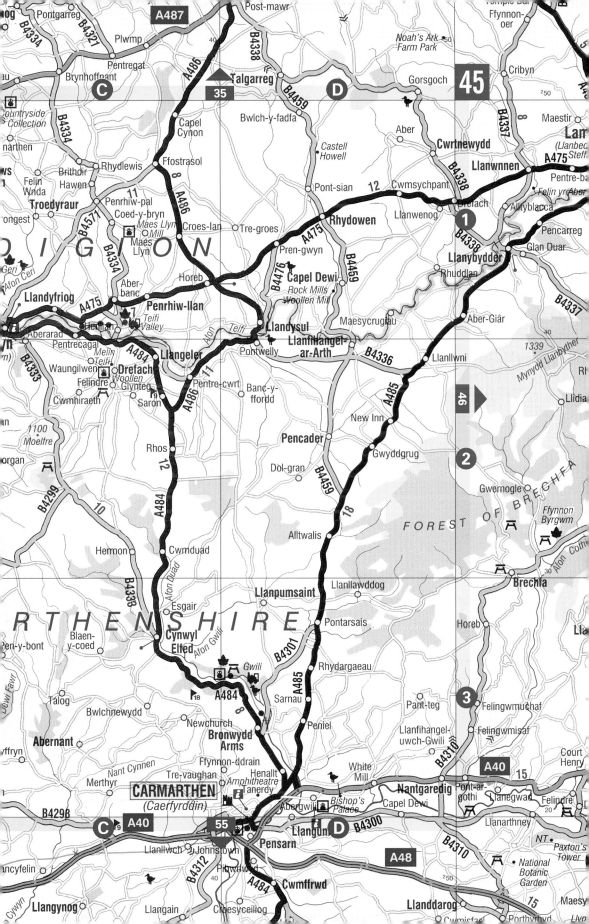

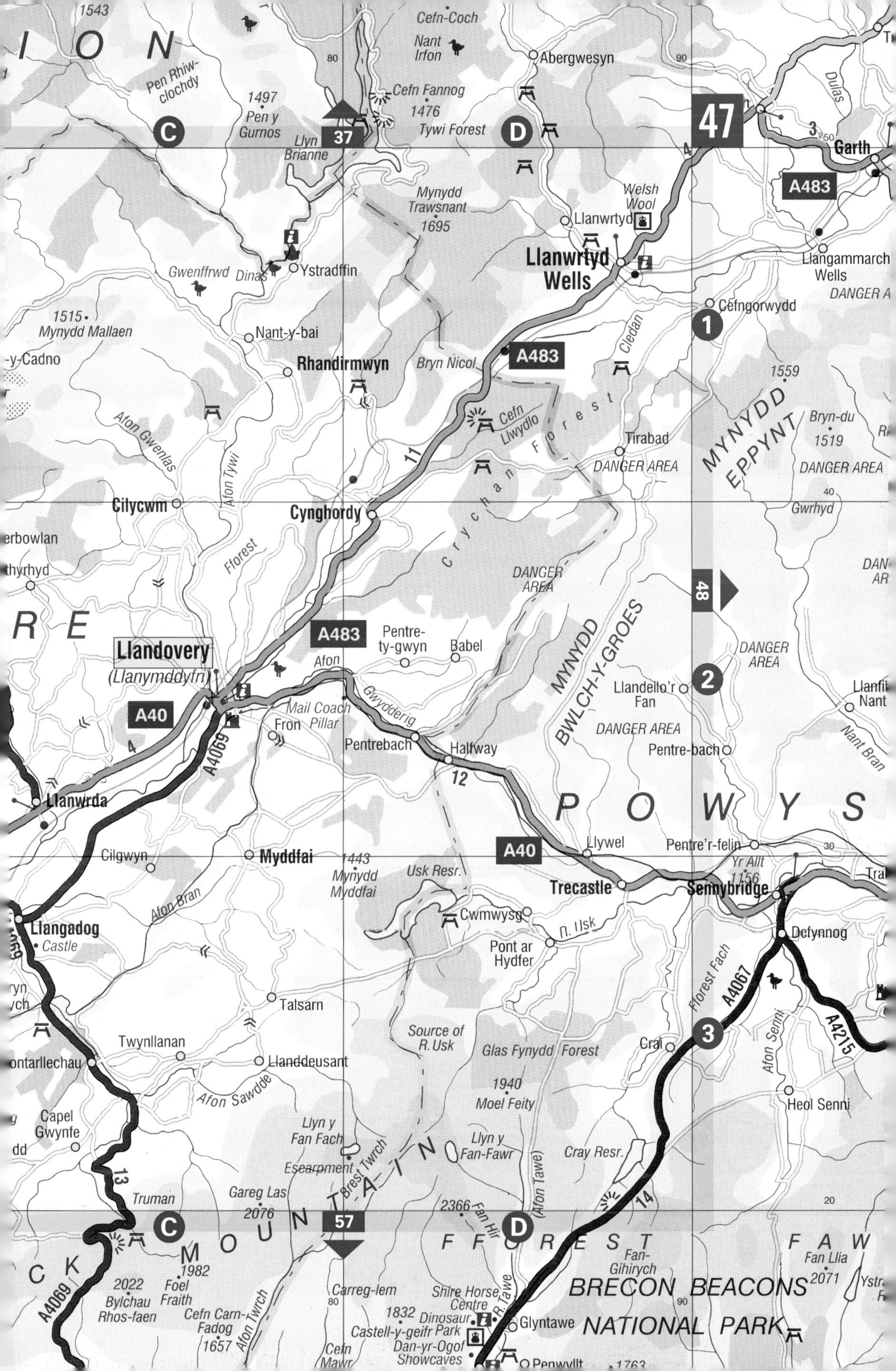
47
37
48
57
C
D
1
2
3
ION
RE
POWYS
MOUNTAIN
FFOREST FAW
BRECON BEACONS NATIONAL PARK
1543
Pen Rhiw-clochdy
1497
Pen y Gurnos
Llyn Brianne
Cefn-Coch
Nant Irfon
Cefn Fannog
1476
Tywi Forest
Abergwesyn
Dulas
Garth
A483
Mynydd Trawsnant
1695
Welsh Wool
Llanwrtyd
Llanwrtyd Wells
Llangammarch Wells
Gwenffrwd
Dinas
Ystradffin
1515
Mynydd Mallaen
Nant-y-bai
Rhandirmwyn
Bryn Nicol
Cefngorwydd
DANGER AREA
Cledan
1559
MYNYDD EPPYNT
Bryn-du
1519
Afon Gwenlas
Afon Tywi
Cefn Llwydlo
Crychan Forest
Tirabad
Cilycwm
Cynghordy
Gwrhyd
Fforest
MYNYDD BWLCH-Y-GROES
Llandovery
(Llanymddyfri)
A40
Pentre-ty-gwyn
Babel
Afon Gwydderig
Mail Coach Pillar
Fron
Pentrebach
Halfway
Llandeilo'r Fan
Pentre-bach
Nant Bran
A4069
Llanwrda
Cilgwyn
Myddfai
1443
Mynydd Myddfai
Usk Resr.
Llywel
Pentre'r-felin
Yr Allt
1156
Trecastle
Sennybridge
Llangadog
Castle
Afon Bran
Cwmwysg
R. Usk
Pont ar Hydfer
Defynnog
Forest Fach
A4067
A4215
Talsarn
Source of R. Usk
Glas Fynydd Forest
Cray
Afon Senni
Twynllanan
Llanddeusant
Pontarllechau
1940
Moel Feity
Heol Senni
Afon Sawdde
Capel Gwynfe
Llyn y Fan Fach
Llyn y Fan-Fawr
Cray Resr.
Escarpment
Brest Twrch
Gareg Las
2076
Afon Tawe
2366
Fan Hir
Truman
Fan-Gihirych
Fan Llia
2071
1982
Foel Fraith
2022
Bylchau Rhos-faen
Cefn Carn-Fadog
1657
Afon Twrch
Carreg-lem
Shire Horse Centre
1832
Dinosaur Park
Castell-y-geifr
Dan-yr-Ogof Showcaves
R. Tawe
Glyntawe
Penwyllt
1763
Cefn Mawr

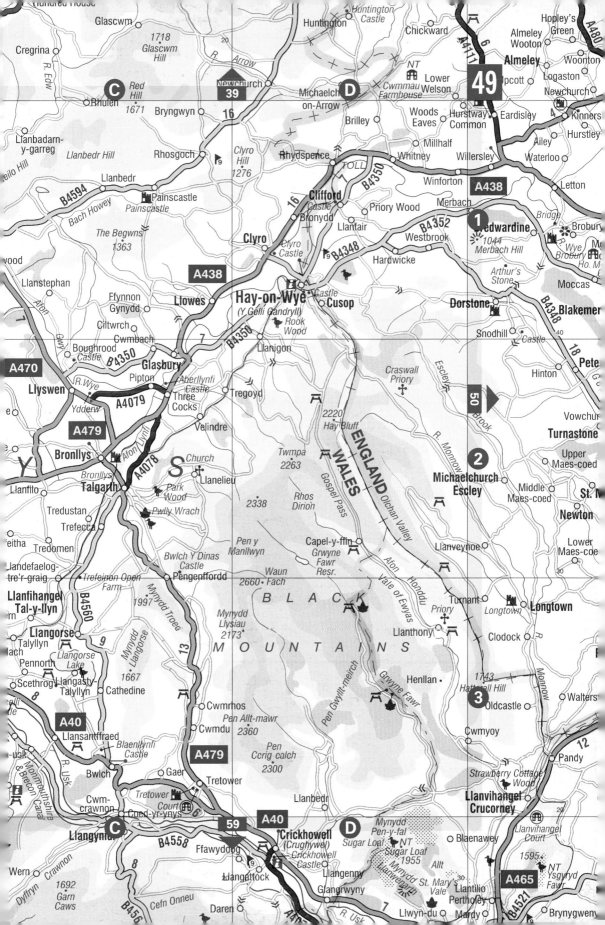

Grid reference letters: C, D (top), 1, 2, 3 (right side), C, D (bottom)
Page number indicators: **49**, **39**, **50**, **59**

Towns and features labelled:

Hundred House, Glascwm, 1718 Glascwm Hill, Huntington, Huntington Castle, Chickward, Hopley's Green, Almeley Wooton, Woonton, Cregrina, R. Edw, Arrow, Lower Welson, Cwmmau Farmhouse, NT, Logaston, Newchurch, Almeley, Bhulen, Red Hill 1671, Newchurch, Michaelchurch on-Arrow, Brilley, Woods Eaves, Hurstway Common, Eardisley, Kinners, Llanbadarn-y-garreg, Llanbedr Hill, Rhosgoch, Clyro Hill 1276, Rhydspence, Whitney, Millhalf, Willersley, Ailey, Hurstley, Waterloo, Llanbedr, B4594, Painscastle, Bach Howey, Clifford, Castle, Bronydd, Priory Wood, Llanfair, Westbrook, Winforton, TOLL, Merbach, Bredwardine, 1044 Merbach Hill, Bridge, Brobury, Letton, A438, B4352, B4350, The Begwns 1363, Clyro, Clyro Castle, B4348, Hardwicke, Arthur's Stone, Wye, Brobury Ho. M, Moccas, Ffynnon Gynydd, Llowes, Hay-on-Wye (Y Gelli Gandryll), Castle, Cusop, Rook Wood, Dorstone, Snodhill, Castle, Blakemer, Ciltwrch, Cwmbach, Boughrood Castle, B4350, Glasbury, Pipton, Llanigon, Craswall Priory, Hinton, Pete, Llyswen, A470, A4079, Ydderw, Three Cocks, Aberllynfi Castle, Tregoyd, Velindre, 2220 Hay Bluff, Escley, Brook, 50, Vowchur, Turnastone, A479, Bronllys, Church, Llanelieu, Twmpa 2263, ENGLAND, WALES, R. Monnow, Michaelchurch Escley, Upper Maes-coed, St. M, Talgarth, Park Wood, Pwlly Wrach, 2338, Rhos Dirion, Gospel Pass, Middle Maes-coed, Newton, Llanfilo, Tredustan, Trefecca, Pen y Manllwyn, Waun Fach 2660, Capel-y-ffin, Grwyne Fawr Resr., Olchan Valley, Afon Honddu, Llanveynoe, Lower Maes-coe, eitha, Tredomen, landefaelog-tre'r-graig, Bwlch Y Dinas Castle, Pengenffordd, B L A C K, Vale of Ewyas, Priory, Turnant, Longtown, Longtown, Llanfihangel Tal-y-llyn, 1997 Mynydd Troed, Mynydd Llysiau 2173, M O U N T A I N S, Llanthony, Clodock, Llangorse, Talyllyn, Mynydd Llangorse, 13, Llangorse Lake, 1667, Cwmrhos, Pen Allt-mawr 2360, Henllan, 1743 Hatterall Hill, Walters, Pennorth, Scethrog, Llangasty-Talyllyn, Cathedine, Cwmdu, Grwyne Fawr, Oldcastle, A40, Llansantffraed, Blaenllynfi Castle, Pen Ccrig calch 2300, Cwmyoy, Pandy, Bwlch, Gaer, Tretower, A479, Llanbedr, Strawberry Cottage Wood, 12, Cwm-crawnon, Tretower Court, Coed-yr-ynys, Llanvihangel Crucorney, Llanvihangel Court, C, 59, A40, Crickhowell (Crughywel), Crickhowell Castle, Mynydd Pen-y-fal Sugar Loaf, NT, D, Blaenawey, 1595, NT, Ysgyryd Fawr, Llangynid, B4558, Ffawyddog, Llangenny, Sugar Loaf 1955, Allt, Llantilio Pertholey, A465, Wern, Crawnon, 1692 Garn Caws, Cefn Onneu, Llangttock, Daren, Glangrwyney, R. Usk, Llwyn-du, Mynydd St. Mary's Vale, Mardy, Brynygwern, A4521, Monmouthshire & Brecon Canal, Dyffryn

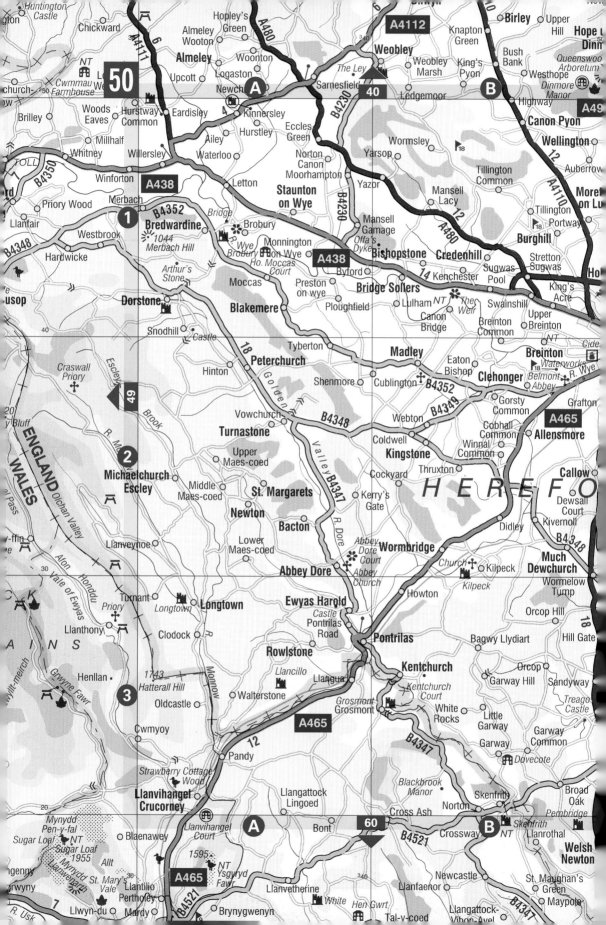

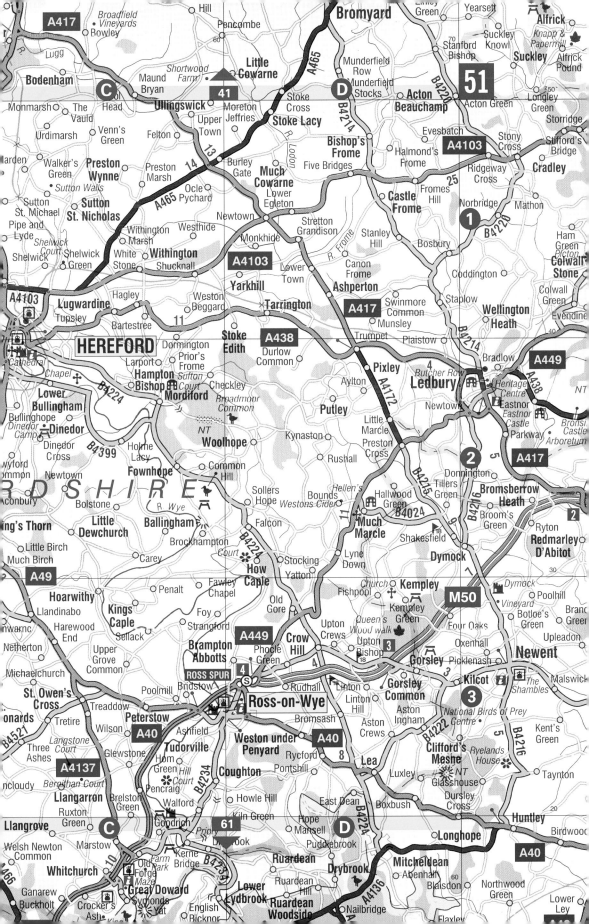

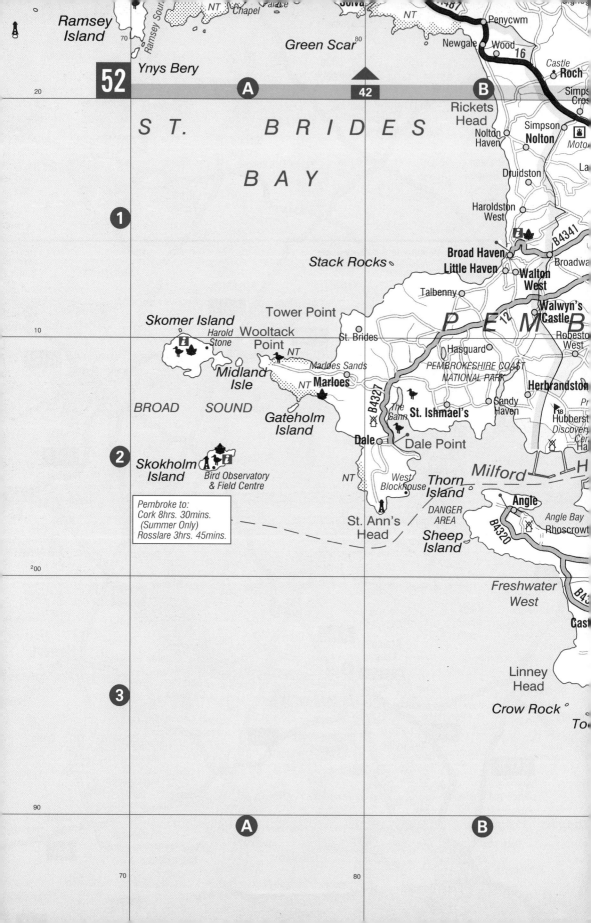

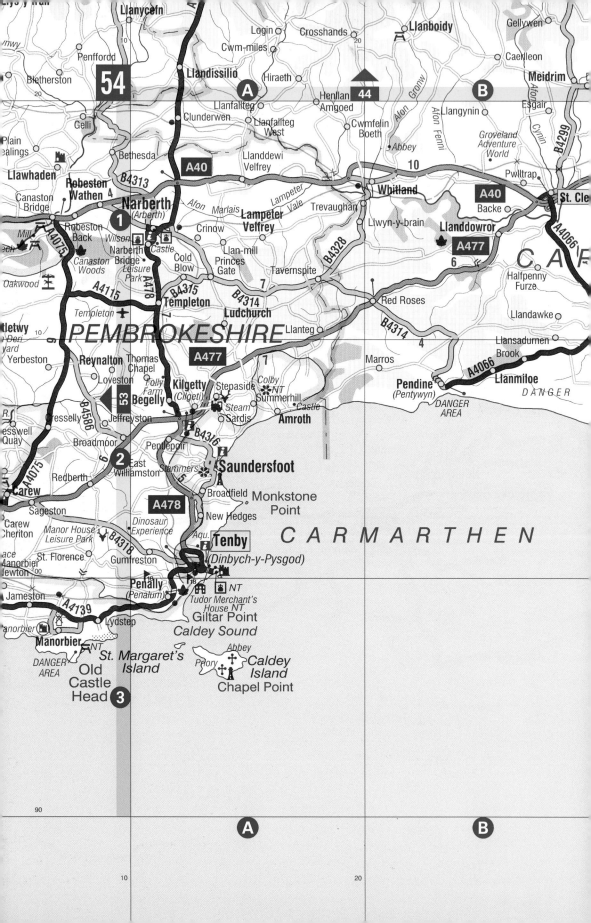

Llanycefn · Llanyfair
Login · Crosshands · Gellywen
Cwm-miles · Llanboidy
Penffordd · Hiraeth · Caerlleon
Bletherston · Llandissilio · Henllan · Meidrim
Llanfallteg · Amgoed · Esgair
Gelli · Clunderwen · Llanfallteg West · Cwmfelin Boeth · Afon Gronw · Llangynin · B4299
Plain Dealings · Llanddewi Velfrey · Abbey · Afon Fenni · Groveland Adventure World

Bethesda · Whitland · Pwlltrap
A40 · Lampeter · Trevaughan · 10 · St. Clé
Robeston Wathen · B4313 · Lampeter Vale · Backe
Narberth (Arberth) · Afon Marlais · Lampeter Velfrey · Llwyn-y-brain · Llanddowror · A4066
Canaston Bridge · Robeston Back · Wilson · Crinow · Llan-mill · 6
Mill · Narberth Bridge · Castle · Cold Blow · Princes Gate · Tavernspite · Halfpenny Furze
Oakwood · Canaston Woods · Leisure Park · A478 · B4315 · Templeton · Ludchurch · B4328 · Red Roses · Llandawke
Templeton · A4115 · Llanteg · B4314 · Llansadurnen
PEMBROKESHIRE · A4075 · Reynalton · Thomas Chapel · A477 · Marros · Brook
Yerbeston · Loveston · Folly Farm · Kilgetty (Cilgeti) · Stepaside · Colby NT · Summerhill · A4066 · Llanmiloe
Cresselly · Begelly · 53 · Steam · Sardis · Castle · Pendine (Pentywyn) · DANGER
Presswell Quay · Jeffreyston · B4586 · Broadmoor · Pentlepoir · Amroth · DANGER AREA
Carew · Redberth · East Williamston · Stammers · **Saundersfoot** · B4316
Sageston · A478 · Broadfield · Monkstone Point
Carew Cheriton · Manor House Leisure Park · Dinosaur Experience · New Hedges · **C A R M A R T H E N**
St. Florence · B4318 · Aqu. · **Tenby** (Dinbych-y-Pysgod)
Jameston · Gumfreston · A4139 · Penally (Penalun) · Tudor Merchant's House NT
Manorbier · Lydstep · **Giltar Point** · Caldey Sound
DANGER AREA · Old Castle Head · 3 · **St. Margaret's Island** · Priory · Abbey · **Caldey Island** · Chapel Point

90

10 · 20

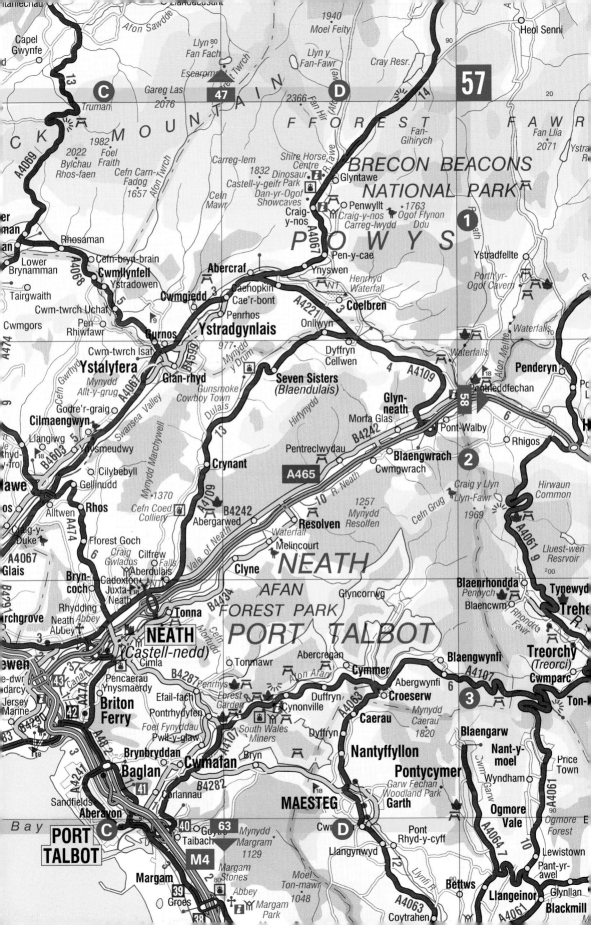

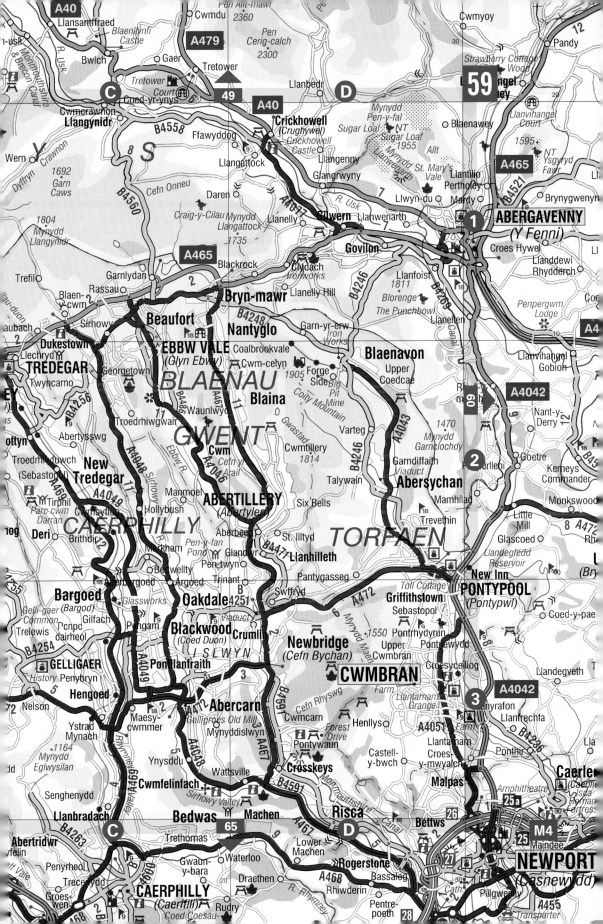

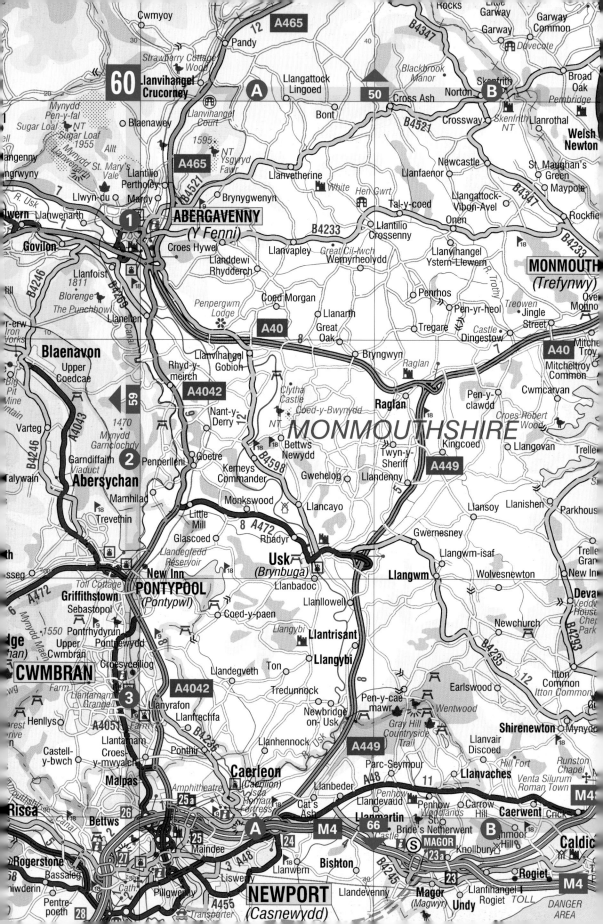

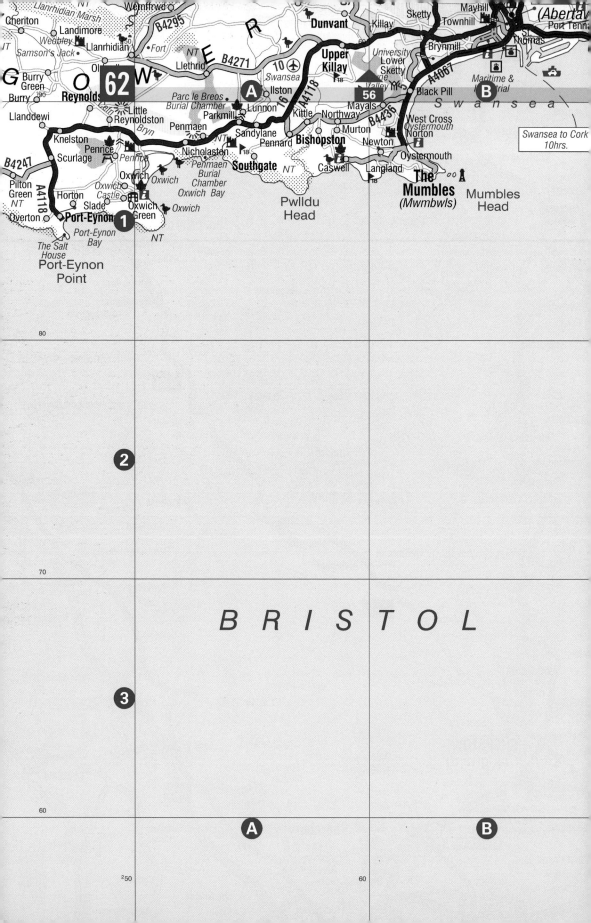

Cheriton
Llanrhidian Marsh
Weobley
Landimore
Samson's Jack
Llanrhidian
Fort
Llethrid
Olds

B4295
Wernffrwd
B4271
Dunvant
Killay
Sketty
Mayhill
Townhill
(Abertaw)
Port Tenn

Upper Killay
Lower Sketty
University
Swansea Valley
Brynmill
St Thomas

G
Burry Green
Burry
Reynolds
Reynoldston
Little Reynoldston

W
E
R
10
Swansea
16
A4118

56
Black Pill
Maritime & Industrial
B

A
Ilston
Parc le Breos Burial Chamber
Lunnon
Parkmill
Kittle
Northway
Mayals
A4067
A4118
B4436
West Cross
Oystermouth
Norton
Swansea
Swansea to Cork 10hrs.

Llanddewi
Knelston
Scurlage
Penrice
Penrice
Penmaen
Nicholaston
Sandylane
Pennard
Bishopston
Murton
Newton
Oystermouth

Penmaen Burial Chamber
Southgate
NT
Caswell
Langland
The Mumbles
(Mwmbwls)
Mumbles Head

B4247
Pilton Green
Horton
Slade
Oxwich Castle
Oxwich
Oxwich Bay
Pwlldu Head

A4118
Overton
Port-Eynon
Oxwich Green
Oxwich
NT

1

The Salt House
Port-Eynon Bay
Port-Eynon Point

80

2

70

B R I S T O L

3

60

A

B

250
60

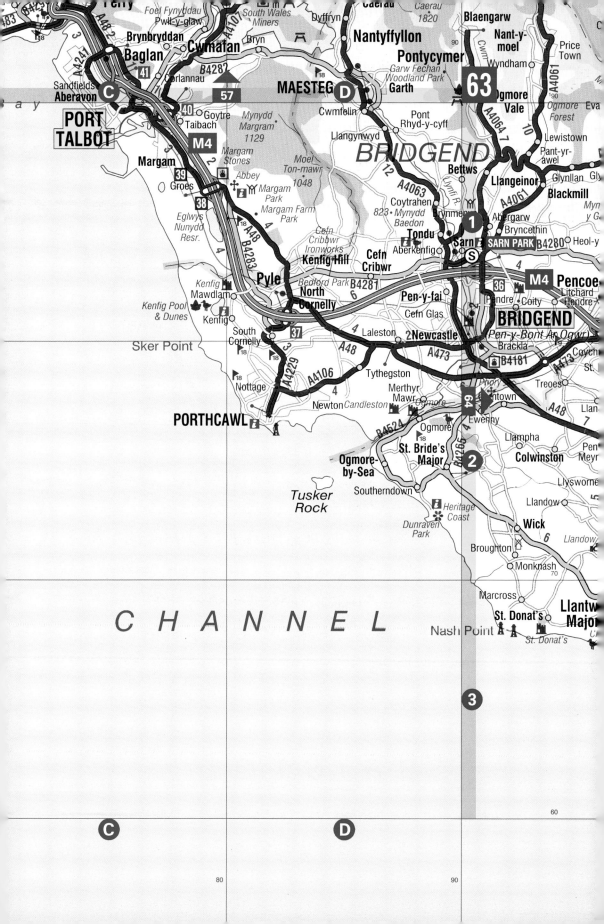

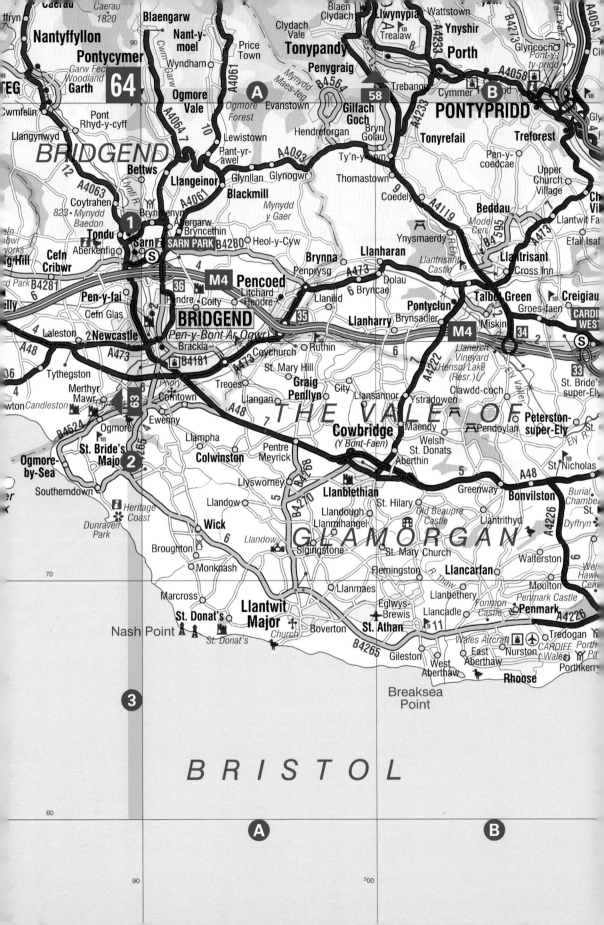

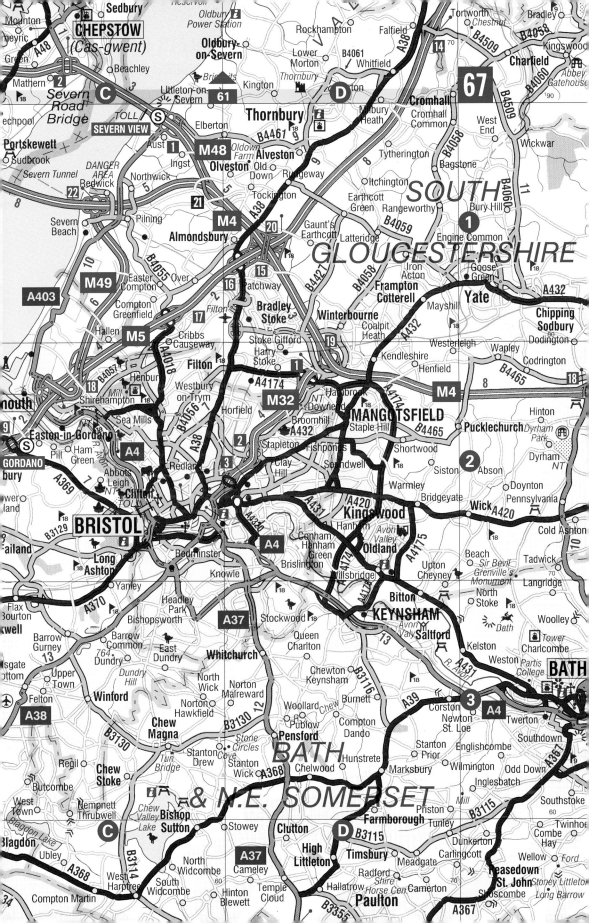

INDEX TO CITIES, TOWNS, VILLAGES, HAMLETS & LOCATIONS
Mynegai i Ddinasoedd, Trefi, Pentrefi, Cymydau a Lleoliadau

(1) A strict alphabetical order is used e.g Ashperton follows Ash Parva but precedes Ashton.

Glynir yn gaeth wrth drefn y wyddor e.e. mae Ashperton yn dilyn Ash Parva ond yn dod cyn Ashton.

(2) The map reference given refers to the actual map square in which the town spot or built-up area is located and not to the place name.

Mae'r cyfeirnod map a roddir yn cyfeirio at yr union sgwaryn ar y map lle mae smotyn y dref neu'r ardal adeiliedig ac nid at enw'r lle.

(3) Where two or more places of the same name occur in the same County or Unitary Authority, the nearest large town is also given;
e.g. Aston. *Ches* —3C **11** (nr. Frodsham) indicates that Aston is located in square 3C on page **11** and is situated near Frodsham in the County of Cheshire.

Os bydd dau le gyda'r un enw'n digwydd yn yr un Sir neu'r un awdurdod Unedol, rhoddir enw'r dref fawr agosaf hefyd;
*e.e. Mae Aston. Ches —3C **11** (nr. Frodsham) yn dangos bod Aston yn sgwaryn 3C ar dudalen **11** a'i bod hi ger Frodsham yn Sydd Gaer.*

COUNTIES and UNITARY AUTHORITIES with the abbreviations used in this index
Siroedd ac Awdurdodau Unedol gyda'r byrfoddau a ddefnyddir yn y mynegai hwn

Bath & N E Somerset : *Bath*
Blaenau Gwent : *Blae*
Bridgend : *B'end*
Bristol (City) : *Bris*
Caerphilly : *Cphy*
Cardiff : *Card*
Carmarthenshire : *Carm*
Ceredigion : *Cdgn*
Cheshire : *Ches*
Conwy : *Cnwy*

Denbighshire : *Den*
Flintshire : *Flin*
Gloucestershire : *Glos*
Greater London : *G Lon*
Greater Manchester : *G Man*
Gwynedd : *Gwyn*
Halton : *Hal*
Herefordshire : *Here*
Isle of Anglesey : *IOA*
Lancashire : *Lanc*

Merseyside : *Mers*
Merthyr Tydfil : *Mer T*
Monmouthshire : *Mon*
Neath Port Talbot : *Neat*
Newport : *Newp*
North Somerset : *N Som*
Pembrokeshire : *Pemb*
Powys : *Powy*
Rhondda Cynon Taff : *Rhon*
Shropshire : *Shrp*

Somerset : *Som*
South Gloucestershire : *S Glo*
Staffordshire : *Staf*
Swansea : *Swan*
Telford & Wrekin : *Telf*
Torfaen : *Torf*
Vale of Glamorgan, The : *V Glam*
Warrington : *Warr*
Worcestershire : *Worc*
Wrexham : *Wrex*

Abberley. *Worc* —2D **41**
Abberley Common. *Worc* —2D **41**
Abbey Dore. *Here* —2A **50**
Abbots Leigh. *N Som* —2C **67**
Abcott. *Shrp* —1A **40**
Abdon. *Shrp* —3C **33**
Abenhall. *Glos* —1D **61**
Aber. *Cdgn* —1D **45**
Aberaeron. *Cdgn* —2D **35**
Aberaman. *Rhon* —2B **58**
Aberangell. *Powy* —3B **23**
Aberarad. *Carm* —2C **45**
Aberarth. *Cdgn* —2D **35**
Aberavon. *Neat* —1C **63**
Aber-banc. *Cdgn* —1C **45**
Aberbargoed. *Cphy* —3C **59**
Aberbechan. *Powy* —2C **31**
Aberbeeg. *Blae* —2D **59**
Aberbowlan. *Carm* —2B **46**
Aberbran. *Powy* —3A **48**
Abercanaid. *Mer T* —2B **58**
Abercarn. *Cphy* —3D **59**
Abercastle. *Pemb* —2B **42**
Abercegir. *Powy* —1D **29**
Abercraf. *Powy* —1D **57**
Abercregan. *Neat* —3D **57**
Abercwmboi. *Rhon* —3B **58**
Abercych. *Pemb* —1B **44**
Abercynon. *Rhon* —3B **58**
Aber-Cywarch. *Gwyn* —3D **23**
Aberdar. *Rhon* —2A **58**
Aberdare. *Rhon* —2A **58**
Aberdaron. *Gwyn* —2A **20**
Aberdaugleddau. *Pemb* —2C **53**
Aberdesach. *Gwyn* —2D **13**
Aberdovey. *Gwyn* —2B **28**
Aberdulais. *Neat* —3C **57**
Aberdyfi. *Gwyn* —2B **28**
Aberedw. *Powy* —1B **48**
Abererch. *Gwyn* —1C **21**
Aberfan. *Mer T* —2B **58**
Aberffraw. *IOA* —1C **13**
Aberffrwd. *Cdgn* —1B **36**
Abergarw. *B'end* —1A **64**
Abergarwed. *Neat* —2D **57**
Abergavenny. *Mon* —1A **60**
Abergele. *Cnwy* —3A **8**
Aber-Giar. *Carm* —1A **46**
Abergorlech. *Carm* —2A **46**
Abergwaun. *Pemb* —2C **43**
Abergwesyn. *Powy* —3D **37**
Abergwili. *Carm* —3D **45**
Abergwynfi. *Neat* —3D **57**
Abergwyngregyn. *Gwyn* —3B **6**
Abergynolwyn. *Gwyn* —1B **28**
Aberhafesp. *Powy* —2B **30**
Aberhonddu. *Powy* —3B **48**

Aberhosan. *Powy* —2D **29**
Aberkenfig. *B'End* —1D **63**
Aberllefenni. *Cdgn* —1C **29**
Abermaw. *Gwyn* —3B **22**
Abermeurig. *Cdgn* —3A **36**
Aber-miwl. *Powy* —2C **31**
Abermule. *Powy* —2C **31**
Abernant. *Carm* —3C **45**
Abernant. *Rhon* —2B **58**
Aber-oer. *Wrex* —3D **17**
Aberpennar. *Rhon* —3B **58**
Aberporth. *Cdgn* —3B **34**
Aberriw. *Powy* —1C **31**
Abersoch. *Gwyn* —2C **21**
Abersychan. *Torf* —2D **59**
Abertawe. *Swan* —3B **56**
Aberteifi. *Cdgn* —1A **44**
Aberthin. *V Glam* —2B **64**
Abertillery. *Blae* —2D **59**
Abertridwr. *Cphy* —3C **59**
Abertridwr. *Powy* —3B **24**
Abertyleri. *Blae* —2D **59**
Abertysswg. *Cphy* —2C **59**
Aber Village. *Powy* —3C **49**
Aberyscir. *Powy* —3B **48**
Aberystwyth. *Cdgn* —3A **28**
Abram. *G Man* —1D **11**
Abson. *S Glo* —2D **67**
Aconbury. *Here* —2C **51**
Acrefair. *Wrex* —3D **17**
Acton. *Ches* —2D **19**
Acton. *Shrp* —3A **32**
Acton. *Wrex* —2A **18**
Acton Beauchamp. *Here* —3D **41**
Acton Bridge. *Ches* —3C **11**
Acton Burnell. *Shrp* —1C **33**
Acton Green. *Here* —3D **41**
Acton Pigott. *Shrp* —1C **33**
Acton Round. *Shrp* —2A **33**
Acton Scott. *Shrp* —3B **32**
Adderley. *Shrp* —1D **27**
Adeney. *Telf* —3D **27**
Adfa. *Powy* —1B **30**
Adforton. *Here* —1B **40**
Admaston. *Telf* —3D **27**
Adpar. *Cdgn* —1C **45**
Afon-wen. *Flin* —3C **9**
Aigburth. *Mers* —2A **10**
Ailey. *Here* —1A **50**
Aintree. *Mers* —1A **10**
Alberbury. *Shrp* —3A **26**
Albert Town. *Pemb* —1C **53**
Albrighton. *Shrp* —3B **26**
Alcaston. *Shrp* —3B **32**
Aldersey Green. *Ches* —2B **18**
Alderton. *Shrp* —2B **26**
Aldford. *Ches* —2B **18**
Aldon. *Shrp* —1B **40**
Alfrick. *Worc* —3D **41**

Alfrick Pound. *Worc* —3D **41**
Alkington. *Shrp* —1C **27**
Allaston. *Glos* —2D **61**
Allensmore. *Here* —2B **50**
Allerton. *Mers* —2B **10**
Allscott. *Shrp* —2D **33**
Allscott. *Telf* —3D **27**
All Stretton. *Shrp* —2B **32**
Allt. *Carm* —2A **56**
Alltami. *Flin* —1D **17**
Alltmawr. *Powy* —1B **48**
Alltwalis. *Carm* —2D **45**
Alltwen. *Neat* —2C **57**
Alltyblacca. *Cdgn* —1A **46**
Allt-y-goed. *Pemb* —1A **44**
Almeley. *Here* —3A **40**
Almeley Wooton. *Here* —3A **40**
Almington. *Staf* —1D **27**
Almondsbury. *S Glo* —1D **67**
Alport. *Powy* —2D **31**
Alpraham. *Ches* —2C **19**
Alvanley. *Ches* —3B **10**
Alveston. *S Glo* —1D **67**
Alvington. *Glos* —2D **61**
Ambleston. *Pemb* —3C **43**
Amlwch. *IOA* —1D **5**
Amlwch Port. *IOA* —1D **5**
Ammanford. *Carm* —1B **56**
Amroth. *Pemb* —2A **54**
Anchor. *Shrp* —3C **31**
Anderton. *Ches* —3D **11**
Anelog. *Gwyn* —2A **20**
Anfield. *Mers* —1A **10**
Angelbank. *Shrp* —1C **41**
Angle. *Pemb* —2B **52**
Annscroft. *Shrp* —1B **32**
Antrobus. *Ches* —3D **11**
Appleton. *Hal* —2C **11**
Appleton Thorn. *Warr* —2D **11**
Arberth. *Pemb* —1A **54**
Arddleen. *Powy* —3D **25**
Argoed. *Cphy* —3C **59**
Argoed Mill. *Powy* —2A **38**
Arleston. *Telf* —3D **27**
Arley. *Ches* —2D **11**
Arlingham. *Glos* —1D **61**
Arthog. *Gwyn* —3B **22**
Ashbrook. *Shrp* —2B **32**
Ashfield. *Here* —3C **51**
Ashfield. *Shrp* —2D **33**
Ashford Bowdler. *Shrp* —1C **41**
Ashford Carbonel. *Shrp* —1C **41**
Ashley Heath. *Staf* —1D **27**
Ashley Moor. *Here* —2B **40**
Ash Magna. *Shrp* —1C **27**
Ash Parva. *Shrp* —1C **27**
Ashperton. *Here* —1D **51**
Ashton. *Ches* —1C **19**
Ashton. *Here* —2C **41**

Ashton-in-Makerfield. *G Man*
—1C **11**
Asterley. *Shrp* —1A **32**
Asterton. *Shrp* —2A **32**
Astley. *G Man* —1D **11**
Astley. *Shrp* —3C **27**
Astley Abbotts. *Shrp* —2D **33**
Aston. *Ches* —3C **11**
(Frodsham)
Aston. *Ches* —3D **19**
(Nantwich)
Aston. *Flin* —1A **18**
Aston. *Here* —2B **40**
Aston. *Shrp* —2C **27**
Aston. *Staf* —3D **19**
Aston. *Telf* —1D **33**
Aston Botterell. *Shrp* —3D **33**
Aston Crews. *Here* —3D **51**
Aston Eyre. *Shrp* —2D **33**
Aston Ingham. *Here* —3D **51**
Aston juxta Mondrum. *Ches*
—2D **19**
Astonlane. *Shrp* —2D **33**
Aston Munslow. *Shrp* —3C **33**
Aston on Clun. *Shrp* —3A **32**
Aston Pigott. *Shrp* —1A **32**
Aston Rogers. *Shrp* —1A **32**
Atcham. *Shrp* —1C **33**
Atherton. *G Man* —1D **11**
Atterley. *Shrp* —2D **33**
Auberrow. *Here* —1B **50**
Audlem. *Ches* —3D **19**
Aulden. *Here* —3B **40**
Aust. *S Glo* —1C **67**
Avonmouth. *Bris* —2C **67**
Awre. *Glos* —2D **61**
Aylburton. *Glos* —2D **61**
Aylburton Common. *Glos* —2D **61**
Aylton. *Here* —2D **51**
Aymestrey. *Here* —2B **40**

Babbinswood. *Shrp* —2A **26**
Babel. *Carm* —2D **47**
Babell. *Flin* —3C **9**
Bachau. *IOA* —2D **5**
Bacheldre. *Powy* —2D **31**
Bachymbyd Fawr. *Den* —1B **16**
Backe. *Carm* —1B **54**
Backford. *Ches* —3B **10**
Backwell. *N Som* —3B **66**
Bacton. *Here* —2A **50**
Bae Cinmel. *Cnwy* —2A **8**
Bae Colwyn. *Cnwy* —3D **7**
Bae Penrhyn. *Cnwy* —2D **7**
Bagginswood. *Shrp* —3D **33**
Bagillt. *Flin* —3D **9**
Baglan. *Neat* —3C **57**
Bagley. *Shrp* —2B **26**

Bagstone. *S Glo* —1D **67**
Bagwy Llydiart. *Here* —3B **50**
Bala. *Gwyn* —1A **24**
Balderton. *Ches* —1A **18**
Ball. *Shrp* —2A **26**
Ballingham. *Here* —2C **51**
Bancffosfelen. *Carm* —1D **55**
Bancycapel. *Carm* —1D **55**
Bancyfelin. *Carm* —1C **55**
Banc-y-ffordd. *Carm* —2D **45**
Bangor. *Gwyn* —3A **6**
Bangor-is-y-coed. *Wrex* —3A **18**
Bank Street. *Worc* —2D **41**
Bank, The. *Shrp* —2D **33**
Banwell. *N Som* —3A **66**
Barbridge. *Ches* —2D **19**
Barewood. *Here* —3A **40**
Bargod. *Cphy* —3C **59**
Bargoed. *Cphy* —3C **59**
Barmouth. *Gwyn* —3B **22**
Barnston. *Ches* —2D **9**
Barnton. *Ches* —3D **11**
Barons Cross. *Here* —3B **40**
Barri. *V Glam* —3C **65**
Barrow. *Shrp* —1D **33**
Barrow Common. *N Som* —3C **67**
Barrow Gurney. *N Som* —3C **67**
Barrow Nook. *Lanc* —1B **10**
Barrow's Green. *Ches* —2C **11**
Barry. *V Glam* —3C **65**
Barry Island. *V Glam* —3C **65**
Bartestree. *Here* —1C **51**
Barton. *Ches* —2B **18**
Baschurch. *Shrp* —2B **26**
Bassaleg. *Newp* —1D **65**
Bate Heath. *Ches* —3D **11**
Bath. *Bath* —3D **67**
Battle. *Powy* —2B **48**
Battlefield. *Shrp* —3C **27**
Bayston Hill. *Shrp* —1B **32**
Bayton. *Worc* —1D **41**
Bayton Common. *Worc* —1D **41**
Beach. *S Glo* —2D **67**
Beachley. *Glos* —3C **61**
Bearstone. *Shrp* —1D **27**
Beaufort. *Blae* —1C **59**
Beaumaris. *IOA* —3B **6**
Bebington. *Mers* —2A **10**
Beddau. *Rhon* —1B **64**
Beddgelert. *Gwyn* —3A **14**
Bedford. *G Man* —1D **11**
Bedlinog. *Mer T* —2D **59**
Bedminster. *Bris* —2C **67**
Bedstone. *Shrp* —1A **40**
Bedwas. *Cphy* —1C **65**
Bedwellty. *Cphy* —2C **59**
Beeston. *Ches* —2C **19**
Began. *Card* —1D **65**
Begelly. *Pemb* —2A **54**
Beggar's Bush. *Powy* —2D **39**
Beguildy. *Powy* —1C **39**
Belgrano. *Cnwy* —3A **8**
Belle Vue. *Shrp* —3B **26**
Benllech. *IOA* —2A **6**
Benthall. *Shrp* —1D **33**
Bentlawn. *Shrp* —1A **32**
Berkeley. *Glos* —3D **61**
Berriew. *Powy* —1C **31**
Berrington. *Shrp* —1C **33**
Berrington. *Worc* —2C **41**
Berrington Green. *Worc* —2C **41**
Berrow Green. *Worc* —3D **41**
Berry Hill. *Glos* —1C **61**
Berry Hill. *Pemb* —1D **43**
Bersham. *Wrex* —3A **18**
Berthengam. *Flin* —3C **9**
Berwyn. *Den* —3C **17**
Bethania. *Cdgn* —2A **36**
Bethania. *Gwyn* —3C **15**
(Blaenau Ffestiniog)
Bethania. *Gwyn* —2B **14**
(Caernarfon)
Bethel. *Gwyn* —1A **24**
(Bala)
Bethel. *Gwyn* —1A **14**
(Caernarfon)
Bethel. *IOA* —3C **5**
Bethesda. *Gwyn* —1B **14**
Bethesda. *Pemb* —1D **53**
Bethlehem. *Carm* —3B **46**
Betley. *Staf* —3D **19**
Bettisfield. *Wrex* —1B **26**
Betton. *Shrp* —1D **27**
Betton Strange. *Shrp* —1C **33**
Bettws. *B'End* —1D **63**
Bettws. *Newp* —3D **59**

Bettws Bledrws. *Cdgn* —3A **36**
Bettws Cedewain. *Powy* —2C **31**
Bettws Gwerfil Goch. *Den* —3B **16**
Bettws Ifan. *Cdgn* —1C **45**
Bettws Newydd. *Mon* —2A **60**
Betws. *Carm* —1B **56**
Betws Garmon. *Gwyn* —2A **14**
Betws-y-Coed. *Cnwy* —2C **15**
Betws-yn-Rhos. *Cnwy* —3A **8**
Beulah. *Cdgn* —1B **44**
Beulah. *Powy* —3A **38**
Bevington. *Glos* —3D **61**
Bickershaw. *G Man* —1D **11**
Bickerton. *Ches* —2C **19**
Bickley Moss. *Ches* —3C **19**
Bicton. *Here* —2B **40**
Bicton. *Shrp* —3D **31**
(Bishop's Castle)
Bicton. *Shrp* —3B **26**
(Shrewsbury)
Bicton Heath. *Shrp* —3B **26**
Bidston. *Mers* —2D **9**
Billinge. *Mers* —1C **11**
Billingsley. *Shrp* —3D **33**
Bilson Green. *Glos* —1D **61**
Bings Heath. *Shrp* —3C **27**
Binweston. *Shrp* —1A **32**
Bircher. *Here* —2B **40**
Birchgrove. *Card* —2C **65**
Birchgrove. *Swan* —3C **57**
Birch Heath. *Ches* —1C **19**
Birch Hill. *Ches* —3C **11**
Birchwood. *Warr* —1D **11**
Birdwood. *Glos* —1D **61**
Birkenhead. *Mers* —2A **10**
Birley. *Here* —3B **40**
Birtley. *Here* —2A **40**
Bishop's Castle. *Shrp* —3A **32**
Bishop's Frome. *Here* —1D **51**
Bishopston. *Swan* —1A **62**
Bishopstone. *Here* —1B **50**
Bishop Sutton. *Bath* —3C **67**
Bishopsworth. *Bris* —3C **67**
Bishton. *Newp* —1A **66**
Bitterley. *Shrp* —1C **41**
Bitton. *S Glo* —3D **67**
Blackbrook. *Mers* —1C **11**
Blackford. *Shrp* —3C **33**
Blackmill. *B'End* —1A **64**
Blackmoor. *G Man* —1D **11**
Black Pill. *Swan* —3B **56**
Blackrock. *Mon* —1D **59**
Black Tar. *Pemb* —2C **53**
Blacktown. *Newp* —1D **65**
Blackwood. *Cphy* —3C **59**
Blacon. *Ches* —1A **18**
Blaenannerch. *Cdgn* —1B **44**
Blaenau Dolwyddelan. *Cnwy* —2B **14**
Blaenau Ffestiniog. *Gwyn* —3C **15**
Blaenavon. *Torf* —2D **59**
Blaenawey. *Mon* —1D **59**
Blaen Celyn. *Cdgn* —3C **35**
Blaen Clydach. *Rhon* —3A **58**
Blaendulais. *Neat* —2D **57**
Blaenffos. *Pemb* —2A **44**
Blaengarw. *B'End* —3A **58**
Blaengeuffordd. *Cdgn* —3B **28**
Blaengwrach. *Neat* —2D **57**
Blaengwynfi. *Neat* —3D **57**
Blaenllechau. *Rhon* —3B **58**
Blaenpennal. *Cdgn* —2B **36**
Blaenplwyf. *Cdgn* —1A **36**
Blaenporth. *Cdgn* —1B **44**
Blaenrhondda. *Rhon* —3A **58**
Blaenwaun. *Carm* —3B **44**
Blaen-y-coed. *Carm* —3B **44**
Blaen-y-cwm. *Blae* —1C **59**
Blaenycwm. *Rhon* —3A **58**
Blagdon. *N Som* —3C **67**
Blaina. *Blae* —2D **59**
Blaisdon. *Glos* —1D **61**
Blakemere. *Here* —1A **50**
Blakeney. *Glos* —2D **61**
Blakenhall. *Ches* —3B **40**
Bleadon. *N Som* —3A **66**
Bleddfa. *Powy* —2D **39**
Bletchley. *Shrp* —1D **27**
Bletherston. *Pemb* —3D **43**
Bliss Gate. *Worc* —1D **41**
Blists Hill. *Telf* —1D **33**
Blue Anchor. *Swan* —3A **56**
Bodedern. *IOA* —2C **5**
Bodelwyddan. *Den* —3B **8**
Bodenham. *Here* —3C **41**
Bodewryd. *IOA* —1C **5**
Bodfari. *Den* —3B **8**

Bodffordd. *IOA* —3D **5**
Bodnant. *Cnwy* —3D **7**
Bodorgan. *IOA* —1C **13**
Boduan. *Gwyn* —1C **21**
Bog, The. *Shrp* —2A **32**
Bold Heath. *Mers* —2D **11**
Bolstone. *Here* —2C **51**
Bomere Heath. *Shrp* —3B **26**
Boncath. *Pemb* —2B **44**
Bont. *Mon* —1A **60**
Bontddu. *Gwyn* —3B **22**
Bont Dolgadfan. *Powy* —1D **29**
Bontgoch. *Cdgn* —3B **28**
Bontnewydd. *Cdgn* —2B **36**
Bont-newydd. *Cnwy* —3B **8**
Bontnewydd. *Gwyn* —1D **13**
(Caernarfon)
Bont Newydd. *Gwyn* —3C **15**
(Ffestiniog)
Bontuchel. *Den* —2B **16**
Bonvilston. *V Glam* —2B **64**
Bon-y-maen. *Swan* —3B **56**
Booley. *Shrp* —2C **27**
Boothstown. *G Man* —1D **11**
Bootle. *Mers* —1A **10**
Boraston. *Shrp* —1D **41**
Boreton. *Shrp* —1C **33**
Borras Head. *Wrex* —2A **18**
Borth. *Cdgn* —3B **28**
Borth-y-Gest. *Gwyn* —1A **22**
Bosbury. *Here* —1D **51**
Bosherston. *Pemb* —3C **53**
Bostock Green. *Ches* —1D **19**
Botloe's Green. *Glos* —3D **51**
Botwnnog. *Gwyn* —1B **20**
Boughrood. *Powy* —2C **49**
Boughspring. *Glos* —3C **61**
Bouldon. *Shrp* —3C **33**
Boulston. *Pemb* —1C **53**
Bounds. *Here* —2D **51**
Bourton. *N Som* —3A **66**
Bourton. *Shrp* —2C **33**
Boverton. *V Glam* —3A **64**
Bowley. *Here* —3C **41**
Bowling Bank. *Wrex* —3B **18**
Bow Street. *Cdgn* —3B **28**
Boxbush. *Glos* —3D **51**
Brackla. *B'End* —2A **64**
Bradfield Green. *Ches* —2D **19**
Bradley. *Ches* —3C **11**
Bradley. *Glos* —3D **61**
Bradley. *Wrex* —2A **18**
Bradley Green. *Ches* —3C **19**
Bradley Stoke. *S Glo* —1D **67**
Bradlow. *Here* —2D **51**
Braichmelyn. *Gwyn* —1B **14**
Brampton Abbotts. *Here* —3D **51**
Brampton Bryan. *Here* —1A **40**
Brand Green. *Glos* —3D **51**
Brandhill. *Shrp* —1A **40**
Bransley. *Shrp* —1D **41**
Bratton. *Telf* —3C **27**
Breaden Heath. *Shrp* —1B **26**
Breadstone. *Glos* —2D **61**
Bream. *Glos* —2D **61**
Bream's Meend. *Glos* —2D **61**
Brechfa. *Carm* —2A **46**
Brecon. *Powy* —3B **48**
Bredenbury. *Here* —3D **41**
Bredwardine. *Here* —1A **50**
Breinton. *Here* —2B **50**
Breinton Common. *Here* —2B **50**
Brelston Green. *Here* —3C **51**
Bretton. *Flin* —1A **18**
Bridell. *Pemb* —1A **44**
Bridgemere. *Ches* —3D **19**
Bridgend. *B'End* —1A **64**
Bridge Sollers. *Here* —1B **50**
Bridge Trafford. *Ches* —3B **10**
Bridgeyate. *S Glo* —2D **67**
Bridgnorth. *Shrp* —2D **33**
Bridstow. *Here* —3C **51**
Brierley. *Glos* —1D **61**
Brierley. *Here* —3B **40**
Brilley. *Here* —1D **49**
Brimaston. *Pemb* —3C **43**
Brimfield. *Here* —2C **41**
Brimstage. *Mers* —2A **10**
Brinsty Common. *Here* —3D **41**
Brislington. *S Glo* —2D **67**
Bristol. *Bris* —2C **67**
Bristol (Lulsgate) Airport. *N Som* —3C **67**
Brithdir. *Cphy* —2C **59**
Brithdir. *Cdgn* —1C **45**
Brithdir. *Gwyn* —3C **23**

Briton Ferry. *Neat* —3C **57**
Broadfield. *Pemb* —2A **54**
Broad Haven. *Pemb* —1B **52**
Broadheath. *Worc* —2D **41**
Broadlay. *Carm* —2C **55**
Broadmoor. *Pemb* —2D **53**
Broad Oak. *Carm* —3A **46**
Broadoak. *Glos* —1D **61**
Broad Oak. *Here* —3B **50**
Broadstone. *Shrp* —3C **33**
Broad, The. *Here* —2B **40**
Broadway. *Carm* —2C **55**
(Kidwelly)
Broadway. *Carm* —1B **54**
(Laugharne)
Broadway. *Pemb* —1B **52**
Broadwell. *Glos* —1C **61**
Brobury. *Here* —1A **50**
Brockhampton. *Here* —2C **51**
Brockley. *N Som* —3B **66**
Brockton. *Shrp* —3A **32**
(Bishop's Castle)
Brockton. *Shrp* —1D **33**
(Madeley)
Brockton. *Shrp* —2C **33**
(Much Wenlock)
Brockton. *Shrp* —1A **32**
(Pontesbury)
Brockton. *Telf* —3D **27**
Brockweir. *Glos* —2C **61**
Bromborough. *Mers* —2A **10**
Bromdon. *Shrp* —3D **33**
Bromfield. *Shrp* —1B **40**
Bromley. *Shrp* —2D **33**
Brompton. *Shrp* —1C **33**
Bromsash. *Here* —3D **51**
Bromsberrow Heath. *Glos* —2D **51**
Bromyard. *Here* —3D **41**
Bromyard Downs. *Here* —3D **41**
Bronaber. *Gwyn* —1C **23**
Broncroft. *Shrp* —3C **33**
Brongest. *Cdgn* —1C **45**
Brongwyn. *Cdgn* —1B **44**
Bronington. *Wrcx* 1B **26**
Bronllys. *Powy* —2C **49**
Bronnant. *Cdgn* —2B **36**
Bronwydd Arms. *Carm* —3D **45**
Bronydd. *Powy* —1D **49**
Bronygarth. *Shrp* —1D **25**
Brook. *Carm* —2B **54**
Brookend. *Glos* —2D **61**
Brookhurst. *Mers* —2A **10**
Brooklands. *Shrp* —3C **19**
Brooks. *Powy* —2C **31**
Broome. *Shrp* —2C **33**
(Cardington)
Broome. *Shrp* —3B **32**
(Craven Arms)
Broomedge. *Warr* —2D **11**
Broomhill. *Bris* —2D **67**
Broom's Green. *Glos* —2D **51**
Broseley. *Shrp* —1D **33**
Broughall. *Shrp* —3C **19**
Broughton. *Flin* —1A **18**
Broughton. *V Glam* —2A **64**
Brownhill. *Shrp* —2B **26**
Brownhills. *Shrp* —1D **27**
Brown Knowl. *Ches* —2B **18**
Broxton. *Ches* —2B **18**
Broxwood. *Here* —3A **40**
Bruera. *Ches* —1B **18**
Brymbo. *Cnwy* —3D **7**
Brymbo. *Wrex* —2D **17**
Bryn. *Carm* —2A **56**
Bryn. *G Man* —1C **11**
Bryn. *Neat* —3D **57**
Bryn. *Shrp* —3D **31**
Brynamman. *Carm* —1C **57**
Brynberian. *Pemb* —2A **44**
Brynbryddan. *Neat* —3C **57**
Bryncae. *Rhon* —1A **64**
Bryncethin. *B'End* —1A **64**
Bryncir. *Gwyn* —3D **13**
Bryn-coch. *Neat* —3C **57**
Bryncroes. *Gwyn* —1B **20**
Bryncrug. *Gwyn* —1B **28**
Bryn Du. *IOA* —3C **5**
Bryn Eden. *Gwyn* —2C **23**
Bryneglwys. *Den* —3C **17**
Bryn Eglwys. *Gwyn* —1B **14**
Brynford. *Flin* —3C **9**
Bryn Gates. *G Man* —1C **11**
Bryn Golau. *Rhon* —1B **64**
Brynwran. *IOA* —3C **5**
Bryngwran. *IOA* —3C **5**
Bryngwyn. *Mon* —2A **60**
Bryngwyn. *Powy* —1C **49**

Bryn-henllan. *Pemb* —2D **43**
Brynhoffnant. *Cdgn* —3C **35**
Bryn-llwyn. *Flin* —2B **8**
Brynllywarch. *Powy* —3C **31**
Bryn-mawr. *Blae* —1C **59**
Bryn-mawr. *Gwyn* —3B **22**
Brynmenyn. *B'End* —1A **64**
Brynmill. *Swan* —3B **56**
Brynna. *Rhon* —1A **64**
Brynrefail. *Gwyn* —1A **14**
Brynrefail. *IOA* —2D **5**
Brynsadler. *Rhon* —1B **64**
Bryn-Saith Marchog. *Den* —2B **16**
Brynsiencyn. *IOA* —1D **13**
Brynteg. *IOA* —2D **5**
Brynteg. *Wrex* —2A **18**
Brynygwenyn. *Mon* —1A **60**
Bryn-y-maen. *Cnwy* —3D **7**
Buckholt. *Here* —1C **61**
Buckland. *Here* —3C **41**
Buckley. *Flin* —1D **17**
Buckley Hill. *Mers* —1A **10**
Buckton. *Here* —1A **40**
Buildwas. *Shrp* —1D **33**
Builth Road. *Powy* —3B **38**
Builth Wells. *Powy* —3B **38**
Bulkeley. *Ches* —2C **19**
Bull Bay. *IOA* —1D **5**
Bullinghope. *Here* —2C **51**
Bunbury. *Ches* —2C **19**
Burcher. *Here* —2A **40**
Burcote. *Shrp* —2D **33**
Burford. *Shrp* —2C **41**
Burghill. *Here* —1B **50**
Burland. *Ches* —2B **19**
Burley Gate. *Here* —1C **51**
Burlingjobb. *Powy* —3D **39**
Burlton. *Shrp* —2B **26**
Burnett. *Bath* —3D **67**
Burnleydam. *Wrex* —3D **19**
Burrington. *Here* —1B **40**
Burrington. *N Som* —3B **66**
Burry. *Swan* —3D **55**
Burry Green. *Swan* —3D **55**
Burry Port. *Carm* —2D **55**
Burton. *Ches* —1C **19**
  (Kelsall)
Burton. *Ches* —3A **10**
  (Neston)
Burton. *Pemb* —2C **53**
Burton. *Wrex* —2A **18**
Burton Green. *Wrex* —2A **18**
Burtonwood. *Warr* —1C **11**
Burwardsley. *Ches* —2C **19**
Burwarton. *Shrp* —3D **33**
Burwen. *IOA* —1D **5**
Bury Hill. *S Glo* —1D **67**
Bush Bank. *Here* —3B **40**
Bushmoor. *Shrp* —3B **32**
Butcombe. *N Som* —3C **67**
Bute Town. *Cphy* —2C **59**
Butt Green. *Ches* —2D **19**
Buttington. *Powy* —1D **31**
Buttonbridge. *Shrp* —1D **41**
Buttonoak. *Shrp* —1D **41**
Bwcle. *Flin* —1D **17**
Bwlch. *Powy* —3C **49**
Bwlchderwin. *Gwyn* —3D **13**
Bwlchgwyn. *Wrex* —2D **17**
Bwlch-Llan. *Cdgn* —3A **36**
Bwlchnewydd. *Carm* —3C **45**
Bwlchtocyn. *Gwyn* —2C **21**
Bwlch-y-cibau. *Powy* —3C **25**
Bwlch-y-fadfa. *Cdgn* —1D **45**
Bwlch-y-ffridd. *Powy* —2A **30**
Bwlch y Garreg. *Powy* —2B **30**
Bwlch-y-groes. *Pemb* —2B **44**
Bwlch-yr-haiarn. *Cnwy* —2C **15**
Bwlch-y-sarnau. *Powy* —1B **38**
Byford. *Here* —1A **50**
Bylchau. *Cnwy* —1A **16**
Byley. *Ches* —1D **19**
Bynea. *Carm* —3A **56**
Byton. *Here* —2A **40**

Cadishead. *G Man* —1D **11**
Cadole. *Flin* —1D **17**
Cadoxton-Juxta-Neath. *Neat*
  —3C **57**
Cadwst. *Den* —1B **24**
Caeathro. *Gwyn* —1A **14**

Caehopkin. *Powy* —1D **57**
Caerau. *B'End* —3D **57**
Caerau. *Card* —2C **65**
Cae'r-bont. *Powy* —1D **57**
Cae'r-bryn. *Carm* —1A **56**
Caerdeon. *Gwyn* —3B **22**
Caerdydd. *Card* —2C **65**
Caerfarchell. *Pemb* —3A **42**
Caerffili. *Cphy* —1C **65**
Caerfyrddin. *Carm* —1D **55**
Caergeiliog. *IOA* —3B **5**
Caergwrle. *Flin* —2A **18**
Caergybi. *IOA* —2B **4**
Caerleon. *Newp* —3A **60**
Caerlleon. *Carm* —3B **44**
Caerllion. *Newp* —3A **60**
Caernarfon. *Gwyn* —1D **13**
Caerphilly. *Cphy* —1C **65**
Caersws. *Powy* —2B **30**
Caerwedros. *Cdgn* —3C **35**
Caerwent. *Mon* —3B **60**
Caerwys. *Flin* —3C **9**
Caim. *IOA* —2B **6**
Caio. *Carm* —3B **46**
Calcott. *Shrp* —3B **26**
Caldicot. *Mon* —1B **66**
Caldy. *Mers* —2D **9**
Caledfwlch. *Carm* —3B **46**
Callaughton. *Shrp* —2D **33**
Callow. *Here* —2B **50**
Callow Hill. *Worc* —1D **41**
Calveley. *Ches* —2C **19**
Calverhall. *Shrp* —1D **27**
Cam. *Glos* —3D **61**
Cambridge. *Glos* —2D **61**
Cameley. *Bath* —3D **67**
Camerton. *Bath* —3D **67**
Camrose. *Pemb* —1C **53**
Canaston Bridge. *Pemb* —1D **53**
Canon Bridge. *Here* —1B **50**
Canon Frome. *Here* —1D **51**
Canon Pyon. *Here* —1B **50**
Cantlop. *Shrp* —1C **33**
Canton. *Card* —2C **65**
Capel Bangor. *Cdgn* —3B **28**
Capel Betws Lleucu. *Cdgn* —3B **36**
Capel Coch. *IOA* —2D **5**
Capel Curig. *Cnwy* —2C **15**
Capel Cynon. *Cdgn* —1C **45**
Capel Dewi. *Carm* —3D **45**
Capel Dewi. *Cdgn* —3B **28**
  (Aberystwyth)
Capel Dewi. *Cdgn* —1D **45**
  (Llandysul)
Capel Garmon. *Cnwy* —2D **15**
Capel Gwyn. *IOA* —3C **5**
Capel Gwynfe. *Carm* —3C **47**
Capel Hendre. *Carm* —1A **56**
Capel Isaac. *Carm* —3A **46**
Capel Iwan. *Carm* —2B **44**
Capel Llanilterne. *Card* —2B **64**
Capel Mawr. *IOA* —3D **5**
Capel Newydd. *Pemb* —2B **44**
Capel Seion. *Carm* —1A **56**
Capel Seion. *Cdgn* —1B **36**
Capel Uchaf. *Gwyn* —3D **13**
Capel-y-ffin. *Powy* —2D **49**
Capenhurst. *Ches* —3A **10**
Cardeston. *Shrp* —3A **26**
Cardiff. *Card* —2C **65**
Cardiff Airport. *V Glam* —3B **64**
Cardigan. *Cdgn* —1A **44**
Cardington. *Shrp* —2C **33**
Carew. *Pemb* —2D **53**
Carew Cheriton. *Pemb* —2D **53**
Carew Newton. *Pemb* —2D **53**
Carey. *Here* —2C **51**
Carlingcott. *Bath* —3D **67**
Carmarthen. *Carm* —1D **55**
Carmel. *Carm* —1A **56**
Carmel. *Flin* —3C **9**
Carmel. *Gwyn* —2D **13**
Carmel. *IOA* —2C **5**
Carnhedryn. *Pemb* —3A **42**
Carno. *Powy* —2A **30**
Carreglefn. *IOA* —2C **5**
Carrington. *G Man* —1D **11**
Carrog. *Cnwy* —3C **15**
Carrog. *Den* —3C **17**
Carrow Hill. *Mon* —3B **60**
Carway. *Carm* —2D **55**
Cascob. *Powy* —2D **39**
Cas-gwent. *Mon* —3C **61**
Cas-Mael. *Pemb* —3D **43**
Casnewydd. *Newp* —1A **66**
Castell. *Cnwy* —1C **15**

Castell. *Den* —1C **17**
Castell Hendre. *Pemb* —3D **43**
Castell-nedd. *Neat* —3C **57**
Castell Newydd Emlyn. *Carm* —1C **45**
Castell-y-bwch. *Torf* —3D **59**
Castlebythe. *Pemb* —3D **43**
Castle Caereinion. *Powy* —1C **31**
Castle Frome. *Here* —1D **51**
Castlemartin. *Pemb* —3C **53**
Castlemorris. *Pemb* —2C **43**
Castleton. *Newp* —1D **65**
Caswell. *Swan* —1A **62**
Catbrook. *Mon* —2C **61**
Cathedine. *Powy* —3C **49**
Catherton. *Shrp* —1D **41**
Cat's Ash. *Newp* —3A **60**
Caynham. *Shrp* —1C **41**
Cefn Berain. *Cnwy* —1A **16**
Cefn-brith. *Cnwy* —2A **16**
Cefn-bryn-brain. *Carm* —1C **57**
Cefn Bychan. *Cphy* —3D **59**
Cefn-bychan. *Flin* —1C **17**
Cefncaeau. *Carm* —3A **56**
Cefn Canol. *Powy* —1D **25**
Cefn-coch. *Powy* —2C **25**
Cefn-coed-y-cymmer. *Mer T* —2B **58**
Cefn Cribwr. *B'End* —1D **63**
Cefn-ddwysarn. *Gwyn* —1A **24**
Cefn Einion. *Shrp* —3D **31**
Cefneithin. *Carm* —1A **56**
Cefn Glas. *B'End* —1D **63**
Cefngorwydd. *Powy* —1A **48**
Cefn Llwyd. *Cdgn* —3B **28**
Cefn-mawr. *Wrex* —3D **17**
Cefn-y-bedd. *Wrex* —2A **18**
Cefn-y-coed. *Powy* —2C **31**
Cefn-y-pant. *Carm* —3A **44**
Cegidfa. *Powy* —3D **25**
Ceinewydd. *Cdgn* —3C **35**
Cellan. *Cdgn* —1B **46**
Cemaes. *IOA* —1C **5**
Cemmaes. *Powy* —1D **29**
Cemmaes Road. *Powy* —1D **29**
Cenarth. *Carm* —1B **44**
Cenin. *Gwyn* —3D **13**
Ceri. *Powy* —3C **31**
Cerist. *Powy* —3A **30**
Cerrigceinwen. *IOA* —3D **5**
Cerrigydrudion. *Cnwy* —3A **16**
Ceunant. *Gwyn* —1A **14**
Chadwick Green. *Mers* —1C **11**
Chancery. *Cdgn* —1A **36**
Chapel Hill. *Mon* —2C **61**
Chapel Lawn. *Shrp* —1A **40**
Charfield. *S Glo* —3D **61**
Charlcombe. *Bath* —3D **67**
Charlton. *Telf* —3C **27**
Chatwall. *Shrp* —2C **33**
Chaxhill. *Glos* —1D **61**
Checkley. *Ches* —3D **19**
Checkley. *Here* —2C **51**
Chelmarsh. *Shrp* —3D **33**
Chelmick. *Shrp* —2B **32**
Chelvey. *N Som* —3B **66**
Chelwood. *Bath* —3D **67**
Cheney Longville. *Shrp* —3B **32**
Chepstow. *Mon* —3C **61**
Cheriton. *Pemb* —3C **53**
Cheriton. *Swan* —3D **55**
Cherrington. *Telf* —2D **27**
Chester. *Ches* —1B **18**
Cheswardine. *Shrp* —2D **27**
Cheswell. *Telf* —3D **27**
Chetton. *Shrp* —2D **33**
Chetwynd Aston. *Telf* —3D **27**
Chew Magna. *Bath* —3C **67**
Chew Stoke. *Bath* —3C **67**
Chewton Keynsham. *Bath* —3D **67**
Chickward. *Here* —3D **39**
Childer Thornton. *Ches* —3A **10**
Child's Ercall. *Shrp* —2D **27**
Childwall. *Mers* —2B **10**
Chipnall. *Shrp* —1D **27**
Chipping Sodbury. *S Glo* —1D **67**
Chirbury. *Shrp* —2D **31**
Chirk. *Wrex* —1D **25**
Cholstrey. *Here* —3B **40**
Chorley. *Ches* —2C **19**
Chorley. *Shrp* —3D **33**
Chorlton. *Ches* —2D **19**
Chorlton Lane. *Ches* —3B **18**
Choulton. *Shrp* —3A **32**
Christchurch. *Glos* —1C **61**
Christleton. *Ches* —1B **18**
Christon. *N Som* —3A **66**
Church Aston. *Telf* —3D **27**

Church End. *Glos* —2D **61**
Church Hill. *Ches* —1D **19**
Churchill. *N Som* —3A **66**
Church Minshull. *Ches* —1D **19**
Church Preen. *Shrp* —2C **33**
Church Pulverbatch. *Shrp* —1B **32**
Church Stoke. *Powy* —2D **31**
Church Stretton. *Shrp* —2B **32**
Churchtown. *Shrp* —3D **31**
Church Village. *Rhon* —1B **64**
Churton. *Ches* —2B **18**
Chwilog. *Gwyn* —1D **21**
Chwitffordd. *Flin* —3C **9**
Cilan Uchaf. *Gwyn* —2B **20**
Cilcain. *Flin* —1C **17**
Cilcennin. *Cdgn* —3A **36**
Cilfrew. *Neat* —2C **57**
Cilfynydd. *Rhon* —3B **58**
Cilgerran. *Pemb* —1A **44**
Cilgeti. *Pemb* —2A **54**
Cilgwyn. *Carm* —3C **47**
Cilgwyn. *Pemb* —2D **43**
Ciliau Aeron. *Cdgn* —3D **35**
Cilmaengwyn. *Neat* —2C **57**
Cilmery. *Powy* —3B **38**
Cilrhedyn. *Pemb* —2B **44**
Cilsan. *Carm* —3A **46**
Ciltalgarth. *Gwyn* —3D **15**
Ciltwrch. *Powy* —1C **49**
Cilybebyll. *Neat* —2C **57**
Cilycwm. *Carm* —2C **47**
Cimla. *Neat* —3C **57**
Cinderford. *Glos* —1D **61**
Cippyn. *Pemb* —1A **44**
City. *Powy* —2D **31**
City. *V Glam* —2A **64**
City Dulas. *IOA* —2D **5**
Clapton-in-Gordano. *N Som* —2B **66**
Clarbeston. *Pemb* —3D **43**
Clarbeston Road. *Pemb* —3D **43**
Clatter. *Powy* —2A **30**
Claughton. *Mers* —2A **10**
Claverham. *N Som* —3B **66**
Clawdd-coch. *V Glam* —2B **64**
Clawdd-newydd. *Den* —2B **16**
Clay Hill. *Bris* —2D **67**
Clearwell. *Glos* —2C **61**
Cleedownton. *Shrp* —3C **33**
Cleehill. *Shrp* —1C **41**
Cleestanton. *Shrp* —1C **41**
Clee St Margaret. *Shrp* —3C **33**
Cleeton St Mary. *Shrp* —1D **41**
Cleeve. *N Som* —3B **66**
Clehonger. *Here* —2B **50**
Cleobury Mortimer. *Shrp* —1D **41**
Cleobury North. *Shrp* —3D **33**
Clevedon. *N Som* —2B **66**
Clifford's Mesne. *Glos* —3D **51**
Clifton. *Bris* —2C **67**
Clifton Hill. *Worc* —2D **41**
Clifton-upon-Teme. *Worc* —2D **41**
Clipiau. *Gwyn* —3D **23**
Clive. *Shrp* —2C **27**
Clocaenog. *Den* —2B **16**
Clock Face. *Mers* —1C **11**
Cloddiau. *Powy* —1D **31**
Clodock. *Here* —3A **50**
Clotton. *Ches* —1C **19**
Clows Top. *Worc* —1D **41**
Cloy. *Wrex* —3A **18**
Cluddley. *Telf* —1D **33**
Clun. *Shrp* —3A **32**
Clunbury. *Shrp* —3A **32**
Clunderwen. *Carm* —1A **54**
Clungunford. *Shrp* —1A **40**
Clunton. *Shrp* —3A **32**
Clutton. *Bath* —3D **67**
Clutton. *Ches* —2B **18**
Clwt-y-bont. *Gwyn* —1A **14**
Clwydfagwyr. *Mer T* —2B **58**
Clydach. *Mon* —1D **59**
Clydach. *Swan* —2B **56**
Clydach Vale. *Rhon* —3A **58**
Clydey. *Pemb* —2B **44**
Clyne. *Neat* —2D **57**
Clynnog-fawr. *Gwyn* —3D **13**
Clyro. *Powy* —1D **49**
Cnwcau. *Pemb* —1B **44**
Cnwch Coch. *Cdgn* —1B **36**
Coalbrookdale. *Telf* —1D **33**
Coalbrookvale. *Blae* —2D **59**
Coalpit Heath. *S Glo* —1D **67**
Coalport. *Telf* —1D **33**
Coalway. *Glos* —1C **61**
Cobhall Common. *Here* —2B **50**
Cobnash. *Here* —2B **40**

Cock Bank. *Wrex* —3A **18**
Cock Gate. *Here* —2B **40**
Cockshutford. *Shrp* —3C **33**
Cockshutt. *Shrp* —2B **26**
Cockyard. *Here* —2B **50**
Coddington. *Ches* —2B **18**
Coddington. *Here* —1D **51**
Codrington. *S Glo* —2D **67**
Coed Duon. *Cphy* —3C **59**
Coedely. *Rhon* —1B **64**
Coedglasson. *Powy* —2B **38**
Coedkernew. *Newp* —1D **65**
Coed Morgan. *Mon* —1A **60**
Coedpoeth. *Wrex* —2D **17**
Coedway. *Powy* —3A **26**
Coed-y-bryn. *Cdgn* —1C **45**
Coed-y-paen. *Mon* —3A **60**
Coed-yr-ynys. *Powy* —3C **49**
Coed Ystumgwern. *Gwyn* —2A **22**
Coelbren. *Powy* —1D **57**
Cogan. *V Glam* —2C **65**
Coity. *B'End* —1A **64**
Cold Ashton. *S Glo* —2D **67**
Cold Blow. *Pemb* —1A **54**
Coldharbour. *Glos* —2C **61**
Cold Hatton. *Telf* —2D **27**
Cold Hatton Heath. *Telf* —2D **27**
Coldwell. *Here* —2B **50**
Colebatch. *Shrp* —3A **32**
Coleford. *Glos* —1C **61**
Colemere. *Shrp* —1B **26**
Colemore Green. *Shrp* —2D **33**
Collins Green. *Warr* —1C **11**
Collins Green. *Worc* —3D **41**
Colwall Green. *Here* —1D **51**
Colwall Stone. *Here* —1D **51**
Colwinston. *V Glam* —2A **64**
Colwyn Bay. *Cnwy* —3D **7**
Combe. *Here* —2A **40**
Combe Hay. *Bath* —3D **67**
Combe Moor. *Here* —2A **40**
Comberbach. *Ches* —3D **11**
Comberton. *Here* —2B **40**
Comins Coch. *Cdgn* —3B **28**
Comley. *Shrp* —2B **32**
Commins. *Powy* —2C **25**
Commins Coch. *Powy* —1D **29**
Common Hill. *Here* —2C **51**
Commonside. *Ches* —3C **11**
Compton Dando. *Bath* —3D **67**
Compton Greenfield. *S Glo* —1C **67**
Compton Martin. *Bath* —3C **67**
Condover. *Shrp* —1B **32**
Congl-y-wal. *Gwyn* —3C **15**
Congresbury. *N Som* —3B **66**
Conham. *S Glo* —2D **67**
Connah's Quay. *Flin* —1D **17**
Conwy. *Cnwy* —3C **7**
Coppenhall. *Ches* —2D **19**
Coppenhall Moss. *Ches* —2D **19**
Coppicegate. *Shrp* —3D **33**
Coptiviney. *Shrp* —1B **26**
Coreley. *Shrp* —1D **41**
Corfton. *Shrp* —3B **32**
Corlannau. *Neat* —3C **57**
Corntown. *V Glam* —2A **64**
Corris. *Gwyn*   1C **29**
Corris Uchaf. *Gwyn* —1C **29**
Corston. *Bath* —3D **67**
Corwen. *Den* —3B **16**
Cosheston. *Pemb* —2D **53**
Cosmeston. *V Glam* —3C **65**
Cotebrook. *Ches* —1C **19**
Cotland. *Mon* —2C **61**
Coton Hill. *Shrp* —3B **26**
Cotonwood. *Shrp* —1D **27**
Coughton. *Here* —3C **51**
Cound. *Shrp* —1C **33**
Court Henry. *Carm* —3A **46**
Cowbridge. *V Glam* —2A **64**
Cowslip Green. *N Som* —3B **66**
Coxall. *Here* —1A **40**
Coxbank. *Ches* —3D **19**
Coychurch. *V Glam* —1A **64**
Coytrahen. *B'End* —1D **63**
Crabtree Green. *Wrex* —3A **18**
Crackleybank. *Shrp* —3D **27**
Cradley. *Here* —1D **51**
Cradoc. *Powy* —2B **48**
Crai. *Powy* —3D **47**
Craig-cefn-parc. *Swan* —2B **56**
Craig-llwyn. *Shrp* —2D **25**
Craignant. *Shrp* —1D **25**
Craig-y-Duke. *Neat* —2C **57**
Craig-y-nos. *Powy* —1D **57**
Cranage. *Ches* —1D **19**

Crank. *Mers* —1C **11**
Craven Arms. *Shrp* —3B **32**
Crawford. *Lanc* —1B **10**
Creamore Bank. *Shrp* —1C **27**
Credenhill. *Here* —1B **50**
Cregrina. *Powy* —3C **39**
Creigiau. *Card* —1B **64**
Cressage. *Shrp* —1C **33**
Cresselly. *Pemb* —2D **53**
Cresswell Quay. *Pemb* —2D **53**
Crewe. *Ches* —2B **18**
(Farndon)
Crewe. *Ches* —2D **19**
(Nantwich)
Crewgreen. *Powy* —3A **26**
Cribbs Causeway. *S Glo* —2C **67**
Cribyn. *Cdgn* —3A **36**
Criccieth. *Gwyn* —1D **21**
Crick. *Mon* —3B **60**
Crickadarn. *Powy* —1B **48**
Crickheath. *Shrp* —2D **25**
Crickhowell. *Powy* —1D **59**
Criggion. *Powy* —3D **25**
Crinow. *Pemb* —1A **54**
Crocker's Ash. *Here* —1C **61**
Croeserw. *Neat* —3D **57**
Croes-Goch. *Pemb* —2B **42**
Croes Hywel. *Mon* —1A **60**
Croes-lan. *Cdgn* —1C **45**
Croesor. *Gwyn* —3B **14**
Croesowallt. *Shrp* —2D **25**
Croesyceiliog. *Carm* —1D **55**
Croesyceiliog. *Torf* —3A **60**
Croes-y-mwyalch. *Newp* —3A **60**
Croesywaun. *Gwyn* —2A **14**
Croft. *Warr* —1D **11**
Crofty. *Swan* —3A **56**
Cromhall. *S Glo* —3D **61**
Cromhall Common. *S Glo* —1D **67**
Cronton. *Mers* —2B **10**
Crosby. *Mers* —1A **10**
Cross Ash. *Mon* —1B **60**
Cross Foxes. *Gwyn* —3C **23**
Crossgates. *Powy* —2B **38**
Cross Hands. *Carm* —1A **56**
(Ammanford)
Crosshands. *Carm* —3A **44**
(Whitland)
Cross Hill. *Glos* —3C **61**
Cross Houses. *Shrp* —1C **33**
Cross Inn. *Cdgn* —2A **36**
(Aberaeron)
Cross Inn. *Cdgn* —3C **35**
(New Quay)
Cross Inn. *Rhon* —1B **64**
Crosskeys. *Cphy* —3D **59**
Cross Lane Head. *Shrp* —2D **33**
Crosslanes. *Shrp* —3A **26**
Cross Lanes. *Wrex* —3A **18**
Cross Oak. *Powy* —3C **49**
Crossway. *Mon* —1B **60**
Crossway. *Powy* —3B **38**
Crossway Green. *Mon* —3C **61**
Crosswell. *Pemb* —2A **44**
Crosswood. *Cdgn* —1B **36**
Crow Hill. *Here* —3D **51**
Crowton. *Ches* —3C **11**
Croxton Green. *Ches* —2C **19**
Cruckmeore. *Shrp* —1B **32**
Cruckton. *Shrp* —3B **26**
Crudgington. *Telf* —2D **27**
Crug. *Powy* —1C **39**
Crughywel. *Powy* —1D **59**
Crugybar. *Carm* —2B **46**
Crug-y-byddar. *Powy* —3C **31**
Crumlin. *Cphy* —3D **59**
Crumpsbrook. *Shrp* —1D **41**
Crundale. *Pemb* —1C **53**
Crwbin. *Carm* —1D **55**
Crymych. *Pemb* —2A **44**
Crynant. *Neat* —2C **57**
Cublington. *Here* —2A **50**
Cuddington. *Ches* —3D **11**
Cuddington Heath. *Ches* —3B **18**
Cuerdley Cross. *Warr* —2C **11**
Culcheth. *Warr* —1D **11**
Culmington. *Shrp* —3B **32**
Cusop. *Here* —1D **49**
Cutiau. *Gwyn* —3B **22**
Cuttybridge. *Pemb* —1C **53**
Cwm. *Blae* —2C **59**
Cwm. *Den* —3B **8**
Cwm. *Powy* —2D **31**
Cwmafan. *Neat* —3C **57**
Cwmaman. *Rhon* —3A **58**
Cwmann. *Carm* —1A **46**

Cwmbach. *Carm* —3B **44**
Cwmbach. *Powy* —2C **49**
Cwmbach. *Rhon* —2B **58**
Cwmbach Llechryd. *Powy* —3B **38**
Cwmbelan. *Powy* —3A **30**
Cwmbran. *Torf* —3D **59**
Cwmbrwyno. *Cdgn* —3C **29**
Cwm Capel. *Carm* —2D **55**
Cwmcarn. *Cphy* —3D **59**
Cwmcarvan. *Mon* —2B **60**
Cwm-celyn. *Blae* —2D **59**
Cwmcerdinen. *Swan* —2B **56**
Cwm-Cewydd. *Gwyn* —3D **23**
Cwmcoy. *Cdgn* —1B **44**
Cwmcrawnon. *Powy* —1C **59**
Cwmcych. *Pemb* —2B **44**
Cwmdare. *Rhon* —2A **58**
Cwmdu. *Carm* —2B **46**
Cwmdu. *Powy* —3C **49**
Cwmduad. *Carm* —2C **45**
Cwm Dulais. *Swan* —2B **56**
Cwmerfyn. *Cdgn* —3B **28**
Cwmfelin. *B'End* —1D **63**
Cwmfelin Boeth. *Carm* —1A **54**
Cwmfelinfach. *Cphy* —3C **59**
Cwmfelin Mynach. *Carm* —3B **44**
Cwmffrwd. *Carm* —1D **55**
Cwmgiedd. *Powy* —1C **57**
Cwmgors. *Neat* —1C **57**
Cwmgwili. *Carm* —1A **56**
Cwmgwrach. *Neat* —2D **57**
Cwmhiraeth. *Carm* —2C **45**
Cwmifor. *Carm* —3B **46**
Cwmisfael. *Carm* —1D **55**
Cwm-Llinau. *Powy* —1D **29**
Cwmllynfell. *Neat* —1C **57**
Cwm-mawr. *Carm* —1A **56**
Cwm-miles. *Carm* —3A **44**
Cwmorgan. *Carm* —2B **44**
Cwmparc. *Rhon* —3A **58**
Cwm Penmachno. *Cnwy* —3C **15**
Cwmpennar. *Rhon* —2B **58**
Cwm Plysgog. *Pemb* —1A **44**
Cwmrhos. *Powy* —3C **49**
Cwmsychpant. *Cdgn* —1D **45**
Cwmsyfiog. *Cphy* —2C **59**
Cwmsymlog. *Cdgn* —3B **28**
Cwmtillery. *Blae* —2D **59**
Cwm-twrch Isaf. *Powy* —2C **57**
Cwm-twrch Uchaf. *Powy* —1C **57**
Cwmwysg. *Powy* —3D **47**
Cwm-y-glo. *Gwyn* —1A **14**
Cwmyoy. *Mon* —3A **50**
Cwmystwyth. *Cdgn* —1C **37**
Cwrt. *Gwyn* —2B **28**
Cwrtnewydd. *Cdgn* —1D **45**
Cwrt-y-Cadno. *Carm* —1B **46**
Cydweli. *Carm* —2D **55**
Cyffylliog. *Den* —2B **16**
Cymau. *Flin* —2D **17**
Cymmer. *Neat* —3D **57**
Cymmer. *Rhon* —3B **58**
Cyncoed. *Card* —1C **65**
Cynghordy. *Carm* —2D **47**
Cynghordy. *Swan* —2B **56**
Cynheidre. *Carm* —2D **55**
Cynonville. *Neat* —3D **57**
Cynwyd. *Den* —3B **16**
Cynwyl Elfed. *Carm* —3C **45**
Cywarch. *Gwyn* —3D **23**

Dafen. *Carm* —2A **56**
Dale. *Pemb* —2B **52**
Danesford. *Shrp* —2D **33**
Daren. *Powy* —1D **59**
Daresbury. *Hal* —2C **11**
Darliston. *Shrp* —1C **27**
Darowen. *Powy* —1D **29**
Davenham. *Ches* —3D **11**
David's Well. *Powy* —1B **38**
Dawley. *Telf* —1D **33**
Dawn. *Cnwy* —3D **7**
Daywall. *Shrp* —1D **25**
Ddol. *Flin* —3C **9**
Ddol Cownwy. *Powy* —3B **24**
Dean Park. *Powy* —2C **41**
Defynnog. *Powy* —3A **48**
Deganwy. *Cnwy* —3C **7**
Deiniolen. *Gwyn* —1A **14**
Delamere. *Ches* —1C **19**
Denbigh. *Den* —2B **16**
Denio. *Gwyn* —1C **21**
Deri. *Cphy* —2C **59**
Derrington. *Shrp* —2D **33**
Derwen. *Den* —2B **16**

Derwen Gam. *Cdgn* —3D **35**
Derwenlas. *Powy* —2C **29**
Deuddwr. *Powy* —3D **25**
Devauden. *Mon* —3B **60**
Devil's Bridge. *Cdgn* —1C **37**
Dewshall Court. *Here* —2B **50**
Diddlebury. *Shrp* —3C **33**
Didley. *Here* —2B **50**
Dihewyd. *Cdgn* —3D **35**
Dilwyn. *Here* —3B **40**
Dinas. *Carm* —2B **44**
Dinas. *Gwyn* —1B **20**
Dinas. *Pemb* —2D **43**
Dinas Dinlle. *Gwyn* —2D **13**
Dinas Mawddwy. *Gwyn* —3D **23**
Dinas Powys. *V Glam* —2C **65**
Dinbych. *Den* —1B **16**
Dinbych-y-Pysgod. *Pemb* —2A **54**
Dinedor. *Here* —2C **51**
Dinedor Cross. *Here* —2C **51**
Dingestow. *Mon* —1B **60**
Dingle. *Mers* —2A **10**
Dinmael. *Cnwy* —3B **16**
Dinorwic. *Gwyn* —1A **14**
Discoed. *Powy* —2D **39**
Disserth. *Powy* —3B **38**
Ditton. *Hal* —2B **10**
Ditton Priors. *Shrp* —3D **33**
Dixton. *Mon* —1C **61**
Dobs Hill. *Flin* —1A **18**
Dobson's Bridge. *Shrp* —1B **26**
Docklow. *Here* —3C **41**
Doc Penfro. *Pemb* —2C **53**
Doddington. *Shrp* —1D **41**
Dodington. *S Glo* —1D **67**
Dodleston. *Ches* —1A **18**
Dolanog. *Powy* —3B **24**
Dolau. *Powy* —2C **39**
Dolau. *Rhon* —1B **64**
Dolbenmaen. *Gwyn* —3A **14**
Doley. *Shrp* —2D **27**
Dol-fach. *Powy* —1A **30**
(Llanbrynmair)
Dolfach. *Powy* —1A **38**
(Llanidloes)
Dolfor. *Powy* —3C **31**
Dolgarrog. *Cnwy* —1C **15**
Dolgellau. *Gwyn* —3C **23**
Dolgoch. *Gwyn* —1B **28**
Dol-gran. *Carm* —2D **45**
Dolhelfa. *Powy* —1A **38**
Dolley Green. *Powy* —2D **39**
Dollwen. *Cdgn* —3B **28**
Dolphin. *Flin* —3C **9**
Dolwen. *Cnwy* —3D **7**
Dolwyddelan. *Cnwy* —2C **15**
Dol-y-Bont. *Cdgn* —3B **28**
Dolyhir. *Powy* —3D **39**
Domgay. *Powy* —3D **25**
Donnington. *Here* —2D **51**
Donnington. *Shrp* —1C **33**
Donnington. *Telf* —3D **27**
Dormington. *Here* —1C **51**
Dorrington. *Shrp* —1B **32**
Dorstone. *Here* —1A **50**
Dovaston. *Shrp* —2A **26**
Dowlais. *Mer T* —2B **58**
Downall Green. *G Man* —1C **11**
Downend. *S Glo* —2D **67**
Down, The. *Shrp* —2D **33**
Downton on the Rock. *Here* —1B **40**
Doynton. *S Glo* —2D **67**
Draethen. *Cphy* —1D **65**
Dreenhill. *Pemb* —1C **53**
Drefach. *Carm* —1A **56**
(Meidrim)
Drefach. *Carm* —2C **45**
(Newcastle Emlyn)
Drefach. *Carm* —3B **44**
(Tumble)
Drefach. *Carm* —1A **46**
Drope. *V Glam* —2C **65**
Druid. *Den* —3B **16**
Druidston. *Pemb* —1B **52**
Drury. *Flin* —1D **17**
Drybrook. *Glos* —1D **61**
Drybrook. *Here* —1C **61**
Dryslwyn. *Carm* —3A **46**
Dryton. *Shrp* —1C **33**
Duckington. *Ches* —2B **18**
Duddon. *Ches* —1C **19**
Dudleston. *Shrp* —1A **26**
Dudleston Heath. *Shrp* —1A **26**
Dudston. *Shrp* —2D **31**
Dudwells. *Pemb* —3C **43**
Duffryn. *Neat* —3D **57**

Dukestown. *Blae* —1C **59**
Dulas. *IOA* —2D **5**
Dundry. *N Som* —3C **67**
Dunham-on-the-Hill. *Ches* —3B **10**
Dunham Town. *G Man* —2D **11**
Dunham Woodhouses. *G Man*
    —2D **11**
Dunkerton. *Bath* —3D **67**
Dunvant. *Swan* —3A **56**
Durlow Common. *Here* —2D **51**
Dursley. *Glos* —3D **61**
Dursley Cross. *Glos* —1D **61**
Dutlas. *Powy* —1D **39**
Dutton. *Ches* —3C **11**
Dwygyfylchi. *Cnwy* —3C **7**
Dwyran. *IOA* —1D **13**
Dyffryn. *B'End* —3D **57**
Dyffryn. *Carm* —3C **45**
Dyffryn. *IOA* —3B **4**
Dyffryn. *Pemb* —2C **43**
Dyffryn. *V Glam* —2B **64**
Dyffryn Ardudwy. *Gwyn* —2A **22**
Dyffryn Castell. *Cdgn* —3C **29**
Dyffryn Ceidrych. *Carm* —3C **47**
Dyffryn Cellwen. *Neat* —1D **57**
Dylife. *Powy* —2D **29**
Dymock. *Glos* —2D **51**
Dyrham. *S Glo* —2D **67**
Dyserth. *Den* —3B **8**

Eardington. *Shrp* —2D **33**
Eardisland. *Here* —3B **40**
Eardisley. *Here* —1A **50**
Eardiston. *Shrp* —2A **26**
Eardiston. *Worc* —2D **41**
Earlestown. *Mers* —1C **11**
Earlswood. *Mon* —3B **58**
Earthcott Green. *S Glo* —1D **67**
East Aberthaw. *V Glam* —3B **64**
East Clevedon. *N Som* —2B **66**
East Dean. *Glos* —3D **51**
East Dundry. *N Som* —3C **67**
East End. *N Som* —3B **66**
Easter Compton. *S Glo* —1C **67**
Eastham. *Mers* —2A **10**
Eastham. *Worc* —2D **41**
Eastham Ferry. *Mers* —2A **10**
Easthampton. *Here* —2B **40**
East Harptree. *Bath* —3C **67**
Easthope. *Shrp* —2C **33**
Eastnor. *Here* —2D **51**
Easton-in-Gordano. *N Som* —2C **67**
East Wall. *Shrp* —2C **33**
East Williamston. *Pemb* —2D **53**
Eaton. *Ches* —1C **19**
Eaton. *Shrp* —3A **32**
  (Bishop's Castle)
Eaton. *Shrp* —2C **33**
  (Church Stretton)
Eaton Bishop. *Here* —2B **50**
Eaton Constantine. *Shrp* —1C **33**
Eaton upon Tern. *Shrp* —3D **27**
Ebbw Vale. *Blae* —2C **59**
Ebnal. *Ches* —3B **18**
Eccles Green. *Here* —1A **50**
Eccleston. *Ches* —1B **18**
Eccleston. *Mers* —1B **10**
Edern. *Gwyn* —1B **20**
Edge. *Shrp* —1A **32**
Edgebolton. *Shrp* —2C **27**
Edge End. *Glos* —1C **61**
Edge Green. *Ches* —2B **18**
Edgeley. *Shrp* —3C **19**
Edgmond. *Telf* —3D **27**
Edgmond Marsh. *Telf* —2D **27**
Edgton. *Shrp* —3A **32**
Edstaston. *Shrp* —1C **27**
Edwardsville. *Mer T* —3B **58**
Edwinsford. *Carm* —2B **46**
Edwyn Ralph. *Here* —3B **41**
Efail-fach. *Neat* —3C **57**
Efail Isaf. *Rhon* —1B **64**
Efailnewydd. *Gwyn* —1C **21**
Efail-rhyd. *Powy* —2C **25**
Efailwen. *Carm* —3A **44**
Efenechtyd. *Den* —2C **17**
Eglwysbach. *Cnwy* —3D **7**
Eglwys Brewis. *V Glam* —3B **64**
Eglwys Fach. *Cdgn* —2B **28**
Eglwyswrw. *Pemb* —2A **44**
Egremont. *Mers* —1A **10**
Eisingrug. *Gwyn* —1B **22**
Elan Village. *Powy* —2A **38**
Elberton. *S Glo* —1D **67**
Ellerdine. *Telf* —2D **27**

Ellerdine Heath. *Telf* —2D **27**
Ellerton. *Shrp* —2D **27**
Ellesmere. *Shrp* —1B **26**
Ellesmere Port. *Ches* —3B **10**
Ellwood. *Glos* —2C **61**
Elton. *Ches* —3B **10**
Elton. *Glos* —1D **61**
Elton. *Here* —1B **40**
Elton Green. *Ches* —3B **10**
Elworth. *Ches* —1D **19**
Ely. *Card* —2C **65**
Enchmarsh. *Shrp* —2C **33**
Engine Common. *S Glo* —1D **67**
Engleseabrook. *Ches* —2D **19**
English Bicknor. *Glos* —1C **61**
Englishcombe. *Bath* —3D **67**
English Frankton. *Shrp* —2B **26**
Ensdon. *Shrp* —3B **26**
Erbistock. *Wrex* —3A **18**
Erwood. *Powy* —1B **48**
Eryrys. *Den* —2D **17**
Esgair. *Carm* —3C **45**
  (Carmarthen)
Esgair. *Carm* —1B **54**
  (St Clears)
Esgairgeiliog. *Powy* —1C **29**
Etloe. *Glos* —2D **61**
Ettiley Heath. *Ches* —1D **19**
Eudon Burnell. *Shrp* —3D **33**
Eudon George. *Shrp* —3D **33**
Evanstown. *B'End* —1A **64**
Evendine. *Here* —1D **51**
Evenjobb. *Powy* —2D **39**
Everton. *Mers* —1A **10**
Evesbatch. *Here* —1D **51**
Ewdness. *Shrp* —2D **33**
Ewenny. *V Glam* —2A **64**
Ewlo. *Flin* —1A **18**
Ewloe. *Flin* —1A **18**
Ewyas Harold. *Here* —3A **50**
Exfords Green. *Shrp* —1B **32**
Eye. *Here* —2B **40**
Eyton. *Here* —2B **40**
Eyton. *Shrp* —3A **32**
  (Bishop's Castle)
Eyton. *Shrp* —3A **26**
  (Shrewsbury)
Eyton. *Wrex* —3A **18**
Eyton on Severn. *Shrp* —1C **33**
Eyton upon the Weald Moors. *Telf*
  —3D **27**

Faddiley. *Ches* —2C **19**
Fagwyr. *Swan* —2B **56**
Failand. *N Som* —2C **67**
Fairbourne. *Gwyn* —3B **22**
Fairwater. *Card* —2C **65**
Falcon. *Here* —2D **51**
Falfield. *S Glo* —3D **61**
Far Forest. *Worc* —1D **41**
Farleigh. *N Som* —3B **66**
Farley. *N Som* —2B **66**
Farley. *Shrp* —1A **32**
  (Shrewsbury)
Farley. *Shrp* —1D **33**
  (Telford)
Farlow. *Shrp* —3D **33**
Farmborough. *Bath* —3D **67**
Far Moor. *G Man* —1C **11**
Farndon. *Ches* —2B **18**
Farnworth. *Hal* —2C **11**
Fauls. *Shrp* —1C **27**
Fawley Chapel. *Here* —3C **51**
Fazakerley. *Mers* —1A **10**
Fearnhead. *Warr* —1D **11**
Felhampton. *Shrp* —3B **32**
Felindre. *Carm* —3A **46**
  (Llandeilo)
Felindre. *Carm* —2B **46**
  (Llandovery)
Felindre. *Carm* —2C **45**
  (Newcastle Emlyn)
Felindre. *Powy* —3C **31**
Felindre. *Swan* —2B **56**
Felindre Farchog. *Pemb* —2A **44**
Felinfach. *Cdgn* —3A **36**
Felinfach. *Powy* —2B **48**
Felinfoel. *Carm* —2A **56**
Felingwmisaf. *Carm* —3A **46**
Felingwmuchaf. *Carm* —3A **46**
Felin Newydd. *Powy* —1B **30**
  (Newtown)
Felin Newydd. *Powy* —2D **25**
  (Oswestry)
Felin Wnda. *Cdgn* —1C **45**

Felinwynt. *Cdgn* —3B **34**
Felton. *Here* —1C **51**
Felton. *N Som* —3C **67**
Felton Butler. *Shrp* —3A **26**
Fenn's Bank. *Wrex* —1C **27**
Ferndale. *Rhon* —3A **58**
Ferryside. *Carm* —1C **55**
Ffairfach. *Carm* —3B **46**
Ffair Rhos. *Cdgn* —2C **37**
Ffaldybrenin. *Carm* —1B **46**
Ffarmers. *Carm* —1B **46**
Ffawyddog. *Powy* —1D **59**
Ffestiniog. *Gwyn* —3C **15**
Fforest. *Carm* —2A **56**
Fforest-fach. *Swan* —3B **56**
Fforest Goch. *Neat* —2C **57**
Ffostrasol. *Cdgn* —1C **45**
Ffos-y-ffin. *Cdgn* —2D **35**
Ffrith. *Den* —3B **26**
Ffrwdgrech. *Powy* —3B **48**
Ffynnon-ddrain. *Carm* —3D **45**
Ffynnongroyw. *Flin* —2C **9**
Ffynnon Gynydd. *Powy* —1C **49**
Ffynnonoer. *Cdgn* —3A **36**
Filton. *Bris* —2D **67**
Fishguard. *Pemb* —2C **43**
Fishponds. *Bris* —2D **67**
Fishpool. *Glos* —3D **51**
Fishpools. *Powy* —2C **39**
Fitz. *Shrp* —3B **26**
Five Bridges. *Here* —1D **51**
Five Roads. *Carm* —2C **55**
Flax Bourton. *N Som* —3C **67**
Flaxley. *Glos* —1D **61**
Flemingston. *V Glam* —2B **64**
Flint. *Flin* —3D **9**
Flint Mountain. *Flin* —3D **9**
Flintsham. *Here* —3A **40**
Flixton. *G Man* —1D **11**
Fochriw. *Cphy* —2C **59**
Foel. *Powy* —3A **24**
Ford. *Shrp* —3B **26**
Forden. *Powy* —1D **31**
Ford Heath. *Shrp* —3B **26**
Forge. *Powy* —2C **29**
Forge Side. *Torf* —2D **59**
Forge, The. *Here* —3A **40**
Forthay. *Glos* —3D **61**
Forton. *Shrp* —2B **26**
Forton. *Staf* —2D **27**
Forton Heath. *Shrp* —3B **26**
Four Alls, The. *Shrp* —1D **27**
Four Crosses. *Powy* —1B **30**
  (Llanerfyl)
Four Crosses. *Powy* —3D **25**
  (Llanymynech)
Four Mile Bridge. *IOA* —3B **4**
Four Oaks. *Glos* —3D **51**
Four Roads. *Carm* —2D **55**
Fowley Common. *Warr* —1D **11**
Fownhope. *Here* —2C **51**
Foxwist Green. *Ches* —1D **19**
Foxwood. *Shrp* —1D **41**
Foy. *Here* —3C **51**
Frampton Cotterell. *S Glo* —1D **67**
Frampton on Severn. *Glos*
  —2D **61**
Frandley. *Ches* —3D **11**
Frankby. *Mers* —2D **9**
Frank's Bridge. *Powy* —3C **39**
Frankwell. *Shrp* —3B **26**
Freshwater East. *Pemb* —3D **53**
Fretherne. *Glos* —2D **61**
Freystrop. *Pemb* —1C **53**
Friog. *Gwyn* —3B **22**
Frith Common. *Worc* —2D **41**
Frochas. *Powy* —1C **31**
Frodesley. *Shrp* —1C **33**
Frodsham. *Ches* —3C **11**
Fromes Hill. *Here* —1D **51**
Fron. *Carm* —2C **47**
Fron. *Gwyn* —2A **14**
  (Caernarfon)
Fron. *Gwyn* —1C **21**
  (Pwllheli)
Fron. *Powy* —2B **38**
  (Llandrindod Wells)
Fron. *Powy* —2C **31**
  (Newtown)
Fron. *Powy* —1D **31**
  (Welshpool)
Froncysyllte. *Den* —3D **17**
Frongoch. *Gwyn* —1A **24**
Fron Isaf. *Wrex* —3D **17**
Fronoleu. *Gwyn* —1C **23**
Fuller's Moor. *Ches* —2B **18**

Furnace. *Carm* —2A **56**
Furnace. *Cdgn* —2B **28**

Gaer. *Powy* —3C **49**
Gaerwen. *IOA* —3D **5**
Gallt Melyd. *Den* —2B **8**
Ganarew. *Here* —1C **61**
Ganllwyd. *Gwyn* —2C **23**
Garden City. *Flin* —1A **18**
Garden Village. *Swan* —3A **56**
Garmston. *Shrp* —1D **33**
Garnant. *Carm* —1B **56**
Garndiffaith. *Torf* —2D **59**
Garndolbenmaen. *Gwyn* —3D **13**
Garnfadryn. *Gwyn* —1B **20**
Garnlydan. *Blae* —1C **59**
Garnswllt. *Swan* —2B **56**
Garn-yr-erw. *Torf* —1D **59**
Garreg. *Gwyn* —3B **14**
Garston. *Mers* —2B **10**
Garswood. *Mers* —1C **11**
Garth. *B'End* —3D **57**
Garth. *Cdgn* —3B **28**
Garth. *Den* —3D **17**
Garth. *Gwyn* —1A **22**
Garth. *Powy* —1A **48**
  (Builth Wells)
Garth. *Powy* —1D **39**
  (Knighton)
Garthbrengy. *Powy* —2B **48**
Gartheli. *Cdgn* —3A **36**
Garthmyl. *Powy* —2C **31**
Garth Owen. *Powy* —2C **31**
Garway. *Here* —3B **50**
Garway Common. *Here* —3B **50**
Garway Hill. *Here* —3B **50**
Gateacre. *Mers* —2B **10**
Gatesheath. *Ches* —1B **18**
Gaufron. *Powy* —2A **38**
Gaunt's Earthcott. *S Glo* —1D **67**
Gayton. *Mers* —2D **9**
Gell. *Cnwy* —1D **15**
Gelli. *Pemb* —1D **53**
Gelli. *Rhon* —3A **58**
Gellifor. *Den* —1C **17**
Gelligaer. *Cphy* —3C **59**
Gellilydan. *Gwyn* —1B **22**
Gellinudd. *Neat* —2C **57**
Gellywen. *Carm* —3B **44**
Geneva. *Cdgn* —3D **35**
Georgetown. *Blae* —2C **59**
Gerlan. *Gwyn* —1B **14**
Gethsemane. *Pemb* —1D **43**
Geuffordd. *Powy* —3D **25**
Gignog. *Pemb* —3B **42**
Gileston. *V Glam* —3B **64**
Gilfach. *Cphy* —3C **59**
Gilfach Goch. *Rhon* —3A **58**
Gilfachreda. *Cdgn* —3D **35**
Gillar's Green. *Mers* —1B **10**
Gilwern. *Mon* —1D **59**
Gladestry. *Powy* —3D **39**
Glais. *Swan* —2C **57**
Glanaman. *Carm* —1B **56**
Glan-Conwy. *Cnwy* —2D **15**
Glan Duar. *Carm* —1A **46**
Glandwr. *Blae* —2D **59**
Glandwr. *Pemb* —3A **44**
Glan-Dwyfach. *Gwyn* —3D **13**
Glandy Cross. *Carm* —3A **44**
Glandyfi. *Cdgn* —2B **28**
Glangrwyney. *Powy* —1D **59**
Glanmule. *Powy* —2C **31**
Glanrhyd. *Gwyn* —1B **20**
Glan-rhyd. *Neat* —2C **57**
Glanrhyd. *Pemb* —1A **44**
  (Cardigan)
Glan-rhyd. *Pemb* —2A **44**
  (Crymmych)
Glan-y-don. *Flin* —3C **9**
Glan-y-nant. *Powy* —3A **30**
Glan-yr-afon. *Gwyn* —3B **16**
Glan-yr-afon. *IOA* —2B **6**
Glan-yr-afon. *Powy* —1B **30**
Glan-y-wern. *Gwyn* —1B **22**
Glasbury. *Powy* —2C **49**
Glascoed. *Den* —3A **8**
Glascoed. *Mon* —2A **60**
Glascwm. *Powy* —3C **39**
Glasfryn. *Cnwy* —2A **16**
Glasinfryn. *Gwyn* —1A **14**
Glaspwll. *Powy* —2C **29**
Glasshouse. *Glos* —3D **51**
Glazebrook. *Warr* —1D **11**
Glazebury. *Warr* —1D **11**

Glazeley. *Shrp* —3D **33**
Gledrid. *Shrp* —1D **25**
Gleiniant. *Powy* —2A **30**
Glewstone. *Here* —3C **51**
Glyn. *Cnwy* —3D **7**
Glynarthen. *Cdgn* —1C **45**
Glynbrochan. *Powy* —3A **30**
Glyn Ceiriog. *Wrex* —1D **25**
Glyncoch. *Rhon* —3B **58**
Glyncorrwg. *Neat* —3D **57**
Glyndyfrdwy. *Den* —3C **17**
Glyn Ebwy. *Blae* —2C **59**
Glynllan. *B'End* —1A **64**
Glyn-neath. *Neat* —2D **57**
Glynogwr. *B'End* —1A **64**
Glyntaff. *Rhon* —1B **64**
Glyntawe. *Powy* —1D **57**
Glynteg. *Carm* —2C **45**
Gobowen. *Shrp* —1A **26**
Godre'r-graig. *Neat* —2C **57**
Goetre. *Mon* —2A **60**
Goginan. *Cdgn* —3B **28**
Golan. *Gwyn* —3A **14**
Golborne. *G Man* —1D **11**
Goldcliff. *Newp* —1A **66**
Golden Grove. *Carm* —1A **56**
Golden Hill. *Pemb* —3C **43**
Golding. *Shrp* —1C **33**
Goldstone. *Shrp* —2D **27**
Golfa. *Powy* —2C **25**
Goodrich. *Here* —1C **61**
Goodwick. *Pemb* —2C **43**
Goose Green. *S Glo* —1D **67**
Gors. *Cdgn* —1B **36**
Gorsedd. *Flin* —3C **9**
Gorseinon. *Swan* —3A **56**
Gorsgoch. *Cdgn* —3D **35**
Gorslas. *Carm* —1A **56**
Gorsley. *Glos* —3D **51**
Gorsley Common. *Here* —3D **51**
Gorstella. *Ches* —1A **18**
Gorsty Common. *Here* —2B **50**
Gossington. *Glos* —2D **61**
Covilon. *Mon*   1D **59**
Gowerton. *Swan* —3A **56**
Goytre. *Neat* —1A **56**
Grafton. *Here* —2B **50**
Grafton. *Shrp* —3B **26**
Grafton. *Worc* —2C **41**
Graianrhyd. *Den* —2D **17**
Graig. *Carm* —2D **55**
Graig. *Cnwy* —3D **7**
Graig. *Den* —3B **8**
Graig-fechan. *Den* —2C **17**
Graig Penllyn. *V Glam* —2A **64**
Grange. *Here* —1B **40**
Grange. *Mers* —2D **9**
Grangetown. *Card* —2C **65**
Granston. *Pemb* —2B **42**
Grappenhall. *Warr* —2D **11**
Grassendale. *Mers* —2A **10**
Gravelhill. *Shrp* —3B **26**
Greasby. *Mers* —2D **9**
Great Barrow. *Ches* —1B **18**
Great Bolas. *Telf* —2D **27**
Great Budworth. *Ches* —3D **11**
Great Crosby. *Mers* —1A **10**
Great Doward. *Here* —1C **61**
Great Lyth. *Shrp* —1B **32**
Great Ness. *Shrp* —3B **26**
Great Oak. *Mon* —2A **60**
Great Ryton. *Shrp* —1B **32**
Great Sankey. *Warr* —2C **11**
Great Sutton. *Ches* —3A **10**
Great Sutton. *Shrp* —3C **33**
Great Wytheford. *Shrp* —3C **27**
Greenfield. *Flin* —3C **9**
Green Lane. *Shrp* —2D **27**
Greenway. *Pemb* —3D **43**
Greenway. *V Glam* —2B **64**
Greete. *Shrp* —1C **41**
Grendon Green. *Here* —3C **41**
Gresford. *Wrex* —2A **18**
Gretton. *Shrp* —2C **33**
Griffithstown. *Torf* —3D **59**
Grimpo. *Shrp* —2A **26**
Grindle. *Shrp* —1D **33**
Grindley Brook. *Shrp* —3C **19**
Grinshill. *Shrp* —2C **27**
Groes. *Cnwy* —1B **16**
Groes. *Neat* —1C **63**
Groes-faen. *Rhon* —1B **64**
Groesffordd. *Gwyn* —1B **20**
Groesffordd. *Powy* —3B **48**
Groeslon. *Gwyn* —2D **13**
Groes-lwyd. *Powy* —3D **25**

Groes-wen. *Cphy* —1C **65**
Gronant. *Flin* —2B **8**
Grosmont. *Mon* —3B **50**
Grovesend. *Swan* —2A **56**
Guilden Down. *Shrp* —3A **32**
Guilden Sutton. *Ches* —1B **18**
Guilsfield. *Powy* —3D **25**
Gumfreston. *Pemb* —2A **54**
Gurnos. *Powy* —1C **57**
Gwaelod-y-garth. *Card* —1C **65**
Gwaenynog Bach. *Den* —1B **16**
Gwaenysgor. *Flin* —2B **8**
Gwalchmai. *IOA* —3C **5**
Gwastad. *Pemb* —3D **43**
Gwaun-Cae-Gurwen. *Neat* —1C **57**
Gwaun-y-bara. *Cphy* —1C **65**
Gwbert. *Cdgn* —3A **34**
Gwehelog. *Mon* —2A **60**
Gwenddwr. *Powy* —1B **48**
Gwernaffield. *Flin* —1D **17**
Gwernesney. *Mon* —2B **60**
Gwernogle. *Carm* —2A **46**
Gwern-y-go. *Powy* —2D **31**
Gwernymynydd. *Flin* —1D **17**
Gwersyllt. *Wrex* —2A **18**
Gwespyr. *Flin* —2C **9**
Gwredog. *IOA* —2D **5**
Gwyddelwern. *Den* —3B **16**
Gwyddgrug. *Carm* —2D **45**
Gwynfryn. *Wrex* —2D **17**
Gwystre. *Powy* —2B **38**
Gwytherin. *Cnwy* —1D **15**
Gyfelia. *Wrex* —3A **18**
Gyffin. *Cnwy* —3C **7**

Habberley. *Shrp* —1A **32**
Hadley. *Telf* —3D **27**
Hadnall. *Shrp* —2C **27**
Hagley. *Here* —1C **51**
Hakin. *Pemb* —2B **52**
Hale. *Hal* —2B **10**
Hale Bank. *Hal* —2B **10**
Hales. *Staf* —1D **27**
Halewood. *Mers* —2B **10**
Halford. *Shrp* —3B **32**
Halfpenny Furze. *Carm* —1B **54**
Halfway. *Carm* —2B **46**
Halfway. *Powy* —2D **47**
Halfway House. *Shrp* —3A **26**
Halkyn. *Flin* —3D **9**
Hallatrow. *Bath* —3D **67**
Hallen. *S Glo* —1C **67**
Hall Green. *Wrex* —3B **18**
Hallowsgate. *Ches* —1C **19**
Hallwood Green. *Glos* —2D **51**
Halmond's Frome. *Here* —1D **51**
Halmore. *Glos* —2D **61**
Halton. *Hal* —2C **11**
Halton. *Wrex* —1A **26**
Ham. *Glos* —3D **61**
Hambrook. *S Glo* —2D **67**
Ham Green. *Here* —1D **51**
Ham Green. *N Som* —2C **67**
Hamperley. *Shrp* —3B **32**
Hampton. *Shrp* —3D **33**
Hampton Bishop. *Here* —2C **51**
Hampton Heath. *Ches* —3C **19**
Hampton Loade. *Shrp* —3D **33**
Handbridge. *Ches* —1B **18**
Handley. *Ches* —2B **18**
Hanham. *S Glo* —2D **67**
Hanham Green. *S Glo* —2D **67**
Hankelow. *Ches* —3D **19**
Hanley Childe. *Worc* —2D **41**
Hanley William. *Worc* —2D **41**
Hanmer. *Wrex* —1B **26**
Hanwood. *Shrp* —1B **32**
Hapsford. *Ches* —3B **10**
Hardwick. *Shrp* —2A **32**
Hardwicke. *Here* —1B **50**
Haresfinch. *Mers* —1C **11**
Harewood End. *Here* —3C **51**
Hargrave. *Ches* —1B **18**
Harlech. *Gwyn* —1A **22**
Harlescott. *Shrp* —3C **27**
Harley. *Shrp* —1C **33**
Harmer Hill. *Shrp* —2B **26**
Harnage. *Shrp* —1C **33**
Haroldston West. *Pemb* —1B **52**
Harpley. *Worc* —2D **41**
Harry Stoke. *S Glo* —2D **67**
Hartford. *Ches* —3D **11**
Harthill. *Ches* —2C **19**
Harton. *Shrp* —3B **32**
Hasguard. *Pemb* —2B **52**

Haslington. *Ches* —2D **19**
Haston. *Shrp* —2C **27**
Hatchmere. *Ches* —3C **11**
Hatfield. *Here* —3C **41**
Hatherton. *Ches* —3D **19**
Hatton. *Shrp* —2B **32**
Hatton. *Warr* —2C **11**
Hatton Heath. *Ches* —1B **18**
Haughton. *Shrp* —2D **33**
 (Bridgnorth)
Haughton. *Shrp* —2A **26**
 (Oswestry)
Haughton. *Shrp* —1D **33**
 (Shifnal)
Haughton. *Shrp* —3C **27**
 (Shrewsbury)
Haughton Moss. *Ches* —2C **19**
Haven. *Here* —3B **40**
Haverfordwest. *Pemb* —1C **53**
Hawarden. *Flin* —1A **18**
Hawen. *Cdgn* —1C **45**
Haybridge. *Shrp* —1D **41**
Haydock. *Mers* —1C **11**
Hay-on-Wye. *Powy* —1D **49**
Hayscastle. *Pemb* —3B **42**
Hayscastle Cross. *Pemb* —3C **43**
Hayton's Bent. *Shrp* —3C **33**
Hazler. *Shrp* —2B **32**
Headley Park. *Bris* —3C **67**
Heartsease. *Powy* —2C **39**
Heatley. *G Man* —2D **11**
Hebden Green. *Ches* —1D **19**
Hebron. *Carm* —3A **44**
Hegdon Hill. *Here* —3C **41**
Helsby. *Ches* —3B **10**
Helygain. *Flin* —3D **9**
Hem, The. *Shrp* —1D **33**
Henallt. *Carm* —3D **45**
Henbury. *Bris* —2C **67**
Hendomen. *Powy* —2D **31**
Hendre. *B'End* —1A **64**
Hendreforgan. *Rhon* —1A **64**
Hendy. *Carm* —2A **56**
Heneglwys. *IOA* —3D **5**
Henfeddau Fawr. *Pemb* —2B **44**
Henfield. *S Glo* —2D **67**
Hengoed. *Cphy* —3C **59**
Hengoed. *Shrp* —1D **25**
Heniarth. *Powy* —1C **31**
Henley. *Shrp* —3B **32**
 (Church Stretton)
Henley. *Shrp* —1C **41**
 (Ludlow)
Henllan. *Cdgn* —1C **45**
Henllan. *Den* —1B **16**
Henllan. *Mon* —3D **49**
Henllan Amgoed. *Carm* —3A **44**
Henllys. *Torf* —3D **59**
Henryd. *Cnwy* —3C **7**
Henry's Moat. *Pemb* —3D **43**
Heol Senni. *Powy* —3A **48**
Heol-y-Cyw. *B'End* —1A **64**
Herbrandston. *Pemb* —2B **52**
Hereford. *Here* —2C **51**
Hermon. *Carm* —3B **46**
 (Llandeilo)
Hermon. *Carm* —2C **45**
 (Newcastle Emlyn)
Hermon. *IOA* —1C **13**
Hermon. *Pemb* —2B **44**
Heswall. *Mers* —2D **9**
Hewelsfield. *Glos* —2C **61**
Hewish. *N Som* —3A **66**
Heyop. *Powy* —1D **39**
Higford. *Shrp* —1D **33**
High Ercall. *Telf* —3C **27**
Higher End. *G Man* —1C **11**
Higher Kinnerton. *Flin* —1A **18**
Higher Shotton. *Flin* —1A **18**
Higher Shurlach. *Ches* —3D **11**
Higher Walton. *Warr* —2C **11**
Higher Whitley. *Ches* —3D **11**
Higher Wincham. *Ches* —3D **11**
Higher Wych. *Ches* —3B **18**
Highgate. *Powy* —2C **31**
High Green. *Shrp* —3D **33**
High Hatton. *Shrp* —2D **27**
Highlands, The. *Shrp* —3D **33**
High Lane. *Here* —2D **41**
High Legh. *Ches* —2D **11**
Highley. *Shrp* —3D **33**
High Littleton. *Bath* —3D **67**
Highmoor Hill. *Mon* —1B **66**
Hightown. *Mers* —1D **9**
Highway. *Here* —1B **50**
Highwood. *Worc* —2D **41**

Hill. *S Glo* —3D **61**
Hillend. *Swan* —3D **55**
Hillersland. *Glos* —1C **61**
Hill Gate. *Here* —3B **50**
Hillside. *Shrp* —3D **33**
Hillside. *Worc* —2D **41**
Hindford. *Shrp* —1A **26**
Hindley Green. *G Man* —1D **11**
Hinstock. *Shrp* —2D **27**
Hinton. *Here* —2A **50**
Hinton. *Shrp* —1B **32**
Hinton. *S Glo* —2D **67**
Hinton Blewett. *Bath* —3C **67**
Hints. *Shrp* —1D **41**
Hiraeth. *Carm* —3A **44**
Hirnant. *Powy* —2B **24**
Hirwaen. *Den* —1C **17**
Hirwaun. *Rhon* —2A **58**
Hoarwithy. *Here* —3C **51**
Hobarris. *Shrp* —1A **40**
Hodgeston. *Pemb* —3D **53**
Hodley. *Powy* —2C **31**
Hodnet. *Shrp* —2D **27**
Holdgate. *Shrp* —3C **33**
Hollinfare. *Warr* —1D **11**
Hollinswood. *Telf* —1D **33**
Hollinwood. *Shrp* —1C **27**
Hollybush. *Cphy* —2C **59**
Hollyhurst. *Ches* —3C **19**
Holme Lacy. *Here* —2C **51**
Holme Marsh. *Here* —3A **40**
Holmer. *Here* —1C **51**
Holt. *Wrex* —2B **18**
Holyhead. *IOA* —2B **4**
Holywell. *Flin* —3C **9**
Homer. *Shrp* —1D **33**
Homer Green. *Mers* —1A **10**
Hom Green. *Here* —3C **51**
Honeyborough. *Pemb* —2C **53**
Honnington. *Telf* —3D **27**
Hook. *Pemb* —1C **53**
Hook-a-Gate. *Shrp* —1B **32**
Hookgate. *Staf* —1D **27**
Hook Street. *Glos* —3D **61**
Hoole. *Ches* —1B **18**
Hooton. *Ches* —3A **10**
Hope. *Flin* —2A **18**
Hope. *Powy* —1D **31**
Hope. *Shrp* —1A **32**
Hope Bagot. *Shrp* —1C **41**
Hope Bowdler. *Shrp* —2B **32**
Hope Mansell. *Here* —1D **61**
Hopesay. *Shrp* —3A **32**
Hope under Dinmore. *Here* —3C **41**
Hopley's Green. *Here* —3A **40**
Hopton. *Powy* —2D **31**
Hopton. *Shrp* —2A **26**
 (Oswestry)
Hopton. *Shrp* —2C **27**
 (Wem)
Hopton Cangeford. *Shrp* —3C **33**
Hopton Castle. *Shrp* —1A **40**
Hoptonheath. *Shrp* —1A **40**
Hopton Wafers. *Shrp* —1D **41**
Horderley. *Shrp* —3B **32**
Hordley. *Shrp* —1A **26**
Horeb. *Carm* —3A **46**
 (Brechfa)
Horeb. *Carm* —2D **55**
 (Llanelli)
Horeb. *Cdgn* —1C **45**
Horfield. *Bris* —2D **67**
Horsecastle. *N Som* —3B **66**
Horsehay. *Telf* —1D **33**
Horseman's Green. *Wrex* —3B **18**
Horsham. *Worc* —2D **41**
Horton. *Shrp* —1B **26**
Horton. *Swan* —1A **62**
Horton Green. *Ches* —3B **18**
Hortonwood. *Telf* —3D **27**
Hough. *Ches* —2D **19**
Hough Green. *Hal* —2B **10**
Houghton. *Pemb* —2C **53**
How Caple. *Here* —2D **51**
Howey. *Powy* —3B **38**
Howle. *Telf* —2D **27**
Howle Hill. *Here* —3D **51**
Howley. *Warr* —2D **11**
Howton. *Here* —3B **50**
Hoylake. *Mers* —2D **9**
Hubberston. *Pemb* —2B **52**
Hughley. *Shrp* —2C **33**
Humber Court. *Here* —3C **41**
Hundleton. *Pemb* —2C **53**
Hundred House. *Powy* —3C **39**
Hundred, The. *Here* —3C **41**

Hungerford. *Shrp* —3C **33**
Hungryhatton. *Shrp* —2D **27**
Hunstrete. *Bath* —3D **67**
Huntington. *Here* —3D **39**
Huntington. *Telf* —1D **33**
Huntley. *Glos* —1D **61**
Hunt's Cross. *Mers* —2B **10**
Huntstrete. *Bath* —3D **67**
Hurdley. *Powy* —2D **31**
Hurst Green. *Ches* —3C **19**
Hurstley. *Here* —1A **50**
Hurstway Common. *Here* —1D **49**
Hutton. *N Som* —3A **66**
Huxley. *Ches* —1C **19**
Huyton. *Mers* —1B **10**
Hwlffordd. *Pemb* —1C **53**
Hyssington. *Powy* —2A **32**

Icelton. *N Som* —3A **66**
Idole. *Carm* —1D **55**
Ifton Heath. *Shrp* —1A **26**
Ightfield. *Shrp* —1C **27**
Ilston. *Swan* —3A **56**
Ince. *Ches* —3B **10**
Ince Blundell. *Mers* —1A **10**
Inglesbatch. *Bath* —3D **67**
Ingst. *S Glo* —1C **67**
Irby. *Mers* —2D **9**
Irlam. *G Man* —1D **11**
Iron Acton. *S Glo* —1D **67**
Ironbridge. *Telf* —1D **33**
Islington. *Telf* —2D **27**
Islwyn. *Cphy* —3D **59**
Itchington. *S Glo* —1D **67**
Itton Common. *Mon* —3B **60**
Ivington. *Here* —3B **40**
Ivington Green. *Here* —3B **40**

Jackfield. *Shrp* —1D **33**
Jameston. *Pemb* —3D **53**
Jeffreyston. *Pemb* —2D **53**
Jersey Marine. *Neat* —3C **57**
Jingle Street. *Mon* —1B **60**
Johnston. *Pemb* —1C **53**
Johnstown. *Carm* —1C **55**
Johnstown. *Wrex* —3A **18**
Jordanston. *Pemb* —2C **43**

Keckwick. *Hal* —2C **11**
Keeston. *Pemb* —1C **53**
Kelsall. *Ches* —1C **19**
Kelsterton. *Flin* —3D **9**
Kelston. *Bath* —3D **67**
Kemberton. *Shrp* —1D **33**
Kempley. *Glos* —3D **51**
Kempley Green. *Glos* —3D **51**
Kempton. *Shrp* —3A **32**
Kenchester. *Here* —1B **50**
Kendleshire. *S Glo* —2D **67**
Kenfig. *B'End* —1D **63**
Kenfig Hill. *B'End* —1D **63**
Kenley. *Shrp* —1C **33**
Kenn. *N Som* —3B **66**
Kenstone. *Shrp* —2C **27**
Kentchurch. *Here* —3B **50**
Kent's Green. *Glos* —3D **51**
Kenwick. *Shrp* —1B **26**
Kenyon. *Warr* —1D **11**
Kerne Bridge. *Here* —1C **61**
Kerry. *Powy* —3C **31**
Kerry's Gate. *Here* —2A **50**
Kewstoke. *N Som* —3A **66**
Keynsham. *Bath* —3D **67**
Kidnal. *Ches* —3B **18**
Kidwelly. *Carm* —2D **55**
Kilcot. *Glos* —3D **51**
Kilgetty. *Pemb* —2A **54**
Killay. *Swan* —3B **56**
Kiln Green. *Here* —1C **61**
Kilpeck. *Here* —2B **50**
Kimbolton. *Here* —2C **41**
Kingcoed. *Mon* —2B **60**
King's Acre. *Here* —1B **50**
Kings Caple. *Here* —3C **51**
Kingsland. *Here* —2B **40**
Kingsland. *IOA* —2B **4**
Kingsley. *Ches* —3C **11**
Kings Moss. *Mers* —1C **11**
King's Pyon. *Here* —3B **40**
King's Thorn. *Here* —2C **51**
Kingstone. *Here* —2B **50**
Kingston Seymour. *N Som* —3B **66**

Kingswood. *Glos* —3D **61**
Kingswood. *Here* —3D **39**
Kingswood. *Powy* —1D **31**
Kingswood. *S Glo* —2D **67**
Kington. *Here* —3A **40**
Kington. *S Glo* —3D **61**
Kinlet. *Shrp* —3D **33**
Kinmel Bay. *Cnwy* —2A **8**
Kinnerley. *Shrp* —2A **26**
Kinnersley. *Here* —1A **50**
Kinnerton. *Powy* —2D **39**
Kinnerton. *Shrp* —2A **32**
Kinsey Heath. *Ches* —3D **19**
Kinsham. *Here* —2A **40**
Kinton. *Here* —1B **40**
Kinton. *Shrp* —3A **26**
Kirkby. *Mers* —1B **10**
Kirkby Industrial Estate. *Mers*
—1B **10**
Kirkdale. *Mers* —1A **10**
Kittle. *Swan* —1A **62**
Kivernoll. *Here* —2B **50**
Knapton Green. *Here* —3B **40**
Knelston. *Swan* —3A **56**
Knightcott. *N Som* —3A **66**
Knighton. *Powy* —1D **39**
Knighton. *Staf* —2D **27**
Knighton Common. *Worc* —1D **41**
Knightwick. *Worc* —3D **41**
Knill. *Here* —2A **40**
Knockin. *Shrp* —2A **26**
Knollbury. *Mon* —1B **66**
Knolton. *Wrex* —1A **26**
Knotty Ash. *Mers* —1B **10**
Knowbury. *Shrp* —1C **41**
Knowle. *Bris* —2D **67**
Knowle. *Shrp* —1C **41**
Knowsley. *Mers* —1B **10**
Knowsley Hall. *Mers* —1B **10**
Knucklas. *Powy* —1D **39**
Knutsford. *Ches* —3D **11**
Kymin. *Mon* —1C **61**
Kynaston. *Here* —2D **51**
Kynaston. *Shrp* —2A **26**
Kynnersley. *Telf* —3D **27**
Kyre Green. *Worc* —2D **41**
Kyre Park. *Worc* —2D **41**
Kyrewood. *Worc* —2D **41**

Lach Dennis. *Ches* —3D **11**
Lache. *Ches* —1A **18**
Laleston. *B'End* —1D **63**
Lambston. *Pemb* —1C **53**
Lampeter. *Cdgn* —1A **46**
Lampeter Velfrey. *Pemb* —1A **54**
Lamphey. *Pemb* —2D **53**
Land Gate. *G Man* —1C **11**
Landimore. *Swan* —3D **55**
Landore. *Swan* —3B **56**
Landshipping. *Pemb* —1D **53**
Lane Head. *G Man* —1D **11**
Langland. *Swan* —1B **62**
Langridge. *Bath* —3D **67**
Larden Green. *Ches* —2C **19**
Larport. *Here* —2C **51**
Latteridge. *S Glo* —1D **67**
Laugharne. *Carm* —1C **55**
Lavister. *Wrex* —2A **18**
Lawrenny. *Pemb* —2D **53**
Lawton. *Here* —3B **40**
Laysters Pole. *Here* —2C **41**
Lea. *Here* —3D **51**
Lea. *Shrp* —3A **32**
(Bishop's Castle)
Lea. *Shrp* —1B **32**
(Shrewsbury)
Leachpool. *Pemb* —1C **53**
Leasowe. *Mers* —1D **9**
Leaton. *Shrp* —3B **26**
Leckwith. *V Glam* —2D **65**
Ledbury. *Here* —2D **51**
Ledgemoor. *Here* —3B **40**
Ledicot. *Here* —2B **40**
Ledsham. *Ches* —3A **10**
Lee. *Shrp* —1B **26**
Leebotwood. *Shrp* —2B **32**
Lee Brockhurst. *Shrp* —2C **27**
Leechpool. *Mon* —1C **67**
Leegomery. *Telf* —3D **27**
Leeswood. *Flin* —2D **17**
Leftwich. *Ches* —3D **11**
Leigh. *G Man* —1D **11**
Leigh. *Shrp* —1A **32**
Leighton. *Powy* —1D **31**
Leighton. *Shrp* —1D **33**

Leinthall Earls. *Here* —2B **40**
Leinthall Starkes. *Here* —2B **40**
Leintwardine. *Here* —1B **40**
Lem Hill. *Worc* —1D **41**
Leominster. *Here* —3B **40**
Letterston. *Pemb* —3C **43**
Letton. *Here* —1A **50**
(Kington)
Letton. *Here* —1A **40**
(Leintwardine)
Leweston. *Pemb* —3C **43**
Lewistown. *B'End* —1A **64**
Libanus. *Powy* —3A **48**
Lightwood Green. *Ches* —3D **19**
Lightwood Green. *Wrex* —3A **18**
Lilleshall. *Telf* —3D **27**
Lilyhurst. *Shrp* —3D **27**
Lindridge. *Worc* —2D **41**
Lingen. *Here* —2A **40**
Lingoed. *Mon* —1A **60**
Linley. *Shrp* —2A **32**
(Bishop's Castle)
Linley. *Shrp* —2D **33**
(Bridgnorth)
Linley Green. *Here* —3D **41**
Linton. *Here* —3D **51**
Linton Hill. *Here* —3D **51**
Lipley. *Shrp* —1D **27**
Liscard. *Mers* —1A **10**
Lisvane. *Card* —1C **65**
Liswerry. *Newp* —1A **66**
Litchard. *B'End* —1A **64**
Litherland. *Mers* —1A **10**
Little Barrow. *Ches* —1B **18**
Little Birch. *Here* —2C **51**
Little Bolas. *Shrp* —2D **27**
Little Bollington. *Ches* —2D **11**
Little Brampton. *Shrp* —3A **32**
Little Budworth. *Ches* —1C **19**
Little Cowarne. *Here* —3D **41**
Little Crosby. *Mers* —1A **10**
Little Dawley. *Telf* —1D **33**
Littledean. *Glos* —1D **61**
Little Dewchurch. *Here* —2C **51**
Little Drayton. *Shrp* —1D **27**
Little Garway. *Here* —3B **50**
Little Green. *Wrex* —3B **18**
Little Haven. *Pemb* —1B **52**
Little Hereford. *Here* —2C **41**
Little Hulton. *G Man* —1D **11**
Little Leigh. *Ches* —3D **11**
Little London. *Powy* —3B **30**
Little Marcle. *Here* —2D **51**
Little Mill. *Mon* —2A **60**
Little Mountain. *Flin* —1D **17**
Little Ness. *Shrp* —3B **26**
Little Neston. *Ches* —3A **10**
Little Newcastle. *Pemb* —3C **43**
Little Reynoldston. *Swan* —3D **55**
Little Ryton. *Shrp* —1B **32**
Little Soudley. *Shrp* —2D **27**
Little Stanney. *Ches* —3B **10**
Little Stretton. *Shrp* —2B **32**
Little Sutton. *Ches* —3A **10**
Littleton. *Ches* —1B **18**
Littleton-upon-Severn. *S Glo* —3C **61**
Little Wenlock. *Telf* —1D **33**
Liverpool. *Mers* —1A **10**
Liverpool Airport. *Mers* —2B **10**
Lixwm. *Flin* —3C **9**
Llaingoch. *IOA* —2B **4**
Llaithddu. *Powy* —3B **30**
Llampha. *V Glam* —2A **64**
Llan. *Powy* —1D **29**
Llanaber. *Gwyn* —3B **22**
Llanaelhaearn. *Gwyn* —3C **13**
Llanaeron. *Cdgn* —3D **35**
Llanafan. *Cdgn* —1B **36**
Llanafan-fawr. *Powy* —3A **38**
Llanafan-fechan. *Powy* —3A **38**
Llanallgo. *IOA* —2D **5**
Llanandras. *Powy* —2D **39**
Llananno. *Powy* —1B **38**
Llanarmon. *Gwyn* —1D **21**
Llanarmon Dyffryn Ceiriog. *Wrex*
—1C **25**
Llanarmon-yn-Ial. *Den* —2C **17**
Llanarth. *Cdgn* —3D **35**
Llanarth. *Mon* —1A **60**
Llanarthney. *Carm* —3A **46**
Llanasa. *Flin* —2C **9**
Llanbabo. *IOA* —2C **5**
Llanbadarn Fawr. *Cdgn* —3B **28**
Llanbadarn Fynydd. *Powy* —1B **38**
Llanbadarn-y-garreg. *Powy* —1C **49**
Llanbadoc. *Mon* —2A **60**

Llanbadrig. *IOA* —1C **5**
Llanbeder. *Newp* —3A **60**
Llanbedr. *Gwyn* —2A **22**
Llanbedr. *Powy* —3D **49**
(Crickhowell)
Llanbedr. *Powy* —1C **49**
(Hay-on-Wye)
Llanbedr-Dyffryn-Clwyd. *Den* —2C **17**
Llanbedrgoch. *IOA* —2A **6**
Llanbedrog. *Gwyn* —1C **21**
Llanbedr Pont Steffan. *Cdgn* —1A **46**
Llanbedr-y-cennin. *Cnwy* —1C **15**
Llanberis. *Gwyn* —1A **14**
Llanbethery. *V Glam* —3B **64**
Llanbister. *Powy* —1C **39**
Llanblethian. *V Glam* —2B **64**
Llanboidy. *Carm* —3B **44**
Llanbradach. *Cphy* —3C **59**
Llanbrynmair. *Powy* —1D **29**
Llancadle. *V Glam* —3B **64**
Llancarfan. *V Glam* —2B **64**
Llancayo. *Mon* —2A **60**
Llancloudy. *Here* —3B **50**
Llancoch. *Powy* —1D **39**
Llancynfelyn. *Cdgn* —2B **28**
Llandaff. *Card* —2C **65**
Llandanwg. *Gwyn* —2A **22**
Llandarcy. *Neat* —3C **57**
Llandawke. *Carm* —1B **54**
Llanddaniel-Fab. *IOA* —3D **5**
Llanddarog. *Carm* —1A **56**
Llanddeiniol. *Cdgn* —1A **36**
Llanddeiniolen. *Gwyn* —1A **14**
Llandderfel. *Gwyn* —1A **24**
Llanddeusant. *Carm* —3C **47**
Llanddeusant. *IOA* —2C **5**
Llanddew. *Powy* —2B **48**
Llanddewi. *Swan* —3D **55**
Llanddewi Brefi. *Cdgn* —3B **36**
Llanddewi'r Cwm. *Powy* —1B **48**
Llanddewi Rhydderch. *Mon* —1A **60**
Llanddewi Velfrey. *Powy* —1A **54**
Llanddewi Ystradenni. *Powy* —2C **39**
Llanddoged. *Cnwy* —1D **15**
Llanddona. *IOA* —3A **6**
Llanddowror. *Carm* —1B **54**
Llanddulas. *Cnwy* —3A **8**
Llanddwywe. *Gwyn* —2A **22**
Llanddyfnan. *IOA* —3A **6**
Llandecwyn. *Gwyn* —1B **22**
Llandefaelog Fach. *Powy* —2B **48**
Llandefaelog-tre'r-graig. *Powy* —2C **49**
Llandefalle. *Powy* —2C **49**
Llandegai. *Gwyn* —3A **6**
Llandegfan. *IOA* —3A **6**
Llandegla. *Den* —2C **17**
Llandegley. *Powy* —2C **39**
Llandegveth. *Mon* —3A **60**
Llandeilo. *Carm* —3B **46**
Llandeilo Graban. *Powy* —1B **48**
Llandeilo'r Fan. *Powy* —2D **47**
Llandeloy. *Pemb* —3B **42**
Llandenny. *Mon* —2B **60**
Llandevaud. *Newp* —3B **60**
Llandevenny. *Newp* —1B **66**
Llandilo. *Pemb* —3A **44**
Llandinabo. *Here* —3C **51**
Llandinam. *Powy* —3B **30**
Llandissilio. *Pemb* —3A **44**
Llandogo. *Mon* —2C **61**
Llandough. *V Glam* —2A **64**
(Cowbridge)
Llandough. *V Glam* —2C **65**
(Penarth)
Llandovery. *Carm* —2C **47**
Llandow. *V Glam* —2A **64**
Llandre. *Cdgn* —3B **28**
Llandrillo. *Den* —1B **24**
Llandrillo-yn-Rhos. *Cnwy* —2D **7**
Llandrindod Wells. *Powy* —2B **38**
Llandrinio. *Powy* —3D **25**
Llandsadwrn. *Carm* —2B **46**
Llandudno. *Cnwy* —2C **7**
Llandudno Junction. *Cnwy* —3C **7**
Llandudoch. *Pemb* —1A **44**
Llandwrog. *Gwyn* —2D **13**
Llandybie. *Carm* —1B **56**
Llandyfaelog. *Carm* —1D **55**
Llandyfan. *Carm* —1B **56**
Llandyfriog. *Cdgn* —1C **45**
Llandyfrydog. *IOA* —2D **5**
Llandygwydd. *Cdgn* —1B **44**
Llandynan. *Den* —3C **17**
Llandyrnog. *Den* —1C **17**
Llandysilio. *Powy* —3D **25**
Llandyssil. *Powy* —2C **31**

Llandysul. *Cdgn* —1D **45**
Llanedeyrn. *Card* —1D **65**
Llaneglwys. *Powy* —2B **48**
Llanegryn. *Gwyn* —1B **28**
Llanegwad. *Carm* —3A **46**
Llaneilian. *IOA* —1D **5**
Llanelian-yn-Rhos. *Cnwy* —3D **7**
Llanelidan. *Den* —2C **17**
Llanelieu. *Powy* —2C **49**
Llanellen. *Mon* —1A **60**
Llanelli. *Carm* —3A **56**
Llanelltyd. *Gwyn* —3C **23**
Llanelly. *Mon* —1D **59**
Llanelly Hill. *Mon* —1D **59**
Llanelwedd. *Powy* —3B **38**
Llanelwy. *Den* —3B **8**
Llanenddwyn. *Gwyn* —2A **22**
Llanerch. *Powy* —2A **32**
Llanerchymedd. *IOA* —2D **5**
Llanerfyl. *Powy* —1B **30**
Llaneuddog. *IOA* —2D **5**
Llanfachraeth. *IOA* —2C **5**
Llanfaelog. *IOA* —3C **5**
Llanfaelrhys. *Gwyn* —2B **20**
Llanfaenor. *Mon* —1B **60**
Llanfaes. *IOA* —3B **6**
Llanfaes. *Powy* —3B **48**
Llanfaethlu. *IOA* —2C **5**
Llanfaglan. *Gwyn* —1D **13**
Llanfair. *Gwyn* —2A **22**
Llanfair. *Here* —1D **49**
Llanfair Caereinion. *Powy* —1C **31**
Llanfair Clydogau. *Cdgn* —3B **36**
Llanfair Dyffryn Clwyd. *Den* —2C **17**
Llanfairfechan. *Cnwy* —3B **6**
Llanfair-Nant-Gwyn. *Pemb* —2A **44**
Llanfair Pwllgwyngyll. *IOA* —3A **6**
Llanfair Talhaiarn. *Cnwy* —3D **8**
Llanfair Waterdine. *Shrp* —1D **39**
Llanfair-ym-Muallt. *Powy* —3B **38**
Llanfairyneubwll. *IOA* —3C **5**
Llanfairynghornwy. *IOA* —1C **5**
Llanfallteg. *Carm*   1A **54**
Llanfallteg West. *Carm* —1A **54**
Llanfaredd. *Powy* —3B **38**
Llanfarian. *Cdgn* —1A **36**
Llanfechain. *Powy* —2C **25**
Llanfechell. *IOA* —1C **5**
Llanfechreth. *Gwyn* —2C **23**
Llanfendigaid. *Gwyn* —1A **28**
Llanferres. *Den* —1C **17**
Llanfflewyn. *IOA* —2C **5**
Llanfihangel Glyn Myfyr. *Cnwy* —3A **16**
Llanfihangel Nant Bran. *Powy* —2A **48**
Llanfihangel-Nant-Melan. *Powy*
      —3C **39**
Llanfihangel Rhydithon. *Powy* —2C **39**
Llanfihangel Rogiet. *Mon* —1B **66**
Llanfihangel Tal-y-llyn. *Powy* —3C **49**
Llanfihangel-uwch-Gwili. *Carm*
      —3D **45**
Llanfihangel-yng-Ngwynfa. *Powy*
      —3B **24**
Llanfihangel yn Nhowyn. *IOA* —3C **5**
Llanfihangel-y-pennant. *Gwyn* —3A **14**
   (Golan)
Llanfihangel-y-pennant. *Gwyn* —1B **28**
   (Tywyn)
Llanfilo. *Powy* —2C **49**
Llanfinhangel-ar-Arth. *Carm* —2D **45**
Llanfinhangel-y-Creuddyn. *Cdgn*
      —1B **36**
Llanfihangel-y-traethau. *Gwyn*
      —1A **22**
Llanfoist. *Mon* —1D **59**
Llanfor. *Gwyn* —1A **24**
Llanfrechfa. *Torf* —3A **60**
Llanfrothen. *Gwyn* —3B **14**
Llanfrynach. *Powy* —3B **48**
Llanfwrog. *Den* —2C **17**
Llanfwrog. *IOA* —2C **5**
Llanfyllin. *Powy* —3C **25**
Llanfynydd. *Carm* —3B **46**
Llanfynydd. *Flin* —2D **17**
Llanfyrnach. *Pemb* —2B **44**
Llangadfan. *Powy* —3B **24**
Llangadog. *Carm* —3C **47**
   (Llandovery)
Llangadog. *Carm* —2D **55**
   (Llanelli)
Llangadwaladr. *IOA* —1C **13**
Llangadwaladr. *Powy* —1C **25**
Llangaffo. *IOA* —1D **13**
Llangain. *Carm* —1C **55**
Llangammarch Wells. *Powy* —1A **48**

Llangan. *V Glam* —2A **64**
Llangarron. *Here* —3C **51**
Llangasty-Talyllyn. *Powy* —3C **49**
Llangathen. *Carm* —3A **46**
Llangattock. *Powy* —1D **59**
Llangattock Lingoed. *Mon* —3A **50**
Llangattock-Vibon-Avel. *Mon*
      —1B **60**
Llangedwyn. *Powy* —2C **25**
Llangefni. *IOA* —3D **5**
Llangeinor. *B'End* —1A **64**
Llangeitho. *Cdgn* —3B **36**
Llangeler. *Carm* —2C **45**
Llangelynin. *Gwyn* —1A **28**
Llangendeirne. *Carm* —1D **55**
Llangennech. *Carm* —2A **56**
Llangennith. *Swan* —3D **55**
Llangenny. *Powy* —1D **59**
Llangernyw. *Cnwy* —1D **15**
Llangian. *Gwyn* —2B **20**
Llangiwg. *Neat* —2C **57**
Llangloffan. *Pemb* —2C **43**
Llanglydwen. *Carm* —3A **44**
Llangoed. *IOA* —3B **6**
Llangoedmor. *Cdgn* —1B **44**
Llangollen. *Den* —3D **17**
Llangolman. *Pemb* —3A **44**
Llangorse. *Powy* —3C **49**
Llangorwen. *Cdgn* —3B **28**
Llangovan. *Mon* —2B **60**
Llangower. *Gwyn* —1A **24**
Llangranog. *Cdgn* —3C **35**
Llangristiolus. *IOA* —3D **5**
Llangrove. *Here* —1C **61**
Llangua. *Mon* —3A **50**
Llangunllo. *Powy* —1D **39**
Llangunnor. *Carm* —3D **45**
Llangurig. *Powy* —1A **38**
Llangwm. *Cnwy* —3A **16**
Llangwm. *Mon* —2B **60**
Llangwm. *Pemb* —2C **53**
Llangwm-isaf. *Mon* —2B **60**
Llangwnnadl. *Gwyn* —1A **20**
Llangwyfan. *Den* —1C **17**
Llangwyfan-isaf. *IOA* —1C **13**
Llangwyllog. *IOA* —3D **5**
Llangwyryfon. *Cdgn* —1A **36**
Llangybi. *Cdgn* —3B **36**
Llangybi. *Gwyn* —1D **13**
Llangybi. *Mon* —3A **60**
Llangyfelach. *Swan* —3B **56**
Llangynhafal. *Den* —1D **17**
Llangynidr. *Powy* —1C **59**
Llangynin. *Carm* —1B **54**
Llangynog. *Carm* —1C **55**
Llangynog. *Powy* —2B **24**
Llangynwyd. *B'End* —1D **63**
Llanhamlach. *Powy* —3B **48**
Llanharan. *Rhon* —1B **64**
Llanharry. *Rhon* —1A **64**
Llanhennock. *Mon* —3A **60**
Llanhilleth. *Blae* —2D **59**
Llanidloes. *Powy* —3A **30**
Llaniestyn. *Gwyn* —1B **20**
Llanigon. *Powy* —1D **49**
Llanilar. *Cdgn* —1B **36**
Llanilid. *Rhon* —1A **64**
Llanishen. *Card* —1C **65**
Llanishen. *Mon* —2B **60**
Llanllawddog. *Carm* —3D **45**
Llanllechid. *Gwyn* —1B **14**
Llanllowell. *Mon* —3A **60**
Llanllugan. *Powy* —1B **30**
Llanllwch. *Carm* —1C **55**
Llanllwchaiarn. *Powy* —2C **31**
Llanllwni. *Carm* —2D **45**
Llanllyfni. *Gwyn* —2D **13**
Llanmadoc. *Swan* —3D **55**
Llanmaes. *V Glam* —3A **64**
Llanmartin. *Newp* —1A **66**
Llanmerwig. *Powy* —2C **31**
Llanmihangel. *V Glam* —2A **64**
Llan-mill. *Pemb* —1A **54**
Llanmiloe. *Carm* —2B **54**
Llanmorlais. *Swan* —3A **56**
Llannefydd. *Cnwy* —3A **8**
Llannon. *Carm* —2A **56**
Llan-non. *Cdgn* —2A **36**
Llannor. *Gwyn* —1C **21**
Llanpumsaint. *Carm* —3D **45**
Llanrhaeadr. *Den* —1B **16**
Llanrhaeadr-ym-Mochnant. *Powy*
      —2C **25**
Llanrhian. *Swan* —3D **55**
Llanrhos. *Cnwy* —2C **7**
Llanrhyddlad. *IOA* —2C **5**

Llanrhystud. *Cdgn* —2A **36**
Llanrian. *Pemb* —2B **42**
Llanrothal. *Here* —1B **60**
Llanrug. *Gwyn* —1A **14**
Llanrumney. *Card* —1D **65**
Llanrwst. *Cnwy* —1C **15**
Llansadurnen. *Carm* —1B **54**
Llansadwrn. *IOA* —3A **6**
Llansaint. *Carm* —2C **55**
Llansamlet. *Swan* —3B **56**
Llansanffraid Glan Conwy. *Cnwy*
      —3D **7**
Llansannan. *Cnwy* —1A **16**
Llansannor. *V Glam* —2A **64**
Llansantffraed. *Cdgn* —2D **35**
Llansantffraed. *Powy* —3C **49**
Llansantffraed Cwmdeuddwr. *Powy*
      —2A **38**
Llansantffraed in Elwel. *Powy* —3C **39**
Llansantffraid-ym-Mechain. *Powy*
      —2D **25**
Llansawel. *Carm* —2B **46**
Llansilin. *Powy* —2D **25**
Llansoy. *Mon* —2B **60**
Llanspyddid. *Powy* —3B **48**
Llanstadwell. *Pemb* —2C **53**
Llansteffan. *Carm* —1C **55**
Llanstephan. *Powy* —1C **49**
Llantarnam. *Torf* —3D **59**
Llanteg. *Pemb* —1A **54**
Llanthony. *Mon* —3D **49**
Llantilio Crossenny. *Mon* —1A **60**
Llantilio Pertholey. *Mon* —1A **60**
Llantood. *Pemb* —1A **44**
Llantrisant. *Mon* —2B **60**
Llantrisant. *Rhon* —1B **64**
Llantrithyd. *V Glam* —2B **64**
Llantwit Fardre. *Rhon* —1B **64**
Llantwit Major. *V Glam* —3A **64**
Llanuwchllyn. *Gwyn* —1D **23**
Llanvaches. *Newp* —2B **60**
Llanvair Discoed. *Mon* —3B **60**
Llanvapley. *Mon* —1A **60**
Llanvetherine. *Mon* —1A **60**
Llanveynoe. *Here* —2A **50**
Llanvihangel Crucorney. *Mon* —3A **50**
Llanvihangel Gobion. *Mon* —2A **60**
Llanvihangel Ystern-Llewern. *Mon*
      —1B **60**
Llanwarne. *Here* —3C **51**
Llanwddyn. *Powy* —3B **24**
Llanwenarth. *Mon* —1D **59**
Llanwenog. *Cdgn* —1D **45**
Llanwern. *Newp* —1A **66**
Llanwinio. *Carm* —3B **44**
Llanwnda. *Gwyn* —2D **13**
Llanwnda. *Pemb* —2C **43**
Llanwnnen. *Cdgn* —1A **46**
Llanwnog. *Powy* —2B **30**
Llanwrda. *Carm* —2C **47**
Llanwrin. *Powy* —1C **29**
Llanwrthwl. *Powy* —2A **38**
Llanwrtyd. *Powy* —1D **47**
Llanwrtyd Wells. *Powy* —1D **47**
Llanwyddelan. *Powy* —1B **30**
Llanyblodwel. *Shrp* —2D **25**
Llanybri. *Carm* —1C **55**
Llanybydder. *Carm* —1A **46**
Llanycefn. *Pemb* —3D **43**
Llanychaer. *Pemb* —2C **43**
Llanycil. *Gwyn* —1A **24**
Llanymawddwy. *Gwyn* —3A **24**
Llanymddyfri. *Carm* —2C **47**
Llanymynech. *Powy* —2D **25**
Llanynghenedl. *IOA* —2C **5**
Llanynys. *Den* —1C **17**
Llan-y-pwll. *Wrex* —2A **18**
Llanyrafon. *Torf* —3A **60**
Llanyre. *Powy* —2B **38**
Llanystumdwy. *Gwyn* —1D **21**
Llanywern. *Powy* —3C **49**
Llawhaden. *Pemb* —1D **53**
Llawndy. *Flin* —2C **9**
Llawnt. *Shrp* —1D **25**
Llawr Dref. *Gwyn* —2B **20**
Llawryglyn. *Powy* —2A **30**
Llay. *Wrex* —2A **18**
Llechfaen. *Powy* —3B **48**
Llechryd. *Cphy* —2C **59**
Llechryd. *Cdgn* —1B **44**
Llechrydau. *Wrex* —1D **25**
Lledrod. *Cdgn* —1B **36**
Llethrid. *Swan* —3A **56**
Llidiad-Nenog. *Carm* —2A **46**
Llidiardau. *Gwyn* —1D **23**
Llidiart y Parc. *Den* —3C **17**

Llithfaen. *Gwyn* —3C **13**
Lloc. *Flin* —3C **9**
Llong. *Flin* —1D **17**
Llowes. *Powy* —1C **49**
Lloyney. *Powy* —1D **39**
Llundain-fach. *Cdgn* —3A **36**
Llwydcoed. *Rhon* —2A **58**
Llwyncelyn. *Cdgn* —3D **35**
Llwyncelyn. *Swan* —2B **56**
Llwyndaffydd. *Cdgn* —3C **35**
Llwynderw. *Powy* —1D **31**
Llwyn-du. *Mon* —1D **59**
Llwyngwril. *Gwyn* —1A **28**
Llwynhendy. *Carm* —3A **56**
Llwynmawr. *Wrex* —1D **25**
Llwyn-on Village. *Mer T* —1B **58**
Llwyn-teg. *Carm* —2A **56**
Llwyn-y-brain. *Carm* —1A **54**
Llwynygog. *Powy* —2D **29**
Llwyn-y-groes. *Cdgn* —3A **36**
Llwynypia. *Rhon* —3A **58**
Llynclys. *Shrp* —2D **25**
Llynfaes. *IOA* —3D **5**
Llysfaen. *Cnwy* —3D **7**
Llyswen. *Powy* —2C **49**
Llysworney. *V Glam* —2A **64**
Llys-y-fran. *Pemb* —3D **43**
Llywel. *Powy* —2D **47**
Llywernog. *Cdgn* —3C **29**
Locking. *N Som* —3A **66**
Lockleywood. *Shrp* —2D **27**
Logaston. *Here* —3A **40**
Loggerheads. *Staf* —1D **27**
Login. *Carm* —3A **44**
Long Ashton. *N Som* —2C **67**
Longden. *Shrp* —1B **32**
Longden Common. *Shrp* —1B **32**
Longdon on Tern. *Telf* —3D **27**
Longford. *Shrp* —1D **27**
Longford. *Telf* —3D **27**
Long Green. *Ches* —3B **10**
Longhope. *Glos* —1D **61**
Long Lane. *Telf* —3D **27**
Longley Green. *Worc* —3D **41**
Long Meadowend. *Shrp* —3B **32**
Longnor. *Shrp* —1B **32**
Longshaw. *G Man* —1C **11**
Longslow. *Shrp* —1D **27**
Longtown. *Here* —3A **50**
Longville in the Dale. *Shrp* —2C **33**
Loppington. *Shrp* —2B **26**
Lostock Gralam. *Ches* —3D **11**
Lostock Green. *Ches* —3D **11**
Loughor. *Swan* —3A **56**
Loughton. *Shrp* —3D **33**
Loveston. *Pemb* —2D **53**
Lowe. *Shrp* —1C **27**
Lower Brynamman. *Neat* —1C **57**
Lower Bullingham. *Here* —2C **51**
Lower Cam. *Glos* —2D **61**
Lower Chapel. *Powy* —2B **48**
Lower Down. *Shrp* —3A **32**
Lower Egleton. *Here* —1D **51**
Lower Failand. *N Som* —2C **67**
Lower Faintree. *Shrp* —3D **33**
Lower Hardwick. *Here* —3B **40**
Lower Hayton. *Shrp* —3C **33**
Lower Hergest. *Here* —3D **39**
Lower Hordley. *Shrp* —2A **26**
Lower Kinnerton. *Ches* —1A **18**
Lower Langford. *N Som* —3B **66**
Lower Ledwyche. *Shrp* —1C **41**
Lower Ley. *Glos* —1D **61**
Lower Llanfadog. *Powy* —2A **38**
Lower Lydbrook. *Glos* —1C **61**
Lower Lye. *Here* —2B **40**
Lower Machen. *Newp* —1D **65**
Lower Maes-coed. *Here* —2A **50**
Lower Meend. *Glos* —2C **61**
Lower Morton. *S Glo* —3D **61**
Lower Mountain. *Flin* —2A **18**
Lower Penarth. *V Glam* —3C **65**
Lower Peover. *Ches* —3D **11**
Lower Sketty. *Swan* —3B **56**
Lower Soudley. *Glos* —1D **61**
Lower Town. *Here* —1D **51**
Lower Town. *Pemb* —2C **43**
Lower Walton. *Warr* —2D **11**
Lower Welson. *Here* —3D **39**
Lower Whitley. *Ches* —3D **11**
Lower Wych. *Ches* —3B **18**
Lowton. *G Man* —1D **11**
Lowton Common. *G Man* —1D **11**
Lucton. *Here* —2B **40**
Ludchurch. *Pemb* —1A **54**
Ludford. *Shrp* —1C **41**

Ludlow. *Shrp* —1C **41**
Lugg Green. *Here* —2B **40**
Lugwardine. *Here* —1C **51**
Lulham. *Here* —1B **50**
Lulsgate Bottom. *N Som* —3C **67**
Lulsley. *Worc* —3D **41**
Lunnon. *Swan* —1A **62**
Lunt. *Mers* —1A **10**
Luston. *Here* —2B **40**
Luxley. *Glos* —3D **51**
Lydbury North. *Shrp* —3A **32**
Lydham. *Shrp* —2A **32**
Lydney. *Glos* —2D **61**
Lydstep. *Pemb* —3D **53**
Lye, The. *Shrp* —2D **33**
Lymm. *Warr* —2D **11**
Lyneal. *Shrp* —1B **26**
Lyne Down. *Here* —2D **51**
Lyonshall. *Here* —3A **40**

Machen. *Cphy* —1D **65**
Machroes. *Gwyn* —2C **21**
Machynlleth. *Powy* —1C **29**
Madeley. *Telf* —1D **33**
Madley. *Here* —2B **50**
Maenaddwyn. *IOA* —2D **5**
Maenclochog. *Pemb* —3D **43**
Maendy. *V Glam* —2B **64**
Maentwrog. *Gwyn* —3B **14**
Maen-y-groes. *Cdgn* —1A **44**
Maerdy. *Carm* —3B **46**
Maerdy. *Cnwy* —3B **16**
Maerdy. *Rhon* —3A **58**
Maesbrook. *Shrp* —2A **26**
Maesbury. *Shrp* —2A **26**
Maesbury Marsh. *Shrp* —2A **26**
Maes-glas. *Flin* —3C **9**
Maesgwyn-Isaf. *Powy* —3C **25**
Maeshafn. *Den* —1D **17**
Maes Llyn. *Cdgn* —1C **45**
Maesmynis. *Powy* —1B **48**
Maesteg. *B'End* —3D **57**
Maestir. *Cdgn* —1A **46**
Maesybont. *Carm* —1A **56**
Maesycrugiau. *Carm* —1D **45**
Maesycwmmer. *Cphy* —3C **59**
Maesyrhandir. *Powy* —2B **30**
Maghull. *Mers* —1A **10**
Magor. *Mon* —1B **66**
Magwyr. *Mon* —1B **66**
Maiden Wells. *Pemb* —3C **53**
Maindee. *Newp* —1A **66**
Mainstone. *Shrp* —3D **31**
Malinslee. *Telf* —1D **33**
Mallwyd. *Gwyn* —3D **23**
Malpas. *Ches* —3B **18**
Malpas. *Newp* —3D **59**
Malswick. *Glos* —3D **51**
Mamble. *Worc* —1D **41**
Mamhilad. *Mon* —2A **60**
Manafon. *Powy* —1C **31**
Mancot. *Flin* —1A **18**
Mangotsfield. *S Glo* —2D **67**
Manley. *Ches* —3C **11**
Manmoel. *Cphy* —2C **59**
Manorbier. *Pemb* —3D **53**
Manorbier Newton. *Pemb* —3D **53**
Manorowen. *Pemb* —2C **43**
Mansell Gamage. *Here* —1A **50**
Mansell Lacy. *Here* —1B **50**
Marbury. *Ches* —3C **19**
Marchamley. *Shrp* —2C **27**
Marchwiel. *Wrex* —3A **18**
Marcross. *V Glam* —3A **64**
Marden. *Here* —1C **51**
Mardu. *Shrp* —3D **31**
Mardy. *Mon* —1A **60**
Marford. *Wrex* —2A **18**
Margam. *Neat* —1C **63**
Marian Cwm. *Den* —3B **8**
Mariandyrys. *IOA* —2B **6**
Marian-glas. *IOA* —2A **6**
Marian-y-de. *Gwyn* —1C **21**
Marion-y-mor. *Gwyn* —1C **21**
Market Drayton. *Shrp* —1D **27**
Markham. *Cphy* —2C **59**
Marksbury. *Bath* —3D **67**
Marley Green. *Ches* —3C **19**
Marloes. *Pemb* —2A **52**
Marlow. *Here* —1B **40**
Marros. *Carm* —2B **54**
Marshbrook. *Shrp* —3B **32**
Marshfield. *Newp* —1D **65**
Marsh Green. *Telf* —3D **27**

Marsh, The. *Powy* —2A **32**
Marsh, The. *Shrp* —2D **27**
Marston. *Ches* —3D **11**
Marston. *Here* —3A **40**
Marston Stannett. *Here* —3C **41**
Marstow. *Here* —1C **61**
Martinscroft. *Warr* —2D **11**
Martletwy. *Pemb* —1D **53**
Marton. *Shrp* —2B **26**
  (Myddle)
Marton. *Shrp* —1D **31**
  (Worthen)
Mathern. *Mon* —3C **61**
Mathon. *Here* —1D **51**
Mathry. *Pemb* —2B **42**
Maund Bryan. *Here* —3C **41**
Mawdlam. *B'End* —1D **63**
Maw Green. *Ches* —2D **19**
Mayals. *Swan* —1B **62**
Mayhill. *Swan* —3B **56**
Maypole. *Mon* —1B **60**
Mayshill. *S Glo* —1D **67**
Meadgate. *Bath* —3D **67**
Meadowbank. *Ches* —1D **19**
Meadow Green. *Here* —3D **41**
Meadowtown. *Shrp* —1A **32**
Medlicott. *Shrp* —2B **32**
Meeson. *Telf* —2D **27**
Meidrim. *Carm* —3B **44**
Meifod. *Powy* —3C **25**
Meinciau. *Carm* —1D **55**
Meliden. *Den* —2B **8**
Melinbyrhedyn. *Powy* —2D **29**
Melincourt. *Neat* —2D **57**
Melin-y-coed. *Cnwy* —1D **15**
Melin-y-ddol. *Powy* —1B **30**
Melin-y-wig. *Den* —3B **16**
Melling. *Mers* —1A **10**
Melling Mount. *Mers* —1B **10**
Melverley. *Shrp* —3A **26**
Melverley Green. *Shrp* —3A **26**
Menai Bridge. *IOA* —3A **6**
Menithwood. *Worc* —2D **41**
Meole Brace. *Shrp* —3B **26**
Meols. *Mers* —2D **9**
Merbach. *Here* —1A **50**
Mere. *Ches* —2D **11**
Mere Heath. *Ches* —3D **11**
Meretown. *Staf* —2D **27**
Merlin's Bridge. *Pemb* —1C **53**
Merrington. *Shrp* —2B **26**
Merrion. *Pemb* —3C **53**
Merthyr. *Carm* —3C **45**
Merthyr Cynog. *Powy* —2A **48**
Merthyr Dyfan. *V Glam* —3C **65**
Merthyr Mawr. *B'End* —2D **63**
Merthyr Tudful. *Mer T* —2B **58**
Merthyr Tydfil. *Mer T* —2B **58**
Merthyr Vale. *Mer T* —2B **58**
Michaelchurch. *Here* —3C **51**
Michaelchurch Escley. *Here* —2A **50**
Michaelchurch-on-Arrow. *Powy*
  —3D **39**
Michaelston-le-Pit. *V Glam* —2C **65**
Michaelston-y-Vedw. *Newp* —1D **65**
Mickle Trafford. *Ches* —1B **18**
Middlehope. *Shrp* —3B **32**
Middle Maes-coed. *Here* —2A **50**
Middleton. *Here* —2C **41**
Middleton. *Shrp* —1C **41**
  (Ludlow)
Middleton. *Shrp* —2A **26**
  (Oswestry)
Middleton. *Swan* —3D **55**
Middleton on the Hill. *Here* —2C **41**
Middleton Priors. *Shrp* —2D **33**
Middleton Scriven. *Shrp* —3D **33**
Middletown. *Powy* —3A **26**
Middlewich. *Ches* —1D **19**
Milbury Heath. *S Glo* —3D **61**
Milebrook. *Powy* —1A **40**
Miles Hope. *Here* —2C **41**
Milford. *Powy* —2B **30**
Milford Haven. *Pemb* —2C **53**
Milkwall. *Glos* —2C **61**
Millend. *Glos* —3D **61**
Mill Green. *Shrp* —2D **27**
Millhalf. *Here* —1D **49**
Milson. *Shrp* —1D **41**
Milton. *N Som* —3A **66**
Milton. *Pemb* —2D **53**
Milton Green. *Ches* —2B **18**
Minera. *Wrex* —2D **17**
Minffordd. *Gwyn* —1A **22**
Minllyn. *Gwyn* —3D **23**
Minsterley. *Shrp* —1A **32**

Minton. *Shrp* —2B **32**
Minwear. *Pemb* —1D **53**
Miskin. *Rhon* —1B **64**
Mitcheldean. *Glos* —1D **61**
Mitchel Troy. *Mon* —1B **60**
Mitcheltroy Common. *Mon* —2B **60**
Moccas. *Here* —1A **50**
Mochdre. *Cnwy* —3D **7**
Mochdre. *Powy* —3B **30**
Moelfre. *Cnwy* —3A **8**
Moelfre. *IOA* —2A **6**
Moelfre. *Powy* —2C **25**
Mold. *Flin* —1D **17**
Mollington. *Ches* —3A **10**
Monachty. *Cdgn* —2A **36**
Monaughty. *Powy* —2D **39**
Monington. *Pemb* —1A **44**
Monkhide. *Here* —1D **51**
Monkhopton. *Shrp* —2D **33**
Monkland. *Here* —3B **40**
Monknash. *V Glam* —2A **64**
Monkswood. *Mon* —2A **60**
Monkton. *Pemb* —2C **53**
Monmarsh. *Here* —1C **51**
Monmouth. *Mon* —1C **61**
Monnington on Wye. *Here* —1A **50**
Montford. *Shrp* —3B **26**
Montford Bridge. *Shrp* —3B **26**
Montgomery. *Powy* —2D **31**
Moorcot. *Here* —3A **40**
Moore. *Hal* —2C **11**
Moorend. *Glos* —2D **61**
Moorhampton. *Here* —1A **50**
Moortown. *Telf* —3D **27**
Morda. *Shrp* —2D **25**
Mordiford. *Here* —2C **51**
More. *Shrp* —2A **32**
Morehouse, The. *Shrp* —2C **33**
Moreton. *Here* —2C **41**
Moreton. *Mers* —1D **9**
Moreton Corbet. *Shrp* —2C **27**
Moreton Jeffries. *Here* —1D **51**
Moreton on Lugg. *Here* —1C **51**
Moreton Say. *Shrp* —1D **27**
Morfa. *Cdgn* —3C **35**
Morfa Bach. *Carm* —1C **55**
Morfa Bychan. *Gwyn* —1A **22**
Morfa Glas. *Neat* —2D **57**
Morfa Nefyn. *Gwyn* —3B **12**
Morganstown. *Card* —1C **65**
Moriah. *Cdgn* —1B **36**
Morriston. *Swan* —3B **56**
Mortimer's Cross. *Here* —2B **40**
Morton. *Shrp* —2D **25**
Morton. *S Glo* —3D **61**
Morton Mill. *Shrp* —2C **27**
Morvil. *Pemb* —2D **43**
Morville. *Shrp* —2D **33**
Mose. *Shrp* —2D **33**
Moss. *Wrex* —2A **18**
Moss Bank. *Mers* —1C **11**
Mossbrow. *G Man* —2D **11**
Mossley Hill. *Mers* —2A **10**
Moss Side. *Mers* —1A **10**
Moston. *Shrp* —2C **27**
Moston Green. *Ches* —1D **19**
Mostyn. *Flin* —2C **9**
Mouldsworth. *Ches* —3C **11**
Moulton. *Ches* —1D **19**
Moulton. *V Glam* —2B **64**
Mountain Ash. *Rhon* —3B **58**
Mountain Water. *Pemb* —3C **43**
Mounton. *Mon* —3C **61**
Moylgrove. *Pemb* —1A **44**
Much Birch. *Here* —2C **51**
Much Cowarne. *Here* —1D **51**
Much Dewchurch. *Here* —2B **50**
Much Marcle. *Here* —2D **51**
Much Wenlock. *Shrp* —1D **33**
Mucklestone. *Staf* —1D **27**
Muckleton. *Shrp* —2C **27**
Muckley. *Shrp* —2D **33**
Mumbles, The. *Swan* —1B **62**
Munderfield Row. *Here* —3D **41**
Munderfield Stocks. *Here* —3D **41**
Munsley. *Here* —1D **51**
Munslow. *Shrp* —3C **33**
Murdishaw. *Hal* —2C **11**
Murton. *Swan* —1A **62**
Muxton. *Telf* —3D **27**
Mwmbwls. *Swan* —1B **62**
Myddfai. *Carm* —2C **47**
Myddle. *Shrp* —2B **26**
Mydroilyn. *Cdgn* —3D **35**
Mynachlog-ddu. *Pemb* —2A **44**
Mynydd-bach. *Mon* —3B **60**

Mynydd Isa. *Flin* —1D **17**
Mynyddislwyn. *Cphy* —3C **59**
Mynydd Llandegai. *Gwyn* —1B **14**
Mynydd-y-briw. *Powy* —2C **25**
Mynyddygarreg. *Carm* —2D **55**
Mynytho. *Gwyn* —1C **21**
Mytton. *Shrp* —3B **26**

Nailbridge. *Glos* —1D **61**
Nailsea. *N Som* —2B **66**
Nanhyfer. *Pemb* —1D **43**
Nannerch. *Flin* —1C **17**
Nant-ddu. *Rhon* —1B **58**
Nanternis. *Cdgn* —3C **35**
Nantgaredig. *Carm* —3D **45**
Nantgarw. *Rhon* —1C **65**
Nant Glas. *Powy* —2A **38**
Nantglyn. *Den* —1B **16**
Nantgwyn. *Powy* —1A **38**
Nantlle. *Gwyn* —2A **14**
Nantmawr. *Shrp* —2D **25**
Nantmel. *Powy* —2B **38**
Nantmor. *Gwyn* —3B **14**
Nant Peris. *Gwyn* —2B **14**
Nantwich. *Ches* —2D **19**
Nant-y-bai. *Carm* —1C **47**
Nant-y-Derry. *Mon* —2A **60**
Nant-y-dugoed. *Powy* —3A **24**
Nant-y-felin. *Cnwy* —3B **6**
Nantyffyllon. *B'End* —3D **57**
Nantyglo. *Blae* —1C **59**
Nant-y-meichiaid. *Powy* —3C **25**
Nant-y-moel. *B'End* —3A **58**
Nant-y-Pandy. *Cnwy* —3B **6**
Narberth. *Pemb* —1A **54**
Narberth Bridge. *Pemb* —1A **54**
Narth, The. *Mon* —2C **61**
Nasareth. *Gwyn* —3D **13**
Nash. *Here* —2A **40**
Nash. *Newp* —1A **66**
Nash. *Shrp* —1D **41**
Neath. *Neat* —3C **57**
Neath Abbey. *Neat* —3C **57**
Nebo. *Cdgn* —2A **36**
Nebo. *Cnwy* —2D **15**
Nebo. *Gwyn* —3D **13**
Nebo. *IOA* —1D **5**
Neen Savage. *Shrp* —1D **41**
Neen Sollars. *Shrp* —1D **41**
Neenton. *Shrp* —3D **33**
Nefyn. *Gwyn* —3C **13**
Nelly Andrews Green. *Powy*
  —1D **31**
Nelson. *Cphy* —3C **59**
Nempnett Thrubwell. *Bath* —3C **67**
Nercwys. *Flin* —1D **17**
Ness. *Ches* —3A **10**
Nesscliffe. *Shrp* —3A **26**
Neston. *Ches* —3D **9**
Netchwood. *Shrp* —2D **33**
Netherend. *Glos* —2C **61**
Netherton. *Here* —3C **51**
Netherton. *Mers* —1A **10**
Netherton. *Shrp* —3D **33**
Netley. *Shrp* —1B **32**
Neuadd. *Carm* —3C **47**
Neuadd. *Powy* —1B **30**
Nevern. *Pemb* —1D **43**
Newborough. *IOA* —1D **13**
Newbridge. *Cphy* —3D **59**
Newbridge. *Cdgn* —3A **36**
Newbridge. *Pemb* —2C **43**
Newbridge. *Wrex* —3D **17**
Newbridge-on-Usk. *Mon* —3A **60**
Newbridge on Wye. *Powy* —3B **38**
New Brighton. *Flin* —1D **17**
New Broughton. *Wrex* —2A **18**
Newcastle. *B'End* —1D **63**
Newcastle. *Mon* —1B **60**
Newcastle. *Shrp* —3D **31**
Newcastle Emlyn. *Carm* —1C **45**
Newchapel. *Pemb* —2B **44**
Newchapel. *Powy* —3A **30**
Newchurch. *Carm* —3C **45**
Newchurch. *Here* —3A **40**
Newchurch. *Mon* —3B **60**
Newchurch. *Powy* —3D **39**
New Cross. *Cdgn* —1B **36**
Newent. *Glos* —3D **51**
New Ferry. *Mers* —2A **10**
Newgate. *Pemb* —3B **42**
Newhall. *Ches* —3D **19**
New Hedges. *Pemb* —2A **54**
New Inn. *Carm* —2D **45**
New Inn. *Mon* —2B **60**

New Inn. *Torf* —3A **60**
New Invention. *Shrp* —1D **39**
Newland. *Glos* —2C **61**
New Lane End. *Warr* —1D **11**
New Marton. *Shrp* —1A **26**
New Mills. *Mon* —2C **61**
New Mills. *Powy* —1B **30**
New Moat. *Pemb* —3D **43**
Newnham. *Glos* —1D **61**
Newnham Bridge. *Worc* —2D **41**
Newport. *Glos* —3D **61**
Newport. *Newp* —1A **66**
Newport. *Pemb* —2D **43**
Newport. *Telf* —3D **27**
New Quay. *Cdgn* —3C **35**
New Radnor. *Powy* —2D **39**
New Row. *Cdgn* —1C **37**
New Street. *Here* —3A **40**
Newstreet Lane. *Shrp* —1D **27**
Newton. *B'End* —2D **63**
Newton. *Ches* —1B **18**
(Chester)
Newton. *Ches* —2C **19**
(Tattenhall)
Newton. *Here* —2A **50**
(Ewyas Harold)
Newton. *Here* —3C **41**
(Leominster)
Newton. *Mers* —2D **9**
Newton. *Shrp* —2D **33**
(Bridgnorth)
Newton. *Shrp* —1B **26**
(Wem)
Newton. *Swan* —1B **62**
Newton Green. *Mon* —3C **61**
Newton-le-Willows. *Mers* —1C **11**
Newton on the Hill. *Shrp* —2B **26**
Newton St Loe. *Bath* —3D **67**
Newtown. *Ches* —3D **19**
Newtown. *Glos* —2D **61**
Newtown. *Here* —2D **51**
(Ledbury)
Newtown. *Here* —2C **51**
(Little Dewchurch)
Newtown. *Here* —1D **51**
(Stretton Grandison)
Newtown. *Powy* —2C **31**
Newtown. *Rhon* —3B **58**
Newtown. *Shrp* —1B **26**
New Tredegar. *Cphy* —2C **59**
Nextend. *Here* —3A **40**
Neyland. *Pemb* —2C **53**
Nib Heath. *Shrp* —3B **26**
Nicholaston. *Swan* —1A **62**
Niwbwrch. *IOA* —1D **13**
Nobold. *Shrp* —3B **26**
Nolton. *Pemb* —1B **52**
Nolton Haven. *Pemb* —1B **52**
No Man's Heath. *Ches* —3C **19**
Noneley. *Shrp* —2B **26**
Norbridge. *Here* —1D **51**
Norbury. *Ches* —3C **19**
Norbury. *Shrp* —2A **32**
Nordley. *Shrp* —2D **33**
Norley. *Ches* —3C **11**
Norris Green. *Mers* —1A **10**
North Cornelly. *B'End* 1D **63**
North End. *N Som* —3B **66**
North Nibley. *Glos* —3D **61**
Northop. *Flin* —1D **17**
Northop Hall. *Flin* —1D **17**
North Stoke. *Bath* —3D **67**
Northway. *Swan* —1A **62**
North Weston. *N Som* —2B **66**
Northwich. *Ches* —3D **11**
North Wick. *Bath* —3C **67**
Northwick. *S Glo* —1C **67**
North Widcombe. *Bath* —3C **67**
Northwood. *Shrp* —1B **26**
Northwood Green. *Glos* —1D **61**
Norton. *Hal* —2C **11**
Norton. *Mon* —3B **50**
Norton. *Powy* —2A **40**
Norton. *Shrp* —3B **32**
(Ludlow)
Norton. *Shrp* —1D **33**
(Madeley)
Norton. *Shrp* —1C **33**
(Shrewsbury)
Norton. *Swan* —1B **62**
Norton Canon. *Here* —1A **50**
Norton Hawkfield. *Bath* —3C **67**
Norton in Hales. *Shrp* —1D **27**
Norton Malreward. *Bath* —3D **67**
Nottage. *B'End* —2D **63**
Nox. *Shrp* —3B **26**

Noyadd Trefawr. *Cdgn* —1B **44**
Nurston. *V Glam* —3B **64**

Oakdale. *Cphy* —3C **59**
Oakengates. *Telf* —3D **27**
Oakenholt. *Flin* —3D **9**
Oakford. *Cdgn* —3D **35**
Oaklands. *Powy* —3B **38**
Oakley Park. *Powy* —3A **30**
Oakmere. *Ches* —1C **19**
Oaks. *Shrp* —1B **32**
Occlestone Green. *Ches* —1D **19**
Ocle Pychard. *Here* —1C **51**
Odd Down. *Bath* —3D **67**
Ogmore. *V Glam* —2D **63**
Ogmore-by-Sea. *V Glam* —2D **63**
Ogmore Vale. *B'End* —1A **64**
Oldbury. *Shrp* —2D **33**
Oldbury-on-Severn. *S Glo* —3D **61**
Oldcastle. *Mon* —3A **50**
Oldcastle Heath. *Ches* —3B **18**
Old Colwyn. *Cnwy* —3D **7**
Old Down. *S Glo* —1D **67**
Oldfield. *Shrp* —3D **33**
Old Forge. *Here* —1C **61**
Old Gore. *Here* —3D **51**
Oldland. *S Glo* —2D **67**
Old Llanberis. *Gwyn* —2B **14**
Oldmixon. *N Som* —3A **66**
Old Park. *Telf* —1D **33**
Old Radnor. *Powy* —3D **39**
Old Swan. *Mers* —1A **10**
Oldwalls. *Swan* —3D **55**
Oldwood Common. *Worc* —2C **41**
Ollerton. *Shrp* —2D **27**
Olmarch. *Cdgn* —3B **36**
Olveston. *S Glo* —1D **67**
Onen. *Mon* —1B **60**
Ongar Street. *Here* —2A **40**
Onibury. *Shrp* —1B **40**
Onllwyn. *Neat* —1D **57**
Onneley. *Shrp* —3D **19**
Orcop. *Here* —3B **50**
Orcop Hill. *Here* —3B **50**
Oreton. *Shrp* —3D **33**
Orford. *Warr* —1D **11**
Orleton. *Here* —2B **40**
Orleton. *Worc* —2D **41**
Orleton Common. *Here* —2B **40**
Orrell. *Mers* —1A **10**
Osbaston. *Shrp* —2A **26**
Oscroft. *Ches* —1C **19**
Oswestry. *Shrp* —2D **25**
Otterspool. *Mers* —2A **10**
Oughtrington. *Warr* —2D **11**
Over. *Ches* —1D **19**
Over. *S Glo* —1C **67**
Over Monnow. *Mon* —1C **61**
Overpool. *Ches* —3A **10**
Overton. *Ches* —3C **11**
Overton. *Shrp* —3D **33**
(Bridgnorth)
Overton. *Shrp* —1C **41**
(Ludlow)
Overton. *Swan* —1A **62**
Ovorton. *Wrox* 3Λ **18**
Owlbury. *Shrp* —2A **32**
Owrytn. *Wrex* —3A **18**
Oxenhall. *Glos* —3D **51**
Oxton. *Mers* —2D **9**
Oxwich. *Swan* —3D **55**
Oxwich Green. *Swan* —1A **62**
Oystermouth. *Swan* —1B **62**

Paddington. *Warr* —2D **11**
Paddolgreen. *Shrp* —1C **27**
Padeswood. *Flin* —1D **17**
Painscastle. *Powy* —1C **49**
Pale. *Gwyn* —1A **24**
Palmerstown. *V Glam* —3C **65**
Pandy. *Gwyn* —2D **23**
(Bala)
Pandy. *Gwyn* —1B **28**
(Tywyn)
Pandy. *Mon* —3A **50**
Pandy. *Powy* —1A **30**
Pandy. *Wrex* —1C **25**
Pandy Tudur. *Cnwy* —1D **15**
Pant. *Shrp* —2D **25**
Pant. *Wrex* —3A **18**
Pantasaph. *Flin* —3C **9**
Pant Glas. *Gwyn* —3D **13**
Pant-glas. *Shrp* —1D **25**
Pantgwyn. *Carm* —3A **46**

Pantgwyn. *Cdgn* —1B **44**
Pant-lasau. *Swan* —3B **56**
Pant-pastynog. *Den* —1B **16**
Pantperthog. *Gwyn* —1C **29**
Pant-teg. *Carm* —3D **45**
Pant-y-Caws. *Carm* —3A **44**
Pant-y-dwr. *Powy* —1A **38**
Pant-y-ffridd. *Powy* —1C **31**
Pantyffynnon. *Carm* —1B **56**
Pantygasseg. *Torf* —2D **59**
Pant-y-llyn. *Carm* —1B **56**
Pant-yr-awel. *B'End* —1A **64**
Pant y Wacco. *Flin* —3C **9**
Parc. *Gwyn* —1D **23**
Parcllyn. *Cdgn* —3B **34**
Parc-Seymour. *Newp* —3B **60**
Parkend. *Glos* —2D **61**
Parkgate. *Ches* —3D **9**
Park Hill. *Mers* —1B **10**
Parkhouse. *Mon* —2B **60**
Parkmill. *Swan* —1A **62**
Parkway. *Here* —2D **51**
Parr. *Mers* —1C **11**
Parrog. *Pemb* —2D **43**
Partington. *G Man* —1D **11**
Patchway. *S Glo* —1D **67**
Paulton. *Bath* —3D **67**
Peasedown St John. *Bath* —3D **67**
Peasley Cross. *Mers* —1C **11**
Peaton. *Shrp* —3C **33**
Peckforton. *Ches* —2C **19**
Pedair-ffordd. *Powy* —2C **25**
Pelcomb Bridge. *Pemb* —1C **53**
Pelcomb Cross. *Pemb* —1C **53**
Pemberton. *Carm* —2A **56**
Pembrey. *Carm* —2D **55**
Pembridge. *Here* —3A **40**
Pembroke. *Pemb* —2C **53**
Pembroke Dock. *Pemb* —2C **53**
Pembroke Ferry. *Pemb* —2C **53**
Penallt. *Mon* —2C **61**
Penally. *Pemb* —3A **54**
Penalt. *Here* —3C **51**
Penalum. *Pemb* —3A **54**
Penarth. *V Glam* —2C **65**
Pen-bont Rhydybeddau. *Cdgn*
—3B **28**
Penbryn. *Cdgn* —3B **34**
Pencader. *Carm* —2D **45**
Pen-cae. *Cdgn* —3D **35**
Pencaenewydd. *Gwyn* —3D **13**
Pencaerau. *Neat* —3C **57**
Pencarnisiog. *IOA* —3C **5**
Pencarreg. *Carm* —1A **46**
Pencelli. *Powy* —3A **48**
Pen-clawdd. *Swan* —3A **56**
Pencoed. *B'End* —1A **64**
Pencombe. *Here* —3C **41**
Pencraig. *Here* —3C **51**
Pencraig. *Powy* —2A **24**
Penderyn. *Rhon* —2A **58**
Pendine. *Carm* —2B **54**
Pendoylan. *V Glam* —2B **64**
Pendre. *B'End* —1A **64**
Penegoes. *Powy* —1C **29**
Penffordd. *Pemb* —3D **43**
Penffordd-Las. *Powy* —2D **29**
Penfro. *Pemb* —2C **53**
Pengam. *Cphy* —3C **59**
Pengam. *Card* —2D **65**
Pengenffordd. *Powy* —2C **49**
Pengorffwysfa. *IOA* —1D **5**
Pengwern. *Den* —3B **8**
Penhelig. *Gwyn* —2B **28**
Penhow. *Newp* —3B **60**
Peniarth. *Gwyn* —1B **28**
Peniel. *Carm* —3D **45**
Penisa'r Waun. *Gwyn* —1A **14**
Penketh. *Warr* —2C **11**
Penley. *Wrex* —1B **26**
Penllech. *Gwyn* —1B **20**
Penllergaer. *Swan* —3B **56**
Pen-llyn. *IOA* —2C **5**
Penmachno. *Cnwy* —2C **15**
Penmaen. *Swan* —1A **62**
Penmaenmawr. *Cnwy* —3C **7**
Penmaenpool. *Gwyn* —3B **22**
Penmaen Rhos. *Cnwy* —3D **7**
Penmark. *V Glam* —3B **64**
Penmon. *IOA* —2B **6**
Penmorfa. *Gwyn* —3A **14**
Penmynydd. *IOA* —3A **6**
Pennal. *Gwyn* —1C **29**
Pennant. *Cdgn* —2A **36**
Pennant. *Den* —1B **24**
Pennant. *Gwyn* —2A **24**

Pennant. *Powy* —2D **29**
Pennant Melangell. *Powy* —2B **24**
Pennar. *Pemb* —2C **53**
Pennard. *Swan* —1A **62**
Pennerley. *Shrp* —2A **32**
Pennington. *G Man* —1D **11**
Pennorth. *Powy* —3C **49**
Pennsylvania. *S Glo* —2D **67**
Penparc. *Cdgn* —1B **44**
Penparcau. *Cdgn* —3A **28**
Penpedairheol. *Cphy* —3C **59**
Penperlleni. *Mon* —2A **60**
Penpont. *Powy* —3A **48**
Penprysg. *B'End* —1A **64**
Penrherber. *Carm* —2B **44**
Penrhiw. *Pemb* —1B **44**
Penrhiwceiber. *Rhon* —3B **58**
Pen Rhiwfawr. *Neat* —1C **57**
Penrhiw-llan. *Cdgn* —1C **45**
Penrhiw-pal. *Cdgn* —1C **45**
Penrhos. *Gwyn* —1C **21**
Penrhos. *Here* —3A **40**
Penrhos. *IOA* —2B **4**
Penrhos. *Mon* —1B **60**
Penrhos. *Powy* —1D **57**
Penrhos garnedd. *Gwyn* —3A **6**
Penrhyn. *IOA* —1C **5**
Penrhyn Bay. *Cnwy* —2D **7**
Penrhyn-coch. *Cdgn* —3B **28**
Penrhyndeudraeth. *Gwyn* —1B **22**
Penrhyn Side. *Cnwy* —2D **7**
Penrice. *Swan* —3D **55**
Pensarn. *Carm* —1D **55**
Pen-sarn. *Gwyn* —2A **22**
Pensax. *Worc* —2D **41**
Pensby. *Mers* —2D **9**
Pensford. *Bath* —3D **67**
Pente-tafarn-y-fedw. *Cnwy* —1D **15**
Pentir. *Gwyn* —1A **14**
Pentlepoir. *Pemb* —2A **54**
Pentraeth. *IOA* —3A **6**
Pentre. *Powy* —2D **31**
(Church Stoke)
Pentre. *Powy* —3C **31**
(Kerry)
Pentre. *Powy* —3B **30**
(Mochdre)
Pentre. *Rhon* —3A **58**
Pentre. *Shrp* —3A **26**
Pentre. *Wrex* —1C **25**
(Llanfyllin)
Pentre. *Wrex* —3D **17**
(Rhosllanerchrugog)
Pentrebach. *Carm* —2D **47**
Pentre-bach. *Cdgn* —1A **46**
Pentrebach. *Mer T* —2B **58**
Pentre-bach. *Powy* —2A **48**
Pentrebach. *Swan* —2B **56**
Pentre Berw. *IOA* —3D **5**
Pentre-bont. *Cnwy* —2C **15**
Pentrecagal. *Carm* —1C **45**
Pentre-celyn. *Den* —2C **17**
Pentre-clawdd. *Shrp* —1D **25**
Pentreclwydau. *Neat* —2D **57**
Pentre-cwrt. *Carm* —2C **45**
Pentre Dolau Honddu. *Powy* —1A **48**
Pentre-du. *Cnwy* —2C **15**
Pentre-dwr. *Neat* —3B **56**
Pentrefelin. *Carm* —3A **46**
Pentrefelin. *Cdgn* —1B **46**
Pentrefelin. *Gwyn* —1D **21**
Pentrefelin. *Gwyn* —1A **22**
Pentrefoelas. *Cnwy* —2D **15**
Pentre Galar. *Pemb* —2A **44**
Pentregat. *Cdgn* —3C **35**
Pentre Gwenlais. *Carm* —1B **56**
Pentre Gwynfryn. *Gwyn* —2A **22**
Pentre Halkyn. *Flin* —3D **9**
Pentre Hodre. *Shrp* —1A **40**
Pentre-Llanrhaeadr. *Den* —1B **16**
Pentre Llifior. *Powy* —2C **31**
Pentrellwyn. *IOA* —2A **6**
Pentre-llwyn-llwyd. *Powy* —3A **38**
Pentre-llyn-cymmer. *Cnwy* —2A **16**
Pentre Meyrick. *V Glam* —2A **64**
Pentre-piod. *Gwyn* —1D **23**
Pentre-poeth. *Newp* —1D **65**
Pentre'r Beirdd. *Powy* —3C **25**
Pentre'r-felin. *Powy* —2A **48**
Pentre-ty-gwyn. *Carm* —2D **47**
Pentre-uchaf. *Gwyn* —1C **21**
Pen-twyn. *Cphy* —2D **59**
(Oakdale)
Pentwyn. *Cphy* —2C **59**
(Rhymney)
Pentwyn. *Card* —1D **65**

Pentyrch. *Card* —1C **65**
Pentywyn. *Carm* —2B **54**
Penuwch. *Cdgn* —2A **36**
Penwyllt. *Powy* —1D **57**
Penybanc. *Carm* —1B **56**
(Ammanford)
Pen-y-banc. *Carm* —3B **46**
(Llandeilo)
Pen-y-bont. *Carm* —3C **45**
Penybont. *Powy* —2C **39**
(Llandrindod Wells)
Pen-y-bont. *Powy* —2D **25**
(Llanfyllin)
Pen-y-Bont Ar Ogwr. *B'End* —1A **64**
Penybontfawr. *Powy* —2B **24**
Penybryn. *Cphy* —3C **59**
Pen-y-bryn. *Pemb* —1A **44**
Pen-y-bryn. *Wrex* —3D **17**
Pen-y-cae. *Powy* —1D **57**
Penycae. *Wrex* —3D **17**
Pen-y-cae-mawr. *Mon* —3B **60**
Penycaerau. *Gwyn* —2A **20**
Pen-y-cefn. *Flin* —3C **9**
Pen-y-clawdd. *Mon* —2B **60**
Pen-y-coedcae. *Rhon* —1B **64**
Penycwm. *Pemb* —3B **42**
Pen-y-darren. *Mer T* —2B **58**
Pen-y-fai. *B'End* —1D **63**
Penyffordd. *Flin* —1A **18**
(Mold)
Pen-y-ffordd. *Flin* —2C **9**
(Prestatyn)
Penyffridd. *Gwyn* —2A **14**
Pen-y-garn. *Cdgn* —3B **28**
Pen-y-garnedd. *IOA* —3A **6**
Penygarnedd. *Powy* —2C **25**
Pen-y-graig. *Gwyn* —1A **20**
Penygraig. *Rhon* —3A **58**
Pen-y-groes. *Carm* —1A **56**
Penygroes. *Gwyn* —2D **13**
Penygroes. *Pemb* —2A **44**
Penymynydd. *Flin* —1A **18**
Penyrheol. *Cphy* —1C **65**
Pen-yr-heol. *Mon* —1B **60**
Penyrheol. *Swan* —3A **56**
Pen-yr-Heolgerrig. *Mer T* —2B **58**
Penysarn. *IOA* —1D **5**
Pen-y-stryt. *Den* —2D **17**
Penywaun. *Rhon* —2A **58**
Peplow. *Shrp* —2D **27**
Perthy. *Shrp* —1A **26**
Peterchurch. *Here* —2A **50**
Peterstone Wentlooge. *Newp*
—1D **65**
Peterston-super-Ely. *V Glam*
—2B **64**
Peterstow. *Here* —3C **51**
Petton. *Shrp* —2B **26**
Phocle Green. *Here* —3D **51**
Pibwrlwyd. *Carm* —1D **55**
Picklenash. *Glos* —3D **51**
Picklescott. *Shrp* —2B **32**
Pickmere. *Ches* —3D **11**
Pickstock. *Telf* —2D **27**
Picton. *Ches* —3B **10**
Picton. *Flin* —2C **9**
Pie Corner. *Here* —2D **41**
Pill. *N Som* —2C **67**
Pilleth. *Powy* —2D **39**
Pillgwenlly. *Newp* —1A **66**
Pillowell. *Glos* —2D **61**
Pill, The. *Mon* —1B **66**
Pilning. *S Glo* —1C **67**
Pilton Green. *Swan* —3D **55**
Pinged. *Carm* —2D **55**
Pinsley Green. *Ches* —3C **19**
Pipe and Lyde. *Here* —1C **51**
Pipe Aston. *Here* —1B **40**
Pipe Gate. *Shrp* —3D **19**
Pipton. *Powy* —2C **49**
Pistyll. *Gwyn* —3C **13**
Pitchford. *Shrp* —1C **33**
Pitt Court. *Glos* —3D **61**
Pitton. *Swan* —3D **55**
Pixley. *Here* —2D **51**
Plain Dealings. *Pemb* —1D **53**
Plaish. *Shrp* —2C **33**
Plaistow. *Here* —1D **51**
Plas Llwyd. *Cnwy* —3A **8**
Plas yn Cefn. *Den* —3B **8**
Platt Bridge. *G Man* —1D **11**
Platt Lane. *Shrp* —1C **27**
Plealey. *Shrp* —1B **32**
Ploughfield. *Here* —1A **50**
Plowden. *Shrp* —3A **32**
Ploxgreen. *Shrp* —1A **32**

Plumley. *Ches* —3D **11**
Plwmp. *Cdgn* —3C **35**
Ponde. *Powy* —2C **49**
Pontamman. *Carm* —1B **56**
Pontantwn. *Carm* —1D **55**
Pontardawe. *Neat* —2C **57**
Pontardulais. *Swan* —2A **56**
Pontarfynach. *Cdgn* —1C **37**
Pont-ar-gothi. *Carm* —3A **46**
Pont ar Hydfer. *Powy* —3D **47**
Pontarllechau. *Carm* —3C **47**
Pontarsais. *Carm* —3D **45**
Pontblyddyn. *Flin* —1D **17**
Pontbren Llwyd. *Rhon* —2A **58**
Pont Cyfyng. *Cnwy* —2C **15**
Pontdolgoch. *Powy* —2B **30**
Ponterwyd. *Cdgn* —3C **29**
Pontesbury. *Shrp* —1B **32**
Pontesford. *Shrp* —1B **32**
Pontfadog. *Wrex* —1D **25**
Pontfaen. *Pemb* —2D **43**
Pont-faen. *Powy* —2A **48**
Pont-Faen. *Shrp* —1D **25**
Pontgarreg. *Cdgn* —3C **35**
Pont-Henri. *Carm* —2D **55**
Ponthir. *Torf* —3A **60**
Ponthirwaun. *Cdgn* —1B **44**
Pontllanfraith. *Cphy* —2C **59**
Pontlliw. *Swan* —2B **56**
Pont Llogel. *Powy* —3B **24**
Pontllyfni. *Gwyn* —2D **13**
Pontlottyn. *Cphy* —2C **59**
Pontneddfechan. *Rhon* —2A **58**
Pont-newydd. *Carm* —2D **55**
Pont-newydd. *Flin* —1C **17**
Pontnewydd. *Torf* —3A **60**
Pont Pen-y-benglog. *Gwyn* —1B **14**
Pontrhydfendigaid. *Cdgn* —2C **37**
Pont Rhyd-y-cyff. *B'End* —1D **63**
Pontrhydyfen. *Neat* —3C **57**
Pont-rhyd-y-groes. *Cdgn* —1C **37**
Pontrhydyrun. *Torf* —3D **59**
Pont Rhythallt. *Gwyn* —1A **14**
Pontrilas. *Here* —3A **50**
Pontrilas Road. *Here* —3A **50**
Pontrobert. *Powy* —3C **25**
Pont-rug. *Gwyn* —1A **14**
Pontshill. *Here* —3D **51**
Pont-Sian. *Cdgn* —1A **45**
Pontsticill. *Mer T* —1B **58**
Pont-Walby. *Neat* —2D **57**
Pontwelly. *Carm* —2D **45**
Pontwgan. *Cnwy* —3C **7**
Pontyates. *Carm* —2D **55**
Pontyberem. *Carm* —1A **56**
Pontybodkin. *Flin* —2D **17**
Pontyclun. *Rhon* —1B **64**
Pontycymer. *B'End* —3A **58**
Pontyglazier. *Pemb* —2A **44**
Pontygwaith. *Rhon* —3B **58**
Pont-y-pant. *Cnwy* —2C **15**
Pontypool. *Torf* —3D **59**
Pontypridd. *Rhon* —3B **58**
Pontypwl. *Torf* —3D **59**
Pontywaun. *Cphy* —3D **59**
Poole Green. *Ches* —2D **19**
Pool Head. *Here* —3C **41**
Poolhill. *Glos* —3D **51**
Poolmill. *Here* —3C **51**
Pool Quay. *Powy* —3D **25**
Pope Hill. *Pemb* —3C **53**
Pope's Hill. *Glos* —1D **61**
Portbury. *N Som* —2C **67**
Port Dinorwig. *Gwyn* —1A **14**
Port-Eynon. *Swan* —1A **62**
Portfield Gate. *Pemb* —1C **53**
Porth. *Rhon* —3B **58**
Porthaethwy. *IOA* —3A **6**
Porthcawl. *B'End* —2D **63**
Porthgain. *Pemb* —2B **42**
Porthill. *Shrp* —3B **32**
Porthkerry. *V Glam* —3B **64**
Porthllechog. *IOA* —1D **5**
Porthmadog. *Gwyn* —1A **22**
Porthmeirion. *Gwyn* —1A **22**
Porth Tywyn. *Carm* —2D **55**
Porth-y-felin. *IOA* —2B **4**
Porthyrhyd. *Carm* —1A **56**
(Carmarthen)
Porthyrhyd. *Carm* —2C **47**
(Llandovery)
Porth-y-waen. *Shrp* —2D **25**
Portishead. *N Som* —2B **66**
Port Lion. *Pemb* —2C **53**
Port Mead. *Swan* —3B **56**
Portskewett. *Mon* —1C **67**

Port Sunlight. *Mers* —2A **10**
Port Talbot. *Neat* —1C **63**
Port Tennant. *Swan* —3B **56**
Portway. *Here* —1B **50**
Post-mawr. *Cdgn* —3D **35**
Pound Bank. *Worc* —1D **41**
Poynton. *Telf* —3C **27**
Poynton Green. *Telf* —3C **27**
Prees. *Shrp* —1C **27**
Prees Green. *Shrp* —1C **27**
Prees Higher Heath. *Shrp* —1C **27**
Prendergast. *Pemb* —1C **53**
Pren-gwyn. *Cdgn* —1D **45**
Prenteg. *Gwyn* —3A **14**
Prenton. *Mers* —2A **10**
Prescot. *Mers* —1B **10**
Prescott. *Shrp* —2B **26**
Prestatyn. *Den* —2B **8**
Presteigne. *Powy* —2A **40**
Presthope. *Shrp* —2C **33**
Preston. *Shrp* —3C **27**
Preston Brockhurst. *Shrp* —2C **27**
Preston Brook. *Hal* —3C **11**
Preston Cross. *Glos* —2D **51**
Preston Gubbals. *Shrp* —3B **26**
Preston Marsh. *Here* —1C **51**
Preston on Wye. *Here* —1A **50**
Preston upon the Weald Moors. *Telf*
—3D **27**
Preston Wynne. *Here* —1C **51**
Price Town. *B'End* —3A **58**
Priest Weston. *Shrp* —2D **31**
Primrose Hill. *Glos* —2D **61**
Princes Gate. *Pemb* —1A **54**
Prion. *Den* —1B **16**
Prior's Frome. *Here* —2C **51**
Priors Halton. *Shrp* —1B **40**
Priorslee. *Telf* —3D **27**
Priory Wood. *Here* —1D **49**
Priston. *Bath* —3D **67**
Publow. *Bath* —3D **67**
Pucklechurch. *S Glo* —2D **67**
Puddinglake. *Ches* —1D **19**
Puddington. *Ches* —3A **10**
Puddlebrook. *Glos* —1D **61**
Pudleston. *Here* —3C **41**
Puleston. *Telf* —2D **27**
Pulford. *Ches* —2A **18**
Pulley. *Shrp* —1B **32**
Pulverbatch. *Shrp* —1B **32**
Pumsaint. *Carm* —1B **46**
Puncheston. *Pemb* —3D **43**
Purlogue. *Shrp* —1D **39**
Purslow. *Shrp* —3A **32**
Purton. *Glos* —2D **61**
(Lydney)
Purton. *Glos* —2D **61**
(Sharpness)
Putley. *Here* —2D **51**
Puxton. *N Som* —3B **66**
Pwll. *Carm* —2D **55**
Pwll. *Powy* —1C **31**
Pwllcrochan. *Pemb* —2C **53**
Pwll-glas. *Den* —2C **17**
Pwllgloyw. *Powy* —2A **48**
Pwllheli. *Gwyn* —1C **21**
Pwllmeyric. *Mon* —3C **61**
Pwlltrap. *Carm* —1B **54**
Pwll-y-glaw. *Neat* —3C **57**
Pye Corner. *Newp* —1A **66**
Pyle. *Neat* —1D **63**

Quabbs. *Shrp* —3D **31**
Quarrybank. *Ches* —1C **19**
Quarry, The. *Glos* —3D **61**
Quatford. *Shrp* —2D **33**
Queen Charlton. *Bath* —3D **67**
Queensferry. *Flin* —1A **18**
Quina Brook. *Shrp* —1C **27**

Raby. *Mers* —3A **10**
Rachub. *Gwyn* —1B **14**
Radford. *Bath* —3D **67**
Radyr. *Card* —1C **65**
Ragdon. *Shrp* —2B **32**
Raglan. *Mon* —2B **60**
Rainford. *Mers* —1A **10**
Rainford Junction. *Mers* —1B **10**
Rainhill. *Mers* —1B **10**
Rangeworthy. *S Glo* —1D **67**
Rassau. *Blae* —1C **59**
Ratlinghope. *Shrp* —2B **32**
Ravenhills Green. *Worc* —3D **41**

Ravensmoor. *Ches* —2D **19**
Rease Heath. *Ches* —2D **19**
Redberth. *Pemb* —2D **53**
Redbrook. *Mon* —1C **61**
Redbrook. *Wrex* —3C **19**
Redcliff Bay. *N Som* —2B **66**
Redhill. *N Som* —3B **66**
Redhill. *Shrp* —3D **27**
Redland. *Bris* —2C **67**
Redmarley D'Abitot. *Glos* —2D **51**
Rednal. *Shrp* —2A **26**
Red Roses. *Carm* —1B **54**
Red Wharf Bay. *IOA* —2A **6**
Redwick. *Newp* —1B **66**
Redwick. *S Glo* —1C **67**
Regil. *N Som* —3C **67**
Reilth. *Shrp* —3D **31**
Resolven. *Neat* —2D **57**
Reynalton. *Pemb* —2D **53**
Reynoldston. *Swan* —3D **55**
Rhadyr. *Mon* —2A **60**
Rhaeadr Gwy. *Powy* —2A **38**
Rhandirmwyn. *Carm* —1C **47**
Rhayader. *Powy* —2A **38**
Rhewl. *Den* —3C **17**
(Llangollen)
Rhewl. *Den* —1C **17**
(Ruthin)
Rhewl. *Shrp* —1A **26**
Rhewl-Mostyn. *Flin* —2C **9**
Rhigos. *Rhon* —2A **58**
Rhiw. *Gwyn* —2B **20**
Rhiwabon. *Wrex* —3A **18**
Rhiwbina. *Card* —1C **65**
Rhiwbryfdir. *Gwyn* —3B **14**
Rhiwderin. *Newp* —1D **65**
Rhiwlas. *Gwyn* —1A **24**
(Bala)
Rhiwlas. *Gwyn* —1A **14**
(Bangor)
Rhiwlas. *Powy* —1C **25**
Rhodiad-y-Brenin. *Pemb* —3A **42**
Rhondda. *Rhon* —1A **64**
Rhoose. *V Glam* —3B **64**
Rhos. *Carm* —2C **45**
Rhos. *Neat* —2C **57**
Rhosaman. *Carm* —1C **57**
Rhoscefnhir. *IOA* —3A **6**
Rhoscolyn. *IOA* —3B **4**
Rhos Common. *Powy* —3D **25**
Rhoscrowther. *Pemb* —2C **53**
Rhos-ddu. *Gwyn* —1B **20**
Rhosdylluan. *Gwyn* —2D **23**
Rhosesmor. *Flin* —1D **17**
Rhos-fawr. *Gwyn* —1C **21**
Rhosgadfan. *Gwyn* —2A **14**
Rhosgoch. *IOA* —2D **5**
Rhosgoch. *Powy* —1C **49**
Rhos Haminiog. *Cdgn* —2A **36**
Rhos-hill. *Pemb* —1A **44**
Rhoshirwaun. *Gwyn* —2A **20**
Rhoslan. *Gwyn* —3D **13**
Rhoslefain. *Gwyn* —1A **28**
Rhosllanerchrugog. *Wrex* —3D **17**
Rhos Lligwy. *IOA* —2D **5**
Rhosmaen. *Carm* —3B **46**
Rhosmeirch. *IOA* —3D **5**
Rhosneigr. *IOA* —3C **5**
Rhos-on-Sea. *Cnwy* —2D **7**
Rhossili. *Swan* —3D **55**
Rhosson. *Pemb* —3A **42**
Rhos, The. *Pemb* —1D **53**
Rhostrenwfa. *IOA* —3D **5**
Rhostryfan. *Gwyn* —2D **13**
Rhostyllen. *Wrex* —3A **18**
Rhoswiel. *Shrp* —1D **25**
Rhosybol. *IOA* —2D **5**
Rhos-y-brithdir. *Powy* —2C **25**
Rhos-y-garth. *Cdgn* —1B **36**
Rhos-y-gwaliau. *Gwyn* —1A **24**
Rhos-y-llan. *Gwyn* —1B **20**
Rhos-y-meirch. *Powy* —2D **39**
Rhuallt. *Den* —3B **8**
Rhuddall Heath. *Ches* —1C **19**
Rhuddlan. *Cdgn* —1D **45**
Rhuddlan. *Den* —3B **8**
Rhulen. *Powy* —3C **39**
Rhuthun. *Den* —2C **17**
Rhyd. *Gwyn* —3B **14**
Rhydaman. *Carm* —1B **56**
Rhydargaeau. *Carm* —3D **45**
Rhydcymerau. *Carm* —2A **46**
Rhyd-Ddu. *Gwyn* —2A **14**
Rhydding. *Neat* —3C **57**
Rhydfudr. *Cdgn* —2A **36**
Rhydlanfair. *Cnwy* —2D **15**

Rhydlewis. *Cdgn* —1C **45**
Rhydlios. *Gwyn* —1A **20**
Rhydlydan. *Cnwy* —2D **15**
Rhyd-meirionydd. *Cdgn* —3B **28**
Rhydowen. *Cdgn* —1D **45**
Rhyd-Rosser. *Cdgn* —2A **36**
Rhydspence. *Powy* —1D **49**
Rhydtalog. *Flin* —2D **17**
Rhyd-uchaf. *Gwyn* —1A **24**
Rhydwyn. *IOA* —2C **5**
Rhyd-y-clafdy. *Gwyn* —1C **21**
Rhydycroesau. *Shrp* —1D **25**
Rhydyfelin. *Cdgn* —1A **36**
Rhydyfelin. *Rhon* —1C **65**
Rhyd-y-foel. *Cnwy* —3A **8**
Rhyd-y-fro. *Neat* —2C **57**
Rhydymain. *Gwyn* —2D **23**
Rhyd-y-meirch. *Mon* —2A **60**
Rhyd-y-meudwy. *Den* —2C **17**
Rhydymwyn. *Flin* —1D **17**
Rhyd-yr-onen. *Gwyn* —1B **28**
Rhyd-y-sarn. *Gwyn* —3B **14**
Rhyl. *Den* —2B **8**
Rhymney. *Cphy* —2C **59**
Rhymni. *Cphy* —2C **59**
Richards Castle. *Here* —2B **40**
Rickford. *N Som* —3B **66**
Ridgebourne. *Powy* —2B **38**
Ridgeway Cross. *Here* —1D **51**
Ridgwardine. *Shrp* —1D **27**
Risbury. *Here* —3C **41**
Risca. *Cphy* —3D **59**
Risley. *Warr* —1D **11**
Roath. *Card* —2C **65**
Robertstown. *Rhon* —2A **58**
Robeston Back. *Pemb* —1D **53**
Robeston Wathen. *Pemb* —1D **53**
Robeston West. *Pemb* —2B **52**
Roch. *Pemb* —3B **42**
Rock. *Worc* —1D **41**
Rock Ferry. *Mers* —2A **10**
Rockfield. *Mon* —1B **60**
Rockgreen. *Shrp* —1C **41**
Rockhampton. *S Glo* —3D **61**
Rodd. *Here* —2A **40**
Roden. *Telf* —3C **27**
Rodington. *Telf* —3C **27**
Rodington Heath. *Telf* —3C **27**
Rodley. *Glos* —1D **61**
Rodway. *Telf* —3D **27**
Rogerstone. *Newp* —1D **65**
Rogiet. *Mon* —1B **66**
Roman Bank. *Shrp* —2C **33**
Rorrington. *Shrp* —1A **32**
Rosebush. *Pemb* —3D **43**
Rosehill. *Shrp* —1D **27**
  (Market Drayton)
Rosehill. *Shrp* —3B **26**
  (Shrewsbury)
Rosemarket. *Pemb* —2C **53**
Rossett. *Wrex* —2A **18**
Ross-on-Wye. *Here* —3D **51**
Rostherne. *Ches* —2D **11**
Round Oak. *Shrp* —3A **32**
Rowberrow. *Som* —3B **66**
Rowen. *Cnwy* —3C **7**
Rowley. *Shrp* —1A **32**
Rowlstone. *Here* —3A **50**
Rowton. *Ches* —1B **18**
Rowton. *Shrp* —3B **32**
  (Ludlow)
Rowton. *Shrp* —3A **26**
  (Shrewsbury)
Rowton. *Telf* —3D **27**
Royal's Green. *Ches* —3D **19**
Ruabon. *Wrex* —3A **18**
Ruardean. *Glos* —1D **61**
Ruardean Hill. *Glos* —1D **61**
Ruardean Woodside. *Glos* —1D **61**
Ruckley. *Shrp* —1C **33**
Rudbaxton. *Pemb* —3C **43**
Rudgeway. *S Glo* —1D **67**
Rudhall. *Here* —3D **51**
Rudheath. *Ches* —3D **11**
Rudheath Woods. *Ches* —3D **11**
Rudry. *Cphy* —1C **65**
Rumney. *Card* —2D **65**
Runcorn. *Hal* —2C **11**
Rushall. *Here* —2D **51**
Rushbury. *Shrp* —2C **33**
Rushton. *Ches* —1C **19**
Rushton. *Shrp* —1D **33**
Ruspidge. *Glos* —1D **61**
Ruthin. *Den* —2C **17**
Ruthin. *V Glam* —2A **64**

Ruxton Green. *Here* —1C **61**
Ruyton-XI-Towns. *Shrp* —2A **26**
Ryeford. *Here* —3D **51**
Ryton. *Glos* —2D **51**

S
Sageston. *Pemb* —2D **53**
Saighton. *Ches* —1B **18**
St Arvans. *Mon* —3C **61**
St Asaph. *Den* —3B **8**
St Athan. *V Glam* —3B **64**
St Briavels. *Glos* —2C **61**
St Brides. *Pemb* —1A **52**
St Bride's Major. *V Glam* —2D **63**
St Bride's Netherwent. *Mon* —1B **66**
St Bride's-super-Ely. *V Glam* —2B **64**
St Brides Wentlooge. *Newp* —1D **65**
St Clears. *Carm* —1B **54**
St David's. *Pemb* —3A **42**
St Dogmaels. *Pemb* —1A **44**
St Donat's. *V Glam* —3A **64**
St Fagans. *Card* —2C **65**
St Florence. *Pemb* —2D **53**
St George. *Cnwy* —3A **8**
St George's. *N Som* —3A **66**
St Georges. *V Glam* —2B **64**
St Harmon. *Powy* —1A **38**
St Helens. *Mers* —1B **10**
St Hilary. *V Glam* —2B **64**
St Illtyd. *Blae* —2D **59**
St Ishmael. *Carm* —2C **55**
St Ishmael's. *Pemb* —2B **52**
St Lythans. *V Glam* —2C **65**
St Margarets. *Here* —2A **50**
St Martin's. *Shrp* —1A **26**
St Mary Church. *V Glam* —2B **64**
St Mary Hill. *V Glam* —2A **64**
St Mary's Grove. *N Som* —3A **66**
St Maughan's Green. *Mon* —1B **60**
St Mellons. *Card* —1D **65**
St Michaels. *Worc* —2C **41**
St Nicholas. *Pemb* —2C **43**
St Nicholas. *V Glam* —2B **64**
St Owen's Cross. *Here* —3C **51**
St Petrox. *Pemb* —3C **53**
St Thomas. *Swan* —3B **56**
St Twynnells. *Pemb* —3C **53**
St Weonards. *Here* —3B **50**
Salem. *Carm* —3B **46**
Salem. *Cdgn* —3B **28**
Salem. *Gwyn* —2A **14**
Salterswall. *Ches* —1D **19**
Saltford. *Bath* —3D **67**
Saltmead. *Card* —2C **65**
Saltney. *Flin* —1A **18**
Sambrook. *Telf* —2D **27**
Sandbach. *Ches* —1D **19**
Sandfields. *Neat* —3C **57**
Sandford. *N Som* —3B **66**
Sandford. *Shrp* —2A **26**
  (Oswestry)
Sandford. *Shrp* —1C **27**
  (Whitchurch)
Sandiway. *Ches* —3D **11**
Sandy. *Carm* —2D **55**
Sandycroft. *Flin* —1A **18**
Sandy Cross. *Here* —3D **41**
Sandy Haven. *Pemb* —2B **52**
Sandylane. *Swan* —1A **62**
Sandyway. *Here* —3B **50**
Sapey Common. *Here* —2D **41**
Sardis. *Carm* —2A **56**
Sardis. *Pemb* —2C **53**
  (Milford Haven)
Sardis. *Pemb* —2A **54**
  (Tenby)
Sarn. *B'End* —1A **64**
Sarn. *Powy* —2D **31**
Sarnau. *Carm* —3D **45**
Sarnau. *Cdgn* —3C **35**
Sarnau. *Gwyn* —1A **24**
Sarnau. *Powy* —2B **48**
  (Brecon)
Sarnau. *Powy* —3D **25**
  (Welshpool)
Sarn Bach. *Gwyn* —2C **21**
Sarnesfield. *Here* —3A **40**
Sarn Meyllteyrn. *Gwyn* —1B **20**
Saron. *Carm* —1B **56**
  (Ammanford)
Saron. *Carm* —2C **45**
  (Newcastle Emlyn)
Saron. *Gwyn* —1A **14**
  (Bethel)
Saron. *Gwyn* —2D **13**
  (Bontnewydd)

Saughall. *Ches* —3A **10**
Saul. *Glos* —2D **61**
Saundersfoot. *Pemb* —2A **54**
Scethrog. *Powy* —3C **49**
School Green. *Ches* —1D **19**
Scleddau. *Pemb* —2C **43**
Scolton. *Pemb* —3C **43**
Scurlage. *Swan* —3D **55**
Seacombe. *Mers* —1A **10**
Seaforth. *Mers* —1A **10**
Sealand. *Flin* —1A **18**
Sea Mills. *Bris* —2C **67**
Sebastopol. *Cphy* —2C **59**
Sebastopol. *Torf* —3D **59**
Sedbury. *Glos* —3C **61**
Sefton. *Mers* —1A **10**
Sefton Park. *Mers* —2A **10**
Seifton. *Shrp* —3B **32**
Selattyn. *Shrp* —1D **25**
Sellack. *Here* —3C **51**
Senghenydd. *Cphy* —3C **59**
Sennybridge. *Powy* —3A **48**
Seven Sisters. *Neat* —2D **57**
Severn Beach. *S Glo* —1C **67**
Shakesfield. *Glos* —2D **51**
Sharpness. *Glos* —2D **61**
Shavington. *Ches* —2D **19**
Shawbirch. *Telf* —3D **27**
Shawbury. *Shrp* —2C **27**
Sheepway. *N Som* —2B **66**
Sheinton. *Shrp* —1D **33**
Shelderton. *Shrp* —1B **40**
Shell Green. *Hal* —2C **11**
Shelsley Beauchamp. *Worc*
  —2D **41**
Shelsley Walsh. *Worc* —2D **41**
Shelton. *Shrp* —3B **26**
Shelve. *Shrp* —2A **32**
Shelwick. *Here* —1C **51**
Shelwick Green. *Here* —1C **51**
Shenmore. *Here* —2A **50**
Shepperdine. *S Glo* —3D **61**
Shifnal. *Shrp* —1D **33**
Shipham. *Som* —3B **66**
Shipton. *Shrp* —2C **33**
Shirehampton. *Bris* —2C **67**
Shirenewton. *Mon* —3B **60**
Shirl Heath. *Here* —3B **40**
Shobdon. *Here* —2A **40**
Shocklach. *Ches* —3B **18**
Shoot Hill. *Shrp* —3B **26**
Shortwood. *S Glo* —2D **67**
Shoscombe. *Bath* —3D **67**
Shotton. *Flin* —1D **17**
Shotwick. *Ches* —3A **10**
Shrawardine. *Shrp* —3A **26**
Shrewsbury. *Shrp* —3B **26**
Shucknall. *Here* —1C **51**
Sibdon Carwood. *Shrp* —3B **32**
Sidbury. *Shrp* —3D **33**
Sidcot. *N Som* —3B **66**
Sigingstone. *V Glam* —2A **64**
Silian. *Cdgn* —3A **36**
Silvington. *Shrp* —3D **33**
Simm's Cross. *Hal* —2C **11**
Simm's Lane End. *Mers* —1C **11**
Simpson. *Pemb* —1B **52**
Simpson Cross. *Pemb* —1B **52**
Sirhowy. *Blae* —1C **59**
Siston. *S Glo* —2D **67**
Six Bells. *Blae* —2D **59**
Skenfrith. *Mon* —3B **50**
Sketty. *Swan* —3B **56**
Skewen. *Neat* —3C **57**
Skyborry Green. *Shrp* —1D **39**
Slade. *Swan* —1A **62**
Sleap. *Shrp* —2B **26**
Slimbridge. *Glos* —2D **61**
Smithies, The. *Shrp* —2D **33**
Smithy Green. *Ches* —3D **11**
Snailbeach. *Shrp* —1A **32**
Snead. *Powy* —2A **32**
Snead Common. *Worc* —2D **41**
Snitton. *Shrp* —1C **41**
Snodhill. *Here* —1A **50**
Soar. *Carm* —3B **46**
Soar. *Gwyn* —1B **22**
Soar. *Powy* —2A **48**
Sodom. *Den* —3B **8**
Sollers Dilwyn. *Here* —3B **40**
Sollers Hope. *Here* —2D **51**
Solva. *Pemb* —3A **42**
Soudley. *Shrp* —2B **32**
  (Church Stretton)
Soudley. *Shrp* —2D **27**
  (Market Drayton)

Soughton. *Flin* —1D **17**
Soundwell. *S Glo* —2D **67**
South Cornelly. *B'End* —1D **63**
Southdown. *Bath* —3D **67**
Southend. *Glos* —3D **61**
Southerndown. *V Glam* —2D **63**
Southgate. *Glos* —3A **28**
Southgate. *Swan* —1A **62**
Southstoke. *Bath* —3D **67**
South Widcombe. *Bath* —3C **67**
Speke. *Mers* —2B **10**
Spital. *Mers* —2A **10**
Spittal. *Pemb* —3C **43**
Sproston Green. *Ches* —1D **19**
Spurstow. *Ches* —2C **19**
Stackpole. *Pemb* —3C **53**
Stackpole Elidor. *Pemb* —3C **53**
Stafford Park. *Telf* —1D **33**
Stamford Bridge. *Ches* —1B **18**
Standford Bridge. *Telf* —2D **27**
St Andrews Major. *V Glam* —2C **65**
Stanford Bishop. *Here* —3D **41**
Stanford Bridge. *Worc* —2D **41**
Stanford on Teme. *Worc* —2D **41**
Stanley. *Shrp* —3D **33**
Stanley Hill. *Here* —1D **51**
Stanlow. *Ches* —3B **10**
Stansbatch. *Here* —2A **40**
Stanthorne. *Ches* —1D **19**
Stanton Drew. *Bath* —3C **67**
Stanton Lacy. *Shrp* —1B **40**
Stanton Long. *Shrp* —2C **33**
Stanton Prior. *Bath* —3D **67**
Stanton upon Hine Heath. *Shrp*
  —2C **27**
Stanton Wick. *Bath* —3D **67**
Stanwardine in the Fields. *Shrp*
  —2B **26**
Stanwardine in the Wood. *Shrp*
  —2B **26**
Stapeley. *Ches* —3D **19**
Staple Hill. *S Glo* —2D **67**
Stapleton. *Bris* —2D **67**
Stapleton. *Here* —2A **40**
Stapleton. *Shrp* —1B **32**
Staplow. *Here* —1D **51**
Star. *Pemb* —2B **44**
Staunton. *Glos* —1C **61**
Staunton on Arrow. *Here* —2A **40**
Staunton on Wye. *Here* —1A **50**
Staylittle. *Powy* —2D **29**
Steel Heath. *Shrp* —1C **27**
Steen's Bridge. *Here* —3C **41**
Stepaside. *Pemb* —2A **54**
Steynton. *Pemb* —2C **53**
Stifford's Bridge. *Here* —1D **51**
Stinchcombe. *Glos* —3D **61**
Stiperstones. *Shrp* —1A **32**
Stirchley. *Telf* —1D **33**
Stoak. *Ches* —3B **10**
Stocking. *Here* —2D **51**
Stockton. *Here* —2C **41**
Stockton. *Shrp* —2D **33**
  (Bridgnorth)
Stockton. *Shrp* —1D **31**
  (Chirbury)
Stockton Cross. *Here* —2C **41**
Stockton Heath. *Warr* —2D **11**
Stockton on Teme. *Worc* —2D **41**
Stockwood. *Bris* —3D **67**
Stoke Bliss. *Worc* —2D **41**
Stoke Cross. *Here* —3D **41**
Stoke Edith. *Here* —1D **51**
Stoke Gifford. *S Glo* —2D **67**
Stoke Heath. *Shrp* —2D **27**
Stoke Lacy. *Here* —1D **51**
Stoke on Tern. *Shrp* —2D **27**
Stoke Prior. *Here* —3C **41**
Stokesay. *Shrp* —3B **32**
Stoke St Milborough. *Shrp* —3C **33**
Stone. *Glos* —3D **61**
Stoneacton. *Shrp* —2C **33**
Stonebridge. *N Som* —3A **66**
Stone-edge-Batch. *N Som* —2B **66**
Stoneley Green. *Ches* —2D **19**
Stoney Stretton. *Shrp* —1A **32**
Stony Cross. *Here* —1D **51**
  (Great Malvern)
Stony Cross. *Here* —2C **41**
  (Leominster)
Storeton. *Mers* —2A **10**
Storridge. *Here* —1D **51**
Stottesdon. *Shrp* —3D **33**
Stowe. *Glos* —2C **61**
Stowe. *Shrp* —1A **40**
Stowey. *Bath* —3C **67**

Strangford. *Here* —3C **51**
Strata Florida. *Cdgn* —2C **37**
Stratford. *G Lon* —1A **66**
Street Dinas. *Shrp* —1A **26**
Strefford. *Shrp* —3B **32**
Stretford. *Here* —3C **41**
Stretton. *Ches* —2B **18**
Stretton. *Warr* —2D **11**
Stretton Grandison. *Here* —1D **51**
Stretton Heath. *Shrp* —3A **26**
Stretton Sugwas. *Here* —1B **50**
Stretton Westwood. *Shrp* —2C **33**
Stroat. *Glos* —3C **61**
Stryd. *IOA* —2B **4**
Stryt-issa. *Wrex* —3D **17**
Suckley. *Worc* —3D **41**
Suckley Knowl. *Worc* —3D **41**
Sudbrook. *Mon* —1C **67**
Sugwas Pool. *Here* —1B **50**
Sully. *V Glam* —3C **65**
Summerhill. *Pemb* —2A **54**
Sutton. *Pemb* —1C **53**
Sutton. *Shrp* —3D **33**
　(Bridgnorth)
Sutton. *Shrp* —1D **27**
　(Market Drayton)
Sutton. *Shrp* —2A **26**
　(Oswestry)
Sutton. *Shrp* —3C **27**
　(Shrewsbury)
Sutton. *Worc* —2D **41**
Sutton Leach. *Mers* —1C **11**
Sutton Maddock. *Shrp* —1D **33**
Sutton St Michael. *Here* —1C **51**
Sutton St Nicholas. *Here* —1C **51**
Sutton Weaver. *Ches* —3C **11**
Swainshill. *Here* —1B **50**
Swanbridge. *V Glam* —3C **65**
Swan Green. *Ches* —3D **11**
Swanwick Green. *Ches* —3C **19**
Sweet Green. *Worc* —2D **41**
Swffyrd. *Cphy* —3D **59**
Swinmore Common. *Here* —1D **51**
Swyddffynnon. *Cdgn* —2B **36**
Swyffrd. *Cphy* —3D **59**
Sycharth. *Powy* —2D **25**
Sychdyn. *Flin* —1D **17**
Sychnant. *Powy* —1A **38**
Sychtyn. *Powy* —1A **30**
Sydney. *Ches* —2D **19**
Sylen. *Carm* —2A **56**
Sylfaen. *Powy* —1C **31**
Symonds Yat. *Here* —1C **61**
Synod Inn. *Cdgn* —3D **35**

Tadwick. *Bath* —2D **67**
Tafarnaubach. *Cphy* —1C **59**
Tafarn-y-bwlch. *Pemb* —2D **43**
Tafarn-y-Gelyn. *Den* —1C **17**
Taff's Well. *Card* —1C **65**
Tafolwern. *Powy* —1D **29**
Taibach. *Neat* —1C **63**
Tai-bach. *Powy* —2C **25**
Tai-Nant. *Wrex* —3D **17**
Tai'n Lon. *Gwyn* —2D **13**
Tairgwaith. *Neat* —1C **57**
Talachddu. *Powy* —2B **48**
Talacre. *Flin* —2C **9**
Talardd. *Gwyn* —2D **23**
Talbenny. *Pemb* —1B **52**
Talbot Green. *Rhon* —1B **64**
Talerddig. *Powy* —1A **30**
Talgarreg. *Cdgn* —3D **35**
Talgarth. *Powy* —2C **49**
Tallarn Green. *Wrex* —3B **18**
Talley. *Carm* —2B **46**
Talog. *Carm* —3C **45**
Talsarn. *Carm* —3C **47**
Talsarn. *Cdgn* —3A **36**
Talsarnau. *Gwyn* —1B **22**
Talwrn. *IOA* —3D **5**
Talwrn. *Wrex* —3D **17**
Tal-y-bont. *Cdgn* —3B **28**
Tal-y-Bont. *Cnwy* —1C **15**
Tal-y-bont. *Gwyn* —3B **6**
　(Bangor)
Tal-y-bont. *Gwyn* —2A **22**
　(Barmouth)
Talybont-on-Usk. *Powy* —3C **49**
Tal-y-cafn. *Cnwy* —3C **7**
Tal-y-coed. *Mon* —1B **60**
Tal-y-llyn. *Gwyn* —1C **29**
Talyllyn. *Powy* —3C **49**

Talysarn. *Gwyn* —2D **13**
Tal-y-waenydd. *Gwyn* —3B **14**
Talywain. *Torf* —2D **59**
Tal-y-Wern. *Powy* —1D **29**
Tanerdy. *Carm* —3D **45**
Tangiers. *Pemb* —1C **53**
Tan-lan. *Cnwy* —1C **15**
Tan-lan. *Gwyn* —3B **14**
Tan-y-bwlch. *Gwyn* —3B **14**
Tan-y-fron. *Cnwy* —1A **16**
Tanyfron. *Wrex* —2D **17**
Tan-y-goes. *Cdgn* —1B **44**
Tanygrisiau. *Gwyn* —3B **14**
Tan-y-pistyll. *Powy* —2B **24**
Tan-yr-allt. *Den* —2B **8**
Tarbock Green. *Mers* —2B **10**
Tarporley. *Ches* —1C **19**
Tarrington. *Here* —1D **51**
Tarvin. *Ches* —1B **18**
Tasley. *Shrp* —2D **33**
Tattenhall. *Ches* —2B **18**
Tavernspite. *Pemb* —1A **54**
Taynton. *Glos* —3D **51**
Tedsmore. *Shrp* —2A **26**
Tedstone Delamere. *Here* —3D **41**
Tedstone Wafer. *Here* —3D **41**
Tegryn. *Pemb* —2A **44**
Telford. *Telf* —3D **27**
Temple Bar. *Carm* —1A **56**
Temple Bar. *Cdgn* —3A **36**
Temple Cloud. *Bath* —3D **67**
Templeton. *Pemb* —1A **54**
Tenbury Wells. *Worc* —2C **41**
Tenby. *Pemb* —2A **54**
Terfyn. *Cnwy* —3A **8**
Ternhill. *Shrp* —1D **27**
Tetchill. *Shrp* —1A **26**
Thatto Heath. *Mers* —1C **11**
Thelwall. *Warr* —2D **11**
Thingwall. *Mers* —2D **9**
Thomas Chapel. *Pemb* —2A **54**
Thomastown. *Rhon* —1B **64**
Thorn. *Powy* —2D **39**
Thornbury. *Here* —3D **41**
Thornbury. *S Glo* —1D **67**
Thornhill. *Cphy* —1C **65**
Thornton. *Mers* —1A **10**
Thornton Hough. *Mers* —2A **10**
Thornton-le-Moors. *Ches* —3B **10**
Threapwood. *Ches* —3B **18**
Three Ashes. *Here* —3C **51**
Three Cocks. *Powy* —2C **49**
Three Crosses. *Swan* —3A **56**
Thruxton. *Here* —2B **50**
Thurstaston. *Mers* —2D **9**
Tibberton. *Telf* —2D **27**
Tickenham. *N Som* —2B **66**
Ticklerton. *Shrp* —2B **32**
Tidenham. *Glos* —3C **61**
Tiers Cross. *Pemb* —1C **53**
Tillers Green. *Glos* —2D **51**
Tilley. *Shrp* —2C **27**
Tillington. *Here* —1B **50**
Tillington Common. *Here* —1B **50**
Tilstock. *Shrp* —1C **27**
Tilston. *Ches* —2B **18**
Tilstone Fearnall. *Ches* —1C **19**
Timsbury. *Bath* —3D **67**
Tintern Parva. *Mon* —2C **61**
Tirabad. *Powy* —1D **47**
Tirnewydd. *Flin* —3C **9**
Tirphil. *Cphy* —2C **59**
Tir-y-dail. *Carm* —1B **56**
Titley. *Here* —3A **40**
Tiverton. *Ches* —1C **19**
Tockington. *S Glo* —1D **67**
Todding. *Here* —1B **40**
Ton. *Mon* —3A **60**
Tondu. *B'End* —1D **63**
Tonfanau. *Gwyn* —1A **28**
Tongwynlais. *Card* —1C **65**
Tonmawr. *Neat* —3D **57**
Tonna. *Neat* —3C **57**
Ton-Pentre. *Rhon* —3A **58**
Tonypandy. *Rhon* —3A **58**
Tonyrefail. *Rhon* —1B **64**
Tortworth. *S Glo* —3D **61**
Tower Hill. *Mers* —1B **10**
Town End. *Mers* —2B **10**
Townhill. *Swan* —3B **56**
Towyn. *Cnwy* —3A **8**
Toxteth. *Mers* —2A **10**
Trallong. *Powy* —3A **48**
Trallwng. *Powy* —1D **31**
Tranmere. *Mers* —2A **10**
Trapp. *Carm* —1B **56**

Trawscoed. *Powy* —2B **48**
Trawsfynydd. *Gwyn* —1C **23**
Trawsgoed. *Cdgn* —1B **36**
Treaddow. *Here* —3C **51**
Trealaw. *Rhon* —3B **58**
Trearddur. *IOA* —3B **4**
Trebanog. *Rhon* —3B **58**
Trebanos. *Neat* —2C **57**
Trecastle. *Powy* —3D **47**
Trecenydd. *Cphy* —1C **65**
Trecwn. *Pemb* —2C **43**
Trecynon. *Rhon* —2A **58**
Tredegar. *Blae* —2C **59**
Trederwen. *Powy* —3D **25**
Tredogan. *V Glam* —3B **64**
Tredomen. *Powy* —2C **49**
Tredunnock. *Mon* —3A **60**
Tredustan. *Powy* —2C **49**
Trefaldwyn. *Powy* —2D **31**
Trefasser. *Pemb* —2B **42**
Trefdraeth. *IOA* —3D **5**
Trefdraeth. *Pemb* —2D **43**
Trefecca. *Powy* —2C **49**
Trefechan. *Mer T* —2B **58**
Trefeglwys. *Powy* —2A **30**
Trefeitha. *Powy* —2C **49**
Trefenter. *Cdgn* —2B **36**
Treffgarne. *Pemb* —2C **43**
Treffynnon. *Flin* —3C **9**
Treffynnon. *Pemb* —3B **42**
Trefil. *Blae* —1C **59**
Trefilan. *Cdgn* —3A **36**
Trefin. *Pemb* —2B **42**
Treflach. *Shrp* —2D **25**
Trefnant. *Den* —3B **8**
Trefonen. *Shrp* —2D **25**
Trefor. *Gwyn* —3C **13**
Trefor. *IOA* —3C **5**
Treforest. *Rhon* —1B **64**
Trefriw. *Cnwy* —1C **15**
Tref-y-Clawdd. *Powy* —1D **39**
Trefynwy. *Mon* —1C **61**
Tregare. *Mon* —1B **60**
Tregaron. *Cdgn* —3B **36**
Tregarth. *Gwyn* —1B **14**
Tregeiriog. *Wrex* —1C **25**
Tregele. *IOA* —1C **5**
Tregoyd. *Powy* —2C **49**
Tre-groes. *Cdgn* —1D **45**
Tregynon. *Powy* —2B **30**
Trehafod. *Rhon* —3B **58**
Treharris. *Mer T* —3C **59**
Treherbert. *Rhon* —3A **58**
Trelawnyd. *Flin* —3B **8**
Trelech. *Carm* —2B **44**
Treleddyd-fawr. *Pemb* —3A **42**
Trelewis. *Mer T* —3C **59**
Trelleck. *Mon* —2C **61**
Trelleck Grange. *Mon* —2B **60**
Trelogan. *Flin* —2C **9**
Trelystan. *Powy* —1D **31**
Tremadog. *Gwyn* —3A **14**
Tremain. *Cdgn* —1C **44**
Tremeirchion. *Den* —3B **8**
Tremorfa. *Card* —2D **65**
Trench. *Telf* —3D **27**
Treoes. *V Glam* —2A **64**
Treorchy. *Rhon* —3A **58**
Treorci. *Rhon* —3A **58**
Tre'r-ddol. *Cdgn* —2B **28**
Tresaith. *Cdgn* —3B **34**
Tre Taliesin. *Cdgn* —2B **28**
Trethomas. *Cphy* —1C **65**
Tretio. *Pemb* —3A **42**
Tretire. *Here* —3C **51**
Tretower. *Powy* —3C **49**
Treuddyn. *Flin* —2D **17**
Trevalyn. *Wrex* —2A **18**
Tre-vaughan. *Carm* —3D **45**
　(Carmarthen)
Trevaughan. *Carm* —1A **54**
　(Whitland)
Trevethin. *Torf* —2D **59**
Trevor. *Den* —3D **17**
Trevor Uchaf. *Den* —3D **17**
Trewern. *Powy* —3D **25**
Trewyddel. *Pemb* —1A **44**
Trimsaran. *Carm* —2D **55**
Trinant. *Cphy* —3D **59**
Trisant. *Cdgn* —1C **37**
Troedrhiwdalar. *Powy* —3A **38**
Troedrhiwfuwch. *Cphy* —2C **59**
Troedrhiwgwair. *Blae* —2C **59**
Troedyraur. *Cdgn* —1C **45**
Troedyrhiw. *Mer T* —2B **58**
Trumpet. *Here* —2D **51**

Tryfil. *IOA* —2D **5**
Tudorville. *Here* —3C **51**
Tudweiliog. *Gwyn* —1B **20**
Tufton. *Pemb* —3D **43**
Tugford. *Shrp* —3C **33**
Tumble. *Carm* —1A **56**
Tunley. *Bath* —3D **67**
Tupsley. *Here* —1C **51**
Turnant. *Here* —3A **50**
Turnastone. *Here* —2A **50**
Tutshill. *Glos* —3C **61**
Tweedale. *Telf* —1D **33**
Twerton. *Bath* —3D **67**
Twinhoe. *Bath* —3D **67**
Twiss Green. *Warr* —1D **11**
Twitchen. *Shrp* —1A **40**
Two Bridges. *Glos* —2D **61**
Twyford Common. *Here* —2C **51**
Twyncarno. *Cphy* —2C **59**
Twynllanan. *Carm* —3C **47**
Twynmynydd. *Carm* —1B **56**
Twyn-y-Sheriff. *Mon* —2B **60**
Tyberton. *Here* —2A **50**
Tycroes. *Carm* —1B **56**
Tycrwyn. *Powy* —3C **25**
Tyddewi. *Pemb* —3A **42**
Ty Issa. *Powy* —1C **25**
Tyldesley. *G Man* —1D **11**
Tyle. *Carm* —3B **46**
Tylorstown. *Rhon* —3B **58**
Tylwch. *Powy* —3A **30**
Ty-nant. *Cnwy* —3A **16**
Tynewydd. *Rhon* —3A **58**
Ty'n-y-bryn. *Rhon* —1B **64**
Tyn-y-celyn. *Wrex* —1C **25**
Tyn-y-cwm. *Swan* —2B **56**
Tyn-y-ffridd. *Powy* —1C **25**
Tynygongl. *IOA* —2A **6**
Tynygraig. *Cdgn* —2B **36**
Tyn-y-groes. *Cnwy* —3C **7**
Ty'n-yr-eithin. *Cdgn* —2B **36**
Tyn-y-rhyd. *Powy* —3B **24**
Tyn-y-wern. *Powy* —2B **24**
Tythegston. *B'End* —2D **63**
Tytherington. *S Glo* —1D **67**
Tywyn. *Cnwy* —3C **7**
Tywyn. *Gwyn* —1A **28**

Ubley. *Bath* —3C **67**
Uckington. *Shrp* —1C **33**
Uffington. *Shrp* —3C **27**
Ullingswick. *Here* —1C **51**
Underdale. *Shrp* —3C **27**
Underton. *Shrp* —2D **33**
Undy. *Mon* —1B **66**
Upcott. *Here* —3A **40**
Uphampton. *Here* —2A **40**
Uphill. *N Som* —3A **66**
Upleadon. *Glos* —3D **51**
Upper Affcot. *Shrp* —3B **32**
Upper Bangor. *Gwyn* —3A **6**
Upper Borth. *Cdgn* —3B **28**
Upper Breinton. *Here* —1B **50**
Upper Brynamman. *Carm* —1C **57**
Upper Chapel. *Powy* —1B **48**
Upper Church Village. *Rhon* —1B **64**
Upper Coedcae. *Torf* —2D **59**
Upper Cound. *Shrp* —1C **33**
Upper Cwmbran. *Torf* —3D **59**
Upper Dinchope. *Shrp* —3B **32**
Upper Framilode. *Glos* —1D **61**
Upper Grove Common. *Here* —3C **51**
Upper Hardwick. *Here* —3B **40**
Upper Hayton. *Shrp* —3C **33**
Upper Heath. *Shrp* —3C **33**
Upper Hengoed. *Shrp* —1D **25**
Upper Hergest. *Here* —3D **39**
Upper Hill. *Here* —3B **40**
Upper Killay. *Swan* —3A **56**
Upper Langford. *N Som* —3B **66**
Upper Longwood. *Shrp* —1D **33**
Upper Lydbrook. *Glos* —1D **61**
Upper Lye. *Here* —2A **40**
Upper Maes-coed. *Here* —2A **50**
Upper Millichope. *Shrp* —3C **33**
Upper Nash. *Pemb* —2D **53**
Upper Netchwood. *Shrp* —2D **33**
Upper Rochford. *Worc* —2D **41**
Upper Sapey. *Here* —2D **41**
Upper Soudley. *Glos* —1D **61**
Upper Town. *Here* —1C **51**
Upper Town. *N Som* —3C **67**
Uppington. *Shrp* —1C **33**
Upton. *Ches* —1B **18**
Upton. *Mers* —2D **9**

Upton. *Pemb* —2D **53**
Upton Bishop. *Here* —3D **51**
Upton Cheyney. *S Glo* —3D **67**
Upton Cressett. *Shrp* —2D **33**
Upton Crews. *Here* —3D **51**
Upton Heath. *Ches* —1B **18**
Upton Magna. *Shrp* —3C **27**
Urdimarsh. *Here* —1C **51**
Urmston. *G Man* —1C **11**
Usk. *Mon* —2A **60**
Uwchmynydd. *Gwyn* —2A **20**
Uzmaston. *Pemb* —1C **53**

Valley. *IOA* —3B **4**
Van. *Powy* —3A **30**
Varteg. *Torf* —2D **59**
Vauld,The. *Here* —1C **51**
Vaynol. *Gwyn* —3A **6**
Vaynor. *Mer T* —1B **58**
Velindre. *Powy* —2C **49**
Vennington. *Shrp* —1A **32**
Venn's Green. *Here* —1C **51**
Vernolds Common. *Shrp* —3B **32**
Viney Hill. *Glos* —2D **61**
Vowchurch. *Here* —2A **50**
Vulcan Village. *Warr* —1C **11**

Waddicar. *Mers* —1A **10**
Waen. *Den* —1B **16**
  (Bodfari)
Waen. *Den* —1C **17**
  (Llandyrnog)
Waen. *Den* —1A **16**
  (Nantglyn)
Waen. *Powy* —2A **30**
Waen Fach. *Powy* —3D **25**
Waen Goleugoed. *Den* —3B **8**
Walcot. *Telf* —3C **27**
Walford. *Here* —1A **40**
  (Leintwardine)
Walford. *Here* —3C **51**
  (Ross-on-Wye)
Walford. *Shrp* —2B **26**
Walford Heath. *Shrp* —3B **26**
Walgherton. *Ches* —3D **19**
Walkden. *G Man* —1D **11**
Walker's Green. *Here* —1C **51**
Wallasey. *Mers* —1A **10**
Wallaston Green. *Pemb* —2C **53**
Wallis. *Pemb* —3D **43**
Wall under Heywood. *Shrp* —2C **33**
Walterston. *V Glam* —2B **64**
Walterstone. *Here* —3A **50**
Walton. *Mers* —1A **10**
Walton. *Powy* —3D **39**
Walton. *Telf* —3C **27**
Walton East. *Pemb* —3D **43**
Walton-in-Gordano. *N Som* —2B **66**
Walton Park. *N Som* —2B **66**
Walton West. *Pemb* —1B **52**
Walwyn's Castle. *Pemb* —1B **52**
Wanswell. *Glos* —2D **61**
Wapley. *S Glo* —2D **67**
Warburton. *G Man* —2D **11**
Wardle. *Ches* —2D **19**
Warmingham. *Ches* —1D **19**
Warmley. *S Glo* —2D **67**
Warren. *Pemb* —3C **53**
Warrington. *Warr* —2D **11**
Waterloo. *Cphy* —1C **65**
Waterloo. *Here* —1A **50**
Waterloo. *Mers* —1A **10**
Waterloo. *Pemb* —2C **53**
Waterloo. *Shrp* —1B **26**
Waterston. *Pemb* —2C **53**
Waters Upton. *Telf* —3D **27**
Wattlesborough Heath. *Shrp*
  —3A **26**
Wattstown. *Rhon* —3B **58**
Wattsville. *Cphy* —3D **59**
Waun. *Powy* —3D **25**
Waunarlwydd. *Swan* —3B **56**
Waun Fawr. *Cdgn* —3A **28**
Waunfawr. *Gwyn* —2A **14**
Waungilwen. *Carm* —2C **45**
Waunlwyd. *Blae* —2C **59**
Waun-y-Clyn. *Carm* —2D **55**
Waverton. *Ches* —1B **18**
Wavertree. *Mers* —2A **10**
Wdig. *Pemb* —2C **43**
Weaverham. *Ches* —3D **11**
Webton. *Here* —2B **50**
Wellington. *Here* —1B **50**
Wellington. *Telf* —3D **27**

Wellington Heath. *Here* —1D **51**
Wellow. *Bath* —3D **67**
Wells Green. *Ches* —2D **19**
Welshampton. *Shrp* —1B **26**
Welsh End. *Shrp* —1C **27**
Welsh Frankton. *Shrp* —1A **26**
Welsh Hook. *Pemb* —3C **43**
Welsh Newton. *Here* —1B **60**
Welsh Newton Common. *Here*
  —1C **61**
Welshpool. *Powy* —1D **31**
Welsh St Donats. *V Glam* —2B **64**
Wem. *Shrp* —2C **27**
Wenallt. *Cdgn* —1B **36**
Wenallt. *Gwyn* —3A **16**
Wentnor. *Shrp* —2A **32**
Wenvoe. *V Glam* —2C **65**
Weobley. *Here* —3B **40**
Weobley Marsh. *Here* —3B **40**
Wern. *Gwyn* —3A **14**
Wern. *Powy* —1C **59**
  (Brecon)
Wern. *Powy* —3D **25**
  (Guilsfield)
Wern. *Powy* —3A **24**
  (Llangadfon)
Wern. *Powy* —2D **25**
  (Llanymynech)
Wernffrwd. *Swan* —3A **56**
Wernyrheolydd. *Mon* —1A **60**
Wervin. *Ches* —3B **10**
West Aberthaw. *V Glam* —3B **64**
West Bank. *Hal* —2C **11**
Westbrook. *Here* —1D **49**
Westbury. *Shrp* —1A **32**
Westbury-on-Severn. *Glos* —1D **61**
Westbury on Trym. *Bris* —2C **67**
West Cross. *Swan* —1B **62**
West Derby. *Mers* —1A **10**
West End. *N Som* —3B **66**
West End. *S Glo* —1D **67**
Westerleigh. *S Glo* —2D **67**
West Felton. *Shrp* —2A **26**
West Harptree. *Bath* —3C **67**
West Hewish. *N Som* —3A **66**
Westhide. *Here* —1C **51**
West Hill. *N Som* —2B **66**
Westhope. *Here* —3B **40**
Westhope. *Shrp* —3B **33**
West Kirby. *Mers* —2D **9**
Westleigh. *G Man* —1D **11**
Westley. *Shrp* —1A **32**
Weston. *Bath* —3D **67**
Weston. *Ches* —2D **19**
Weston. *Hal* —2C **11**
Weston. *Here* —3A **40**
Weston. *Shrp* —2C **33**
  (Bridgnorth)
Weston. *Shrp* —1A **40**
  (Knighton)
Weston. *Shrp* —2C **27**
  (Wem)
Weston Beggard. *Here* —1C **51**
Westoncommon. *Shrp* —2B **26**
Weston-in-Gordano. *N Som* —2B **66**
Weston Lullingfields. *Shrp* —2B **26**
Weston Rhyn. *Shrp* —1D **25**
Weston-super-Mare. *N Som* —3A **66**
Weston under Penyard. *Here*
  —3D **51**
Westra. *V Glam* —2C **65**
West Town. *Bath* —3C **67**
West Town. *N Som* —3B **66**
West Wick. *N Som* —3A **66**
West Williamston. *Pemb* —2D **53**
Wettenhall. *Ches* —1D **19**
Weythel. *Powy* —3D **39**
Wharton. *Ches* —1D **19**
Wharton. *Here* —3C **41**
Whatmore. *Shrp* —1D **41**
Wheathill. *Shrp* —3D **33**
Wheelock. *Ches* —2D **19**
Wheelock Heath. *Ches* —2D **19**
Whelston. *Flin* —3D **9**
Whiston. *Mers* —1B **10**
Whitbourne. *Here* —3D **41**
Whitby. *Ches* —3A **10**
Whitbyheath. *Ches* —3A **10**
Whitchurch. *Bath* —3D **67**
Whitchurch. *Card* —2C **65**
Whitchurch. *Here* —1C **61**
Whitchurch. *Pemb* —3A **42**
Whitchurch. *Shrp* —3D **19**
Whitcot. *Shrp* —2A **32**
Whitcott Keysett. *Shrp* —3D **31**
Whitebrook. *Mon* —2C **61**

Whitechurch. *Pemb* —2A **44**
Whitecroft. *Glos* —2D **61**
Whitegate. *Ches* —1D **19**
White Mill. *Carm* —3D **45**
White Rocks. *Here* —3B **50**
White Stone. *Here* —1C **51**
Whitfield. *S Glo* —3D **61**
Whitford. *Flin* —3C **9**
Whitland. *Carm* —1B **54**
Whitney. *Here* —1D **49**
Whitson. *Newp* —1A **66**
Whittingslow. *Shrp* —3B **32**
Whittington. *Shrp* —1A **26**
Whitton. *Powy* —2D **39**
Whitton. *Shrp* —1C **41**
Whixall. *Shrp* —1C **27**
Whyle. *Here* —2C **41**
Wibdon. *Glos* —3C **61**
Wick. *S Glo* —2D **67**
Wick. *V Glam* —2A **64**
Wick St Lawrence. *N Som* —3A **66**
Wickwar. *S Glo* —1D **67**
Widnes. *Hal* —2C **11**
Wigmore. *Here* —2B **40**
Wilcott. *Shrp* —3A **26**
Wilderspool. *Warr* —2D **11**
Wilkesley. *Ches* —3D **19**
Willaston. *Ches* —2D **19**
  (Crewe)
Willaston. *Ches* —3A **10**
  (Neston)
Willersley. *Here* —1A **50**
Willey. *Shrp* —2D **33**
Willington Corner. *Ches* —1C **19**
Willoughbridge. *Staf* —3D **19**
Willsbridge. *S Glo* —2D **67**
Wilmington. *Bath* —3D **67**
Wilson. *Here* —3C **51**
Wincham. *Ches* —3D **11**
Windle Hill. *Ches* —3A **10**
Winford. *N Som* —3C **67**
Winforton. *Here* —1D **49**
Winnal Common. *Here* —2B **50**
Winnington. *Ches* —3D **11**
Winnington. *Staf* —1D **27**
Winscombe. *N Som* —3B **66**
Winsford. *Ches* —1D **19**
Winsh-wen. *Swan* —3B **56**
Winterbourne. *S Glo* —1D **67**
Winterley. *Ches* —2D **19**
Winwick. *Warr* —1D **11**
Wirswall. *Ches* —3A **19**
Wistanstow. *Shrp* —3B **32**
Wistanswick. *Shrp* —2D **27**
Wistaston. *Ches* —2D **19**
Wiston. *Pemb* —1D **53**
Withington. *Here* —1C **51**
Withington. *Shrp* —3C **27**
Withington Marsh. *Here* —1C **51**
Wixhill. *Shrp* —2C **27**
Wolferlow. *Here* —2D **41**
Wolf's Castle. *Pemb* —3C **43**
Wolfsdale. *Pemb* —3C **43**
Wollaston. *Shrp* —3A **26**
Wollerton. *Shrp* —1D **27**
Wolverley. *Shrp* —1B **26**
Wolvcnowton. *Mon* —3B **60**
Womaston. *Powy* —2D **39**
Wood. *Pemb* —3B **42**
Woodbank. *Ches* —3A **10**
Woodchurch. *Mers* —2D **9**
Woodcroft. *Glos* —3C **61**
Woodford. *Glos* —3D **61**
Woodhill. *N Som* —2B **66**
Woodhill. *Shrp* —3D **33**
Woodhouses. *Ches* —3C **11**
Woodlane. *Shrp* —2D **27**
Woods Eaves. *Here* —1D **49**
Woodseaves. *Shrp* —1D **27**
Woodstock Slop. *Pemb* —3D **43**
Woofferton. *Shrp* —2C **41**
Woolaston. *Glos* —3C **61**
Woolhope. *Here* —2D **51**
Woollard. *Bath* —3D **67**
Woolley. *Bath* —3D **67**
Woolstaston. *Shrp* —2B **32**
Woolston. *Shrp* —3B **32**
  (Church Stretton)
Woolston. *Shrp* —2A **26**
  (Oswestry)
Woolston. *Warr* —1D **11**
Woolton. *Mers* —2B **10**
Woonton. *Here* —3A **40**
  (Kington)
Woonton. *Here* —2C **41**
  (Leominster)

Woore. *Shrp* —3D **19**
Wootton. *Shrp* —1B **40**
  (Ludlow)
Wootton. *Shrp* —2A **26**
  (Oswestry)
Worldsend. *Shrp* —2B **32**
Worle. *N Som* —3A **66**
Worleston. *Ches* —2D **19**
Wormbridge. *Here* —2B **50**
Wormelow Tump. *Here* —2B **50**
Wormsley. *Here* —1B **50**
Worsley. *G Man* —1D **11**
Worthen. *Shrp* —1A **32**
Worthenbury. *Wrex* —3B **18**
Wotherton. *Shrp* —1D **31**
Wraxall. *N Som* —2B **66**
Wrecsam. *Wrex* —2A **18**
Wrenbury. *Ches* —3C **19**
Wrentnall. *Shrp* —1B **32**
Wrexham. *Wrex* —2A **18**
Wrexham Industrial Estate. *Wrex*
  —3A **18**
Wrickton. *Shrp* —3D **33**
Wrinehill. *Staf* —3D **19**
Wrington. *N Som* —3B **66**
Wrockwardine. *Telf* —3D **27**
Wroxeter. *Shrp* —1C **33**
Wybunbury. *Ches* —3D **19**
Wyesham. *Mon* —1C **61**
Wyke. *Shrp* —1D **33**
Wyke, The. *Shrp* —1D **33**
Wykey. *Shrp* —2A **26**
Wyndham. *B'End* —3A **58**
Wyson. *Here* —2C **41**

Yanley. *N Som* —3C **67**
Yardro. *Powy* —3D **39**
Yarkhill. *Here* —1D **51**
Yarpole. *Here* —2B **40**
Yarsop. *Here* —1B **50**
Yate. *S Glo* —1D **67**
Yatton. *Here* —2B **40**
  (Leominster)
Yatton. *Here* —2D **51**
  (Ross-on-Wye)
Yatton. *N Som* —3B **66**
Yazor. *Here* —1B **50**
Y Bala. *Gwyn* —1A **24**
Y Bont-Faen. *V Glam* —2A **64**
Y Dref. *Gwyn* —1D **21**
Y Drenewydd. *Powy* —2C **31**
Yearsett. *Here* —3D **41**
Yeaton. *Shrp* —3B **26**
Yerbeston. *Pemb* —2D **53**
Y Felinheli. *Gwyn* —1A **14**
Y Fenni. *Mon* —1A **60**
Y Ferwig. *Cdgn* —1A **44**
Y Fflint. *Flin* —3D **9**
Y Ffor. *Gwyn* —1C **21**
Y Gelli Gandryll. *Powy* —1D **49**
Ynysboeth. *Rhon* —3B **58**
Ynysddu. *Cphy* —3D **59**
Ynysforgan. *Swan* —3B **56**
Ynyshir. *Rhon* —3B **58**
Ynyslas. *Cdgn* —2B **28**
Ynysmaerdy. *Neat* —3C **57**
Ynysmaerdy. *Rhon* —1B **64**
Ynysmeudwy. *Neat* —2C **57**
Ynystawe. *Swan* —2B **56**
Ynyswen. *Powy* —1D **57**
Ynys-wen. *Rhon* —3A **58**
Ynys y Barri. *V Glam* —3C **65**
Ynysybwl. *Rhon* —3B **58**
Yockleton. *Shrp* —3B **26**
Yorkley. *Glos* —2D **61**
Yorton. *Shrp* —2C **27**
Yorton Heath. *Shrp* —2C **27**
Yr Hob. *Flin* —2A **18**
Yr Wyddgrug. *Flin* —1D **17**
Ysbyty Cynfyn. *Cdgn* —1C **37**
Ysbyty Ifan. *Cnwy* —3D **15**
Ysbyty Ystwyth. *Cdgn* —1C **37**
Ysceifiog. *Flin* —3C **9**
Yspitty. *Carm* —3A **56**
Ystalyfera. *Neat* —2C **57**
Ystrad. *Rhon* —3A **58**
Ystrad Aeron. *Cdgn* —3A **36**
Ystradfellte. *Powy* —1A **58**
Ystradffin. *Carm* —1C **47**
Ystradgynlais. *Powy* —1C **57**
Ystradmeurig. *Cdgn* —2C **37**
Ystrad Mynach. *Cphy* —3C **59**
Ystradowen. *Neat* —1C **57**
Ystradowen. *V Glam* —2B **64**
Ystumtuen. *Cdgn* —1C **37**

Selected Places of Interest and other features
Mynegai i Lefydd Dethol o Ddiddordeb a nodweddion eraill

❏ Opening times for Places of Interest vary greatly; while some open all year, others open only for the summer season, some only open certain days or even part days. We recommend, to avoid disappointment, you check with the nearest Tourist Information Centre (see pages 95/96) before starting your journey.

❏ This is an index to selected features shown on the map pages, it is not a comprehensive guide.

❏ To keep the maps as clear as possible, descriptive words like 'Castle', 'Museum' etc. are omitted, a key to the various map symbols used can be found on page 1 in the reference. Features within very congested areas and town centres are indicated as space allows, wherever possible, at least with the appropriate symbol; in some instances the text may fall into an adjacent map square.

❏ Every possible care has been taken to ensure that the information given in this publication is accurate and whilst the publishers would be grateful to learn of any errors, they regret they cannot accept any responsibility for loss thereby caused.

❏ *Bydd oriau agor llefydd o ddiddordeb yn amrywio'n fawr; tra bo rhai'n agor drwy'r flwyddyn, dim ond yn agor yn ystod yr haf y bydd eraill, a rhai dim ond ar ddiwrnodau arbennig neu am rai oriau'n unig hyd yn oed. Fel nad ydych chi'n cael eich siomi, awgrymwn eich bod chi'n cysylltu â'r Ganolfan Groeso agosaf (gweler tudalennau 95/96) cyn cychwyn ar eich taith.*

❏ *Mynegai i nodweddion dethol ar dudalennau'r mapiau yw hwn a dyna i gyd. Nid yw'n rhestr gynhwysfawr.*

❏ *Er mwyn i'r mapiau fod mor glir ag y bo modd, hepgorir geiriau disgrifiadol fel 'Castell' 'Amgueddfa' ayb a gellir gweld allwedd i'r gwahanol symbolau a ddefnyddir ar y map ar dudalen 1 yn y nodiadau cyfeiriol. Bydd angen gwasgu llawer o wybodaeth i rai ardaloedd ar y map a chanol trefi ac efallai y bydd rhaid addasu'r cynnwys yn ôl y lle sydd ar gael, ond lle bynnag y bo modd, byddwn yn ceisio rhoi'r symbol priodol o leiaf; weithiau, efallai y bydd yr ysgrifen yn ymddangos yn y sgwaryn nesaf ar y map.*

❏ *Cymerwyd pob gofal i sicrhau bod y wybodaeth a gynhwysir yn y cyhoeddiad hwn yn gywir, ac er y byddai'r cyhoeddwyr yn ddiolchgar o glywed am unrhyw gamgymeriad, maent yn ymddiheuro na allant dderbyn unrhyw gyfrifoldeb dros unrhyw golled a achosir trwy hynny.*

Abbey/Friary/Priory
Abaty/Mynachlog/Priordy

Abbey Dore Abbey Church —2A **50**
Basingwerk Abbey, Greenfield
        (Maes-Glas) —3C **9**
Bath Abbey Church —3D **67**
Belmont Abbey, Hereford —2B **50**
Buildwas Abbey —1D **33**
Caldey Island Priory —3A **54**
Craswall Priory, Michaelchurch
        Escley —2D **49**
Cwmhir Abbey, Abbey-cwm-hir
        —1B **38**
Cymer Abbey, Llanelltyd —3C **23**
Denbigh Friary —1B **16**
Ewenny Priory —2A **64**
Haughmond Abbey, Haughton
        —3C **27**
Haverfordwest Priory —1C **53**
Leominster Priory Church —3B **40**
Lilleshall Abbey —3D **27**
Llanthony Priory —3D **49**
Margam Abbey —1D **63**

Neath Abbey —3C **57**
Norton Priory, Halton —2C **11**
Penmon Priory —2B **6**
St Dogmaels Abbey —1A **44**
Shrewsbury Abbey Church —3B **26**
Strata Florida Abbey —2C **37**
Talley Abbey —2B **46**
Tintern Abbey —2C **61**
Valle Crucis Abbey, Llangollen
        —3D **17**
Wenlock Priory, Much Wenlock
        —1D **33**
Woodspring Priory, Worle —3A **66**

Aquarium
Acwariwm

Aberaeron Sea Aquarium —2D **35**
Anglesey Sea Zoo, Brynsiencyn
        —1D **13**
Beaumaris Marine World —3B **6**
Conwy Aquarium —3C **7**
Oceanarium, St David's (Tyddewi)
        —3A **42**

Rhyl Sea Life Centre —2B **8**
St David's Marine Life Centre
        —3A **42**
Silent World Aquarium, Tenby
        (Dinbych-y-Pysgod) —2A **54**
Weston-super-Mare Sea Life Centre
        —3A **66**

Arboretum
Arboretum

See also Garden
Gweler hefyd Gardd
Afan Forest Park Forest Garden,
        Pontrhydyfen —3D **57**
Cae'n y Coed Forest Garden,
        Betws-y-Coed —2C **15**
Eastnor Castle Arboretum —2D **51**
Gelli Aur Country Park Arboretum,
        Golden Grove —1A **56**
Glasdir Forest Garden, Llanfachreth
        —2C **23**
Queenswood Arboretum,
        Hope under Dinmore —3C **41**

Speech House Arboretum,
              Cinderford —1D **61**

Aviary/Bird Garden
Adarfa/Gardd Adar

See also Farm Park, Wildlife Park,
Zoo / Gweler hefyd Parc Fferm,
Parc Bywyd Gwyllt, Sw
Anglesey Birds of Prey &
  Conservation Centre, Llanrhyddlad
                    —2C **5**
Brean Down Tropical Bird Garden
                    —3D **65**
Dyfed Bird of Prey Centre, Cilgerran
                    —1B **44**
National Birds of Prey Centre,
          Newent —3D **51**
Welsh Hawking Centre, Barry
               (Barri) —3B **64**

Botanical Garden
Gardd Fotanegol

Ness Botanic Gardens —3A **10**
Swansea Plantasia —3B **56**
University of Bristol Botanical
            Gardens —2C **67**

Butterfly Farm
Fferm Gloynod Byw

Berkeley Castle Butterfly Farm
                    —3D **61**
Conwy Butterfly House —3C **7**
Felinwynt Rainforest &
        Butterfly Centre —3B **34**
Jubilee Park World of Butterflies,
     Symonds Yat (West) —1C **61**
Pili Palas Butterfly & Bird Palace,
  Menai Bridge (Porthaethwy) —3A **6**

Castle
Castell

See also Castle & Garden
Gweler hefyd Castell a Gardd
Abergavenny Castle —1D **59**
Aberystwyth Castle —3A **28**
Acton Burnell Castle —1C **33**
Beaumaris Castle —3B **6**
Beeston Castle —2C **19**
Bishop's Castle Castle —3A **32**
Bredwardine Castle —1A **50**
Bridgnorth Castle —2D **33**
Bronllys Castle —2C **49**
Builth Castle, Builth Wells
    (Llanfair-ym-Muallt) —2A **54**

Caernarfon Castle —1D **13**
Caerphilly Castle —1C **65**
Caldicot Castle —1B **66**
Camlais Castle, Defynnog —3A **48**
Candleston Castle, Merthyr Mawr
                    —2D **63**
Cardiff Castle —2C **65**
Cardigan Castle —1A **44**
Carew Castle —2D **53**
Carmarthen Castle —3D **45**
Carreg Cennen Castle, Trapp
                    —1B **56**
Castell Coch, Tongwynlais
                    —1C **65**
Castell Dinas Bran, Llangollen
                    —3D **17**
Castell y Bere, Llanfihangel-y-
              pennant —1B **28**
Chepstow Castle —3C **61**
Chester Castle (Agricola Tower)
                    —1B **18**
Cilgerran Castle —1A **44**
Clun Castle —3D **31**
Coity Castle —1A **64**
Conwy Castle —3C **7**
Criccieth Castle —1D **21**
Croft Castle, Cock Gate —2B **40**
Deganwy Castle —3C **7**
Denbigh Castle —1B **16**
Dolbadarn Castle, Llanberis
                    —2A **14**
Dolforwyn Castle —2C **31**
Dolwyddelan Castle —2C **15**
Dorstone Castle —1A **50**
Dryslwyn Castle —3A **46**
Dymock Castle (Castle Tump),
       Botloe's Green —3D **51**
Ellesmere Castle —1B **26**
Ewloe Castle —1D **17**
Flint Castle —3D **9**
Goodrich Castle —1C **61**
Grosmont Castle —3B **50**
Harlech Castle —1A **22**
Haverfordwest Castle —1C **53**
Hopton Castle —1A **40**
Kenfig Castle, Mawdlam —1D **63**
Kidwelly Castle —2D **55**
Kilpeck Castle —2B **50**
Knucklas Castle —1D **39**
Laugharne Castle —1C **55**
Llanblethian Castle —2A **64**
Llancillo Castle, Rowlestone
                    —3A **50**
Llandovery Castle —2C **47**
Llangibby Castle, Llangybi —3A **60**
Llansteffan Castle —1C **55**
Llawhaden Castle —1D **53**
Longtown Castle —3A **50**

Loughor Castle —3A **56**
Ludlow Castle —1C **41**
Lydney Castle —2D **61**
Lyonshall Castle —3A **40**
Mold Castle —1D **17**
Monmouth Castle —1C **61**
Montgomery Castle —2D **31**
Moreton Corbet Castle —2C **27**
Neath Castle —3C **57**
Newcastle (Bridgend) Castle
                    —1A **64**
Newport Castle —1A **66**
Ogmore Castle —2D **63**
Oystermouth Castle —1B **62**
Painscastle Castle —1C **49**
Peckforton Castle —2C **19**
Pembridge Castle, Welsh Newton
                    —1B **60**
Pembroke Castle —2C **53**
Penhow Castle —3B **60**
Pennard Castle, Southgate
                    —1A **62**
Penrice Castle —3D **55**
Pentrefoelas Castle —2D **15**
Pulverbatch Castle —1B **32**
Quatford Castle —2D **33**
Raglan Castle —2B **60**
Rhuddlan Castle —3B **8**
Richard's Castle Castle —1B **40**
Ruyton-XI-Towns Castle —2A **26**
St Briavels Castle —2C **61**
St Donat's Castle —3A **64**
Shrewsbury Castle —3B **26**
Skenfrith Castle —3B **50**
Stokesay Castle —3B **32**
Swansea Castle —3B **56**
Sycharth Castle —2D **25**
Tenby Castle —2A **54**
Thornbury Castle —3D **61**
Tomen-y-mur Castle, Gellilydan
                    —1C **23**
Tretower Castle —3C **49**
Twt Hill, Rhuddlan —3B **8**
Usk Castle —2A **60**
Weobley Castle —3B **40**
Weobley Castle, Oldwalls —3D **55**
Whitchurch Castle —3C **19**
White Castle, Llantilio Crossenny
                    —1A **60**
Whittington Castle —1A **26**

Castle & Garden
Castell a Gardd

See also Castle
Gweler hefyd Castell
Berkeley Castle —3D **61**
Chirk Castle —1D **25**

Manorbier Castle —3D **53**
Picton Castle, The Rhos —1D **53**
Powis Castle, Welshpool (Trallwng)
—1D **31**

Cathedral
Eglwys Gadeiriol

Bangor Cathedral —3A **6**
Brecon Cathedral —3B **48**
Bristol Cathedral —2C **67**
Cardiff RC Cathedral —2C **65**
Chester Cathedral —1B **18**
Clifton RC Cathedral —2C **67**
Hereford Cathedral —2C **51**
Liverpool Cathedral —2A **10**
Liverpool RC Cathedral —1A **10**
Llandaff Cathedral —2C **65**
Newport Cathedral —1A **66**
St Asaph Cathedral —3B **8**
St David's Cathedral —3A **42**
Shrewsbury RC Cathedral
—3B **26**
Swansea RC Cathedral —3B **56**
Wrexham RC Cathedral —2A **18**

Cave/Mine
Ogof/Safle Mwyngloddio

Aveline's Hole, Burrington —3B **66**
Big Pit Mine, Blaenavon —2D **59**
Bog Mine, The, The Bog —2A **32**
Bryn Tail Lead Mine, Llanidloes
—3A **30**
Chwarel Wynne Mine, Glyn Ceiriog
—1C **25**
Clearwell Caves —2C **61**
Dan-yr-Ogof Showcaves, Glyntawe
—1D **57**
Dolaucothi Gold Mines, Plumsaint
—1B **46**
Gloddfa Ganol Slate Mine,
Blaenau Ffestiniog —3B **14**
Great Orme Mines, Llandudno
—2C **7**
King Arthur's Cave & Merlins Cave,
Crocker's Ash —1C **61**
Kynaston's Cave, Nesscliffe
—3A **26**
Llanfair Slate Caverns —2A **22**
Llechwedd Slate Caverns,
Blaenau Ffestiniog —3C **15**
Llywernog Silver-Lead Mine
—3C **29**
Porth'yr-Ogof Cavern, Ystradfellte
—1A **58**
Sygun Copper Mine, Beddgelert
—3B **14**

Country Park
Parc Gwledig

Afan Argoed Country Park,
Cynonville —3D **57**
Alyn Waters Country Park,
Gwersyllt —2A **18**
Arrowe Country Park, Woodchurch
—2D **9**
Avon Valley Country Park,
Keynsham —3D **67**
Breakwater Country Park, Holyhead
(Caergybi) —2B **4**
Bryn Bach Country Park, Tredegar
—2C **59**
Bryngarw Country Park, Brynmenyn
—1A **64**
Caldicot Castle Country Park
—1B **66**
Clyne Valley Country Park,
Lower Sketty —3B **56**
Colemere Country Park —1B **26**
Cosmeston Lakes Country Park
—3C **65**
Craig Gwladus Country Park,
Cilfrew —3C **57**
Craig-y-nos Country Park —1D **57**
Croxteth Country Park, West Derby
—1B **10**
Dare Valley Country Park, Aberdare
(Aberdar) —2A **58**
Eastham Woods Country Park,
Eastham Ferry —2A **10**
Erddig Park Country Park,
Wrexham (Wrecsam) —3A **18**
Forest Farm Country Park,
Whitchurch —1C **65**
Gelli Aur Country Park,
Golden Grove —3B **46**
Glynllifon Country Park, Llandwrog
—2D **13**
Gnoll Estate Country Park, Neath
(Castell-nedd) —3C **57**
Granville Country Park, Muxton
—3D **27**
Great Orme Country Park,
Llandudno —2C **7**
Greenfield Valley Heritage Park,
Greenfield (Maes-Glas) —3C **9**
Halewood Triangle Country Park
—2B **10**
Henblas Country Park, Capel Mawr
—3D **5**
Joys of Life Country Park, Bethesda
—1B **14**
Little Budworth Common
Country Park —1C **19**
Llyn Llech Owain Country Park,
Gorslas —1A **56**

Llys-y-fran Reservoir Country Park
—3D **43**
Loggerheads Country Park, Cadole
—1C **17**
Lyth Hill Country Park, Great Lyth
—1B **32**
Marbury Park Country Park,
Comberbach —3D **11**
Margam Park —1D **63**
Moel Famau Country Park,
Llanbedr-Dyffryn-Clwyd —1C **17**
Nesscliffe Hill Country Park
—3A **26**
Padarn Country Park, Llanberis
—1A **14**
Parc Cefn Onn Country Park,
Thornhill —1C **65**
Parc Cwm Darran Country Park,
Deri —2C **59**
Pembrey Country Park —2D **55**
Pennington Flash Country Park
—1D **11**
Pen-y-fan Pond Country Park,
Pen-twyn —2C **59**
Pex Hill Country Park, Cronton
—2C **11**
Pickering's Pasture Country Park,
Hale Bank —2B **10**
Porthkerry Country Park —3B **64**
Queenswood Country Park,
Hope under Dinmore —3C **41**
Rivacre Valley Country Park,
Overpool —3A **10**
Sankey Valley Park,
Newton-le-Willows / St Helens
—1C **11**
Scolton Manor Country Park
—3C **43**
Severn Valley Country Park,
Highley —3D **33**
Sirhowy Valley Country Park,
Crosskeys —3C **59**
Stadt Moers Country Park, Whiston
—1B **10**
Stanney Woods Country Park,
Whitbyheath —3A **10**
Tatton Country Park, Knutsford
—2D **11**
Tredegar House Country Park,
Newport (Casnewydd) —1D **65**
Ty Mawr Country Park, Newbridge
—3D **17**
Waun-y-Llyn Country Park,
Caergwrle —2D **17**
Wepre Country Park,
Connah's Quay —1D **17**
Wirral Country Park, Thurstaston /
Willaston —2D **9**

Farm Park/Working Farm
Parc Fferm/Fferm Weithio

See also Wildlife Park
Gweler hefyd Parc Bywyd Gwyllt
Acton Scott Historic Working Farm
—3B **32**
Bunny Farm Park, Corwen —3B **16**
Cae Dafydd Rare Breeds Farm,
Nantmor —3B **14**
Cardiff City Farm —2C **65**
Cardigan Island Coastal Farm Park,
Gwbert —3A **34**
Carreg Cennen Castle Farm Park,
Trapp —1B **56**
Court Farm, Stonebridge —3A **66**
Croxteth Home Farm, West Derby
—1B **10**
Dan-yr-Ogof Shire Horse Centre,
Glyntawe —1D **57**
Dwyfor Ranch Rabbit Farm &
Farm Park, Llanystumdwy —1D **21**
Dyfed Shire Horse Farm,
Eglwyswrw —2A **44**
Farm World (Wrexham), Rhostyllen
—3A **18**
Fferm Glyneithinog, Penrherber
—2B **44**
Foel Farm Park, Brynsiencyn
—1D **13**
Folly Farm, Begelly —2A **54**
Gigrin Farm Trail, Rhayader
(Rhaeadr Gwy) —2A **38**
Green Acres Farm Park, Mancot
—1A **18**
Greenmeadow Community Farm,
Cwmbran —3D **59**
Gwaynynog Country World,
Gwaenynog Bach —1B **16**
Hall Farm Park, Pengwern —3B **8**
Henblas Farm Park, Capel Mawr
—3D **5**
Hoo Farm Animal Kingdom,
Preston upon the Weald Moors
—3D **27**
Llangloffan Farmhouse
Cheese Centre —2C **43**
Margam Park Farm Park —1D **63**
Moors Collection, Buttington
—1D **31**
Noah's Ark Farm Park, Cribyn
—3D **35**
Oaklands Small Breeds Farm, The,
Kingswood —3D **39**
Oldown Farm & Forest, Olveston
—1D **67**
Rays Farm Country Matters,
High Green —3D **33**

St Augustine's Farm, Arlingham
—1D **61**
St David's Farm Park —3A **42**
Salem Farm Rural Resource Park
—3B **46**
Shortwood Working Farm,
Pencombe —3C **41**
Stockley Farm, Arley —2D **11**
Tatton Dale Home Farm,
Knutsford —2D **11**
Trefeinon Open Farm, Llangorse
—2C **49**
Wernlas Collection, Onibury
—1B **40**
Windmill Hill City Farm, Bedminster
—2C **67**
Woodlands Farm Park, Wiston
—1D **53**
Wye Valley Farm Park, Goodrich
—1C **61**

Forest Park
Parc Coedwig

See also National Park
Gweler hefyd Parc Cenedlaethol
Afan Forest Park —3D **57**
Coed y Brenin Forest Park —2C **23**
Delamere Forest Park —3C **11**
Forest of Dean —2D **61**
Gwydyr Forest Park —2C **15**

Forest Enterprise Visitor Centre
Canolfannau gwybodaeth
Menter Coedwigaeth

See also National Park and
Tourist Information Centre
NOTE: Telephone numbers are
given in Italics
Gweler hefyd Parc Cenedlaethol a
Canolfan Groeso
Afan Argoed Countryside Centre,
Cynonville —3D **57** 01639 850564
Betws-y-Coed Y Stablau
Visitor Centre —2C **15**
01690 710426
Bod Petrual Visitor Centre,
Clawdd-newydd —1B **16**
Coed y Brenin Forest Park
Visitor Centre, Bryn Eden —2C **23**
Cwmcarn Visitor Centre —3D **59**
01495 272001
Delamere Forest Visitor Centre,
Hatchmere —3C **11**
Garwnant Forest Centre,
Llwyn-on Village —1B **58**
01685 723060

Nant-yr-Arian Visitor Centre,
Llywernog —3C **29**
Wyre Forest Visitor Centre,
Callow Hill —1D **41**
01299 266302

Fortress
Caer

Gun Tower, The, Pembroke Dock
(Doc Penfro) —2C **53**
Perch Rock Fort, New Brighton
—1A **10**

Garden
Gardd

See also Historic Building & Garden
Gweler hefyd Adeilad hanesyddol
a Gardd
Abbey Dore Court Gardens —2A **50**
Bath Georgian Garden —3D **67**
Bodnant Garden —3D **7**
Bridgemere Garden World, Woore
—3D **19**
Brobury House Garden —1A **50**
Bro Meigan Gardens, Llanfair-Nant-
Gwyn —2A **44**
Burford House Gardens —2C **41**
Cholmondeley Castle Gardens,
Hampton Heath —2C **19**
Colby Woodland Garden, Stepaside
—2A **54**
Dunraven Park, Southerndown
—2D **63**
Dyffryn Gardens —2B **64**
Festival Park, Ebbw Vale
(Glyn Ebwy) —2C **59**
Gerddi Gardens, Pontfaen —2D **43**
Goldstone Hall Garden —2D **27**
Happy Valley, Llandudno —2C **7**
Haulfre Gardens, Llandudno —2C **7**
Hergest Croft Gardens, Kington
—3D **39**
Hill Court Gardens, Walford
—3C **51**
Hodnet Hall Gardens —2D **27**
How Caple Court Gardens —2D **51**
Kenchester Water Garden,
Pipe and Lyde —1C **51**
Liverpool Festival Gardens,
Otterspool —2A **10**
Llanerchaeron, Llanaeron —2D **35**
Lydney Park Gardens —2D **61**
Maenllwyd Isaf Garden, Llanmerwig
—2C **31**
Penlan-uchaf Gardens, Crymych
—2B **44**

Penpergwm Lodge Garden,
Llanvihangel Gobion —1A **60**
Picton Gardens
(Old Court Nurseries),
Colwall Stone —1D **51**
Plas Brondanw Gardens, Garreg
—3B **14**
Plas Tan-y-Bwlch Gardens,
Tan-y-Bwlch —3B **14**
Prior Park, Bath —3D **67**
Ryelands House Garden, Taynton
—3D **51**
Stammers Gardens, Saundersfoot
—2A **54**
Stapeley Water Gardens,
Butt Green —2D **19**
Staunton Park Gardens,
Staunton on Arrow —2A **40**
Upton Castle Grounds —2D **53**
Walton Hall Gardens,
Higher Walton —2D **11**
Weir, The, Swainshill —1B **50**
Westbury Court Garden,
Westbury-on-Severn —1D **61**
Wye Valley Herb Garden, Tintern
—2C **61**

Hill Fort
Caer ar Fryn

Bury Ditches Hill Fort, Lower Down
—3A **32**
Cadbury Camp, Tickenham
—2B **66**
Caer Caradoc, Chapel Lawn
—1A **40**
Caer Caradoc, Church Stretton
—2B **32**
Caer y Twr Hill Fort, Holyhead
(Caergybi) —2B **4**
Carn Goch Hill Fort, Bethlehem
—3B **46**
Castell Henllys Iron Age Fort,
Felindre Farchog —2A **44**
Cilifor Top Hill Fort, Llanrhidian
—3A **56**
Coed-y-Bwynydd Hill Fort,
Bettws Newydd —2A **60**
Croft Ambrey Hill Fort, Yatton
—2B **40**
Dinedor Camp, Dinedor Cross
—2C **51**
Herefordshire Beacon Hill Fort,
Ledbury —1D **51**
Llanmelin Hill Fort, Llanvair-Discoed
—3B **60**
Midsummer Hill Hill Fort, Ledbury
—2D **51**

Moel Goedog Hill Fort, Eisingrug
—1B **22**
Nordy Bank Hill Fort, Cockshutford
—3C **33**
Norton Camp, Craven Arms
—3B **32**
Old Oswestry Hill Fort, Oswestry
(Croesoswallt) —1D **25**
Pen-y-crug Hill Fort, Brecon
(Aberhonddu) —2B **48**
Pen-y-Gaer Hill Fort, Llanbedr-y-
cennin —1C **15**
Rath, The, Crundale —1C **53**
Sutton Walls, Sutton St Michael
—1C **51**
Tre'r Ceiri Hill Fort, Llanaelhaeam
—3C **13**

Historic Building
Adeilad Hanesyddol

See also Historic Building & Garden
Gweler hefyd Adeilad hanesyddol
a Gardd
Abberley Hall —2D **41**
Aberconwy House, Conwy —3C **7**
Acton Round Hall —2D **33**
Adcote, Little Ness —3B **26**
Attingham Park, Atcham —1C **33**
Bath Assembly Rooms —3D **67**
Bath Guildhall —3D **67**
Bear Steps Hall, Shrewsbury
—3B **26**
Beaumaris Courthouse —3B **6**
Bridgnorth Town Hall —2D **33**
Bristol Georgian House —2C **67**
Burton Court, Eardisland —3B **40**
Butcher Row House, Ledbury
—2D **51**
Cardiff City Hall —2C **65**
Cardiff Mansion House —2C **65**
Carswell Medieval House,
St Florence —2D **53**
Castle Lodge, Ludlow —1C **41**
Chester Water Tower —1B **18**
Council House, The, Shrewsbury
—3B **26**
Cwmmau Farmhouse, Brilley
—3D **39**
Dorfold Hall, Acton —2D **19**
Dylan Thomas' Boathouse,
Laugharne —1C **55**
Eastnor Castle —2D **51**
Garway Dovecote —3B **50**
Great Aberystwyth Camera Obscura
—3A **28**
Great Castle House, Monmouth
(Trefynwy) —1C **61**

Gwrych Castle, Abergele —3A **8**
Hellen's, Much Marcle —2D **51**
Hereford Old House —1C **51**
King Charles Tower, Chester
—1B **18**
Kingswood Abbey Gatehouse
—3D **61**
Lamphey Bishop's Palace —2D **53**
Longnor Moat House —1B **32**
Lower Brockhampton,
Bringsty Common —3D **41**
Moccas Court —1A **50**
Much Wenlock Guildhall —2D **33**
Nantyglo Roundhouse Towers
—1C **59**
Old Beaupre Castle, St Hilary
—2B **64**
Oxwich Castle —3D **55**
Penarth Fawr Medieval House,
Chwilog —1D **21**
Penmon Dovecot —2B **6**
Penrhos Cottage, Maenclochog
—3A **44**
Plas Mawr, Conwy —3C **7**
Plas Newydd, Llangollen —3D **17**
Red Lodge, Bristol —2C **67**
Rosehill House, Coalbrookdale
—1D **33**
Royal Crescent, No. 1, Bath
—3D **67**
St David's Bishop's Palace —3A **42**
St Georges Hall, Liverpool —1A **10**
Smallest House, The, Conwy
—3C **7**
Sufton Court, Mordiford —2C **51**
Tabley House Collection, Knutsford
—3D **11**
Tudor Merchant's House, Tenby
(Dinbych-y-Pysgod) —2A **54**
Ty Mawr Wybrnant, Penmachno
—2C **15**
Ty'n-y-coed, Penmachno —2D **15**
Upton Cressett Hall —2D **33**
Wilderhope Manor, Longville in
the Dale —2C **33**

Historic Building & Garden
Adeilad hanesyddol a Gardd

See also Historic Building
Gweler hefyd Adeilad hanesyddol
Arley Hall —2D **11**
Benthall Hall —1D **33**
Berrington Hall, Ashton —2C **41**
Bodelwyddan Castle —3A **8**
Bodrhyddan Hall, Dyserth —3B **8**
Bryn Bras Castle, Llanrug —1A **14**
Clevedon Court —2B **66**

Croxteth Hall, West Derby —1B **10**
Dinefwr Park, Llandeilo —3B **46**
Dinmore Manor,
      Hope under Dinmore —3B **40**
Dudmaston Hall, Quatford —3D **33**
Dunham Massey, Dunham Town
        —2D **11**
Dyrham Park —2D **67**
Erddig, Wrexham (Wrecsam)
        —3A **18**
Gregynog, Tregynon —2B **30**
Gwydir Castle, Llanrwst —1C **15**
Hawkstone Hall, Weston —2C **27**
Highgate Cottage, Llanystumdwy
        —1D **21**
Kinnersley Castle —1A **50**
Littledean Hall —1D **61**
Penrhyn Castle, Llandegai —3B **6**
Plas Newydd, Llanfair Pwllgwyngyll
        —1A **14**
Plas yn Rhiw —2B **20**
St Fagans Castle —2C **65**
Shipton Hall —2C **33**
Speke Hall —2B **10**
Tatton Park, Knutsford —2D **11**
Tredegar House, Newport
      (Casnewydd) —1D **65**
Tretower Court —3C **49**
Walcot Hall, Lydbury North —3A **32**

Horse Racecourse
Maes rasio ceffylau

Aintree Racecourse —1A **10**
Bangor Racecourse,
      Bangor-is-y-coed —3A **18**
Bath & Somerset County
      Racecourse —3D **67**
Chepstow Racecourse —3C **61**
Chester (Roodee) Racecourse
        —1A **18**
Haydock Park Racecourse,
      Ashton-in-Makerfield —1C **11**
Hereford Racecourse —1C **51**
Ludlow Racecourse, Bromfield
        —1B **40**

Industrial Monument
Heneb Ddiwydiannol

See also Windmill
Gweler hefyd Melin wynt
Aberdulais Falls Watermills
        —3C **57**
Anderton Boat Lift —3D **11**
Audlem Lock Flight —3D **19**
Bedlam Furnaces, Ironbridge
        —1D **33**

Bersham Ironworks —3A **18**
Blackpool Mill & Caverns,
      Canaston Bridge —1D **53**
Blaenavon Ironworks —2D **59**
Brynkir Woollen Mill, Golan —3A **14**
Bunbury Staircase Locks —2C **19**
Bunbury Watermill —2C **19**
Carew Tidal Mill —2D **53**
Cefn Cribbwr Ironworks,
      Cefn Cribbwr —1D **63**
Cenarth Falls Flour Mill —1B **44**
Clydach Ironworks —1D **59**
Cochwillan Mill, Tal-y-bont —1B **14**
Daniel's Mill, Bridgnorth —2D **33**
Denant Mill Inn, Dreenhill —1C **53**
Dunham Massey Sawmill,
      Dunham Town —2D **11**
Dyfi Furnace —2B **28**
Felin Crewi Watermill, Penegoes
        —1C **29**
Felin Faesog Watermill, Tai'n Lon
        —2D **13**
Felin Geri Watermill, Cwm-cou
        —1C **45**
Felin Isaf Watermill, Pentrefelin
        —3D **7**
Felin Newydd Watermill, Crugybar
        —2B **46**
Felin yr Aber, Llanwnnen —1A **46**
Fourteen Locks, Rogerstone
        —1D **65**
Gelligroes Old Mill, Pontllanfraith
        —3C **59**
Hay Inclined Plane, Coalport
        —1D **33**
Ironbridge —1D **33**
Melin Howell, Llanddeusant —2C **5**
Melin Teifi, Drefach —2C **45**
Middle Mill Woollen Mill,
      Whitchurch —3B **42**
Mortimer's Cross Watermill —2B **40**
Penmachno Woollen Mill —2D **15**
Pentre Watermill, Cadole —1C **17**
Priston Mill —3D **67**
Rock Mills Woollen Mill, Capel Dewi
        —1D **45**
Salt House, The, Port Eynon
        —1A **62**
Shore Road Pumping Station,
      Birkenhead —2A **10**
Stretton Watermill —2B **18**
Tintern Abbey Furnace —2C **61**
Tintern Abbey Mill —2C **61**
Trefriw Woollen Mills —1C **15**
Tregwynt Woollen Mill, Granston
        —2B **42**
Welsh Frankton Lock Flight —1A **26**
Y Felin, St Dogmaels —1A **44**

Motor Racing Circuit
Trac Rasio Ceir

Llandow Motor Circuit —2A **64**
Oulton Park Motor Circuit,
      Little Budworth —1C **19**
Pembrey Motor Circuit —2D **55**

Museum & Art Gallery
Amgueddfa a Oriel Gelf

1st The Queen's Dragoon Guards
      Museum, Cardiff (Caerdydd)
        —2C **65**
Abbey Farm Museum, Greenfield
      (Maes-Glas) —3C **9**
Aberaeron Honey Bee Exhibition
        —2D **35**
Abergavenny & District Museum
        —1D **59**
Aberystwyth Arts Centre —3A **28**
Aberystwyth Yesterday —3A **28**
Albion Art Gallery, St David's
      (Tyddewi) —3A **42**
Andrew Logan Museum of
      Sculpture, Berriew —1C **31**
Anglesey Heritage Gallery,
      Llangefni —3D **5**
Bangor Museum & Art Gallery
        —3A **6**
Barmouth Lifeboat Museum
        —3B **22**
Bath Book Museum —3D **67**
Bath Postal Museum —3D **67**
Bath Roman Bath Museum
        —3D **67**
Beaumaris Gaol —3B **6**
Beaumaris Museum of Childhood
      Memories —3B **6**
Beckford's Tower Museum, Bath
        —3D **67**
Bersham Heritage Centre —3A **18**
Betws-y-Coed Motor Museum
        —2C **15**
Big Pit Mining Museum, Blaenavon
        —2D **59**
Birkenhead Priory Interpetive
      Centre —2A **10**
Birkenhead Tramway Museum
        —2A **10**
Bishop's Castle Railway Museum
        —3A **32**
Blaise Castle House Museum,
      Henbury —2C **67**
Blists Hill Open Air Museum
        —1D **33**
Bluecoat Chambers Art Gallery,
      Liverpool —1A **10**

Boat Museum, The, Ellesmere Port —3B **10**

Brecknock Museum, Brecon (Aberhonddu) —3B **48**

Bridgnorth Childhood & Costume Museum —2D **33**

Bristol City Museum & Art Gallery —2C **67**

Bristol Industrial Museum —2C **67**

British Folk Art Collection, Bath —3D **67**

Bromyard Heritage Centre —3D **41**

Building of Bath Museum —3D **67**

Button Museum, The, Ross-on-Wye —3C **51**

Caerleon Roman Legionary Museum —3A **60**

Caernarfon Air World, Dinas Dinlle —2D **13**

Carmarthen Heritage Centre —1D **55**

Carmarthen Museum, Abergwili —3D **45**

Catalyst Museum, West Bank —2C **11**

Cefn Coed Colliery Museum, Crynant —2C **57**

Ceredigion Museum, Aberystwyth —3A **28**

Char Bazaar Teapot Museum, Conwy —3C **7**

Chepstow Museum —3C **61**

Cheshire Military Museum, Chester —1B **18**

Chester Heritage Centre —1B **18**

Chester Toy Museum —1B **18**

Childhood & Home, Museum of, Abergavenny (Y Fenni) —1D **59**

Churchill Gardens Museum & Brian Hatton Gallery, Hereford —1C **51**

Chwarel Wynne Mine Museum, Glyn Ceiriog —1C **25**

Clive House Museum, Shrewsbury —3B **26**

Clive of India Museum, Welshpool (Trallwng) —1D **31**

Clun Local History Museum —3A **32**

Coalport China Museum —1D **33**

Coleford Great Western Railway Museum —1C **61**

Conwy Valley Railway Museum, Betws-y-Coed —2C **15**

Corris Railway Museum —1C **29**

Costume, Museum of, Bath —3D **67**

Cyfarthfa Castle Museum & Art Gallery, Merthyr Tydfil —2B **58**

Dan-yr-Ogof Museum, Glyntawe —1D **57**

Darby Furnace & Museum of Iron, Coalbrookdale —1D **33**

Davies Memorial Gallery, Newtown (Y Drenewydd) —2C **31**

Dinham House Exhibition Centre, Ludlow —1C **41**

Doctor Who Exhibition, Llangollen —3D **17**

Drenewydd Museum, Bute Town —2C **59**

East Asian Art, Museum of, Bath —3D **67**

Elton Gallery, Coalbrookdale —1D **33**

Felin Geri Watermill Museum, Cwm-cou —1C **45**

Forge House Gallery, Brimfield —2C **41**

Gloddfa Ganol Narrow Gauge Railway Museum, Blaenau Ffestiniog —3B **14**

Glynn Vivian Art Gallery, Swansea (Abertawe) —3B **56**

Golden Sheaf Gallery, The, Narberth (Arberth) —1A **54**

Graham Sutherland Gallery, The Rhos —1D **53**

Grosvenor Museum, Chester —1B **18**

Gwent Rural Life Museum, Usk (Brynbuga) —2A **60**

Harveys Wine Museum, Bristol —2C **67**

Hereford Cider Museum & King Offa Distillery —2C **51**

Hereford City Museum & Art Gallery —2C **51**

Herefordshire Rural Heritage Museum, Great Doward —1C **61**

Herefordshire Waterworks Museum, Hereford —2B **50**

Herschel House Museum, Bath —3D **67**

HM Customs & Excise National Museum, Liverpool —2A **10**

Holburne Museum & Craft Study Centre, Bath —3D **67**

Home, The Museum of the, Pembroke (Penfro) —2C **53**

International Helicopter Museum, Locking —3A **66**

Ironbridge Gorge Museum —1D **33**

Including —

Bedlam Furnaces

Blists Hill Open Air Museum

Coalport China Museum

Darby Furnace

Elton Gallery

Hay Inclined Plane

Ironbridge and Tollhouse

Jackfield Tile Museum

Museum of Iron

Museum of the River and Visitor Centre

Rosehill House

Tar Tunnel

Ironbridge Teddybear Museum —1D **33**

Ironbridge Tollhouse —1D **33**

Ironbridge Toy Museum —1D **33**

Jackfield Tile Museum —1D **33**

Jenner Museum, Berkeley —3D **61**

Joseph Parry's Cottage, Merthyr Tydfil —2B **58**

Jubilee Park Museum of Mazes, Symonds Yat (West) —1C **61**

Junction Cottage, Pontypool (Pontypwl) —2D **59**

Kidwelly Industrial Museum —2D **55**

Kington Museum —3D **39**

Knutsford Heritage Centre —3D **11**

Lady Lever Art Gallery, Port Sunlight —2A **10**

Leominster Folk Museum —3B **40**

Liverpool Football Club Visitor Centre Museum, Anfield —1A **10**

Liverpool Life, Museum of —1A **10**

Liverpool Museum —1A **10**

Llancaiach Fawr - Living History Museum, Nelson —3C **59**

Llandrindod Wells Museum —2B **38**

Llandudno Museum —2C **7**

Llanelli Public Library Gallery —2A **56**

Llangollen Canal Exhibition Centre —3D **17**

Llangollen Model Railway World —3D **17**

Llangollen Motor Museum —3D **17**

Llangollen Victorian School Museum —3D **17**

Llanidloes Museum —3A **30**

Llantarnam Grange Arts Centre, Cwmbran —3D **59**

Llanyrafon Farm Museum, Cwmbran —3A **60**

Lleithyr Farm Museum, Treleddyd-fawr —3A **42**

Lleyn Historical & Maritime Museum, Nefyn —3C **13**

Lloyd George Memorial Museum, Llanystumdwy —1D **21**

Llwyfan Cerrig Station Railway Museum, Bronwydd Arms —3D **45**

Llys Llywelyn, Aberffraw —1C **13**

Lost Street Museum, Ross-on-Wye —3D **51**

Ludlow Museum —1C **41**

Lydney Park Roman Temple Museum —2D **61**

Madog Motor Museum, Porthmadog —1A **22**

Maes Artro Village, Llanbedr —2A **22**

Maesllyn Mill Museum —1C **45**

Magical Machines, Museum of, Cardiff (Caerdydd) —2C **65**

Margam Stones Museum —1D **63**

Merseyside Maritime Museum, Liverpool —2A **10**

Midland Motor Museum, Bridgnorth —2D **33**

Milford Haven Museum —2C **53**

Model Farm Folk Collection, Wolvesnewton —3B **60**

Mold Museum & Art Gallery —1D **17**

Mouldsworth Motor Museum —3C **11**

Mr Bowler's Business, Bath —3D **67**

Much Wenlock Museum —2D **33**

Nantgarw China Works Museum —1C **65**

Nantwich Museum —2D **19**

Nant-y-Coy Mill Museum, Wolf's Castle —3C **43**

National Coracle Centre, Cenarth —1B **44**

National Library of Wales, Aberystwyth —3A **28**

National Museum of Wales (Main Building), Cardiff (Caerdydd) —2C **65**

Neath Museum & Art Gallery —3C **57**

Nelson Museum & Local History Centre, Monmouth (Trefynwy) —1C **61**

Newport Museum & Art Gallery —1A **66**

Newtown Textile Museum —2C **31**

Norchard Steam Centre Museum, Lydney —2D **61**

Norton Priory Museum, Halton —2C **11**

Old Bell Museum, Montgomery (Trefaldwyn) —2D **31**

Old Chapel Gallery, Pembridge —3A **40**

Old Welsh Country Life, Museum of, Tai'n Lon —2D **13**

'On the Air' The, Broadcasting Museum, Chester —1B **18**

Oriel Mostyn, Llandudno —2C **7**

Oriel Pendeitsh Gallery, Caernarfon —1D **13**

Oswestry Transport Museum —2D **25**

Outward Bound Museum, Aberdovey (Aberdyfi) —2B **28**

Owain Glyndwr Museum (Parliament House), Machynlleth —1C **29**

Owen Memorial Museum, Newtown (Y Drenewydd) —2C **31**

Parc Howard Museum & Art Gallery, Llanelli —2A **56**

Park Hall Working Farm Museum, Oswestry (Croesoswallt) —1A **26**

Pembroke Farm Museum —2C **53**

Pembrokeshire Motor Museum, Keeston —1B **52**

Penbontbren Countryside Collection, Glynarthen —1C **45**

Penrhyn Castle Industrial Railway Museum, Llandegai —3B **6**

Pilkington Glass Museum, St Helens —1B **10**

Pontypridd Historical & Cultural Centre —3B **58**

Porthmadog Harbour Station Railway Museum —1A **22**

Porthmadog Maritime Museum —1A **22**

Port Sunlight Heritage Centre —2A **10**

Powysland Museum & Montgomery Canal Centre, Welshpool (Trallwng) —1D **31**

Prescot Museum of Clock & Watch Making —1B **10**

Presteigne (Shire Hall) Museum —2A **40**

Primitive Methodism, Museum of, Englesea-brook —2D **19**

Railway Age, The, Crewe —2D **19**

Rainhill Trails Exhibition —1B **10**

Rhondda Heritage Park, Trehafod —3B **58**

River & Visitor Centre, Museum of the, Ironbridge —1D **33**

Rob Piercy Gallery, Porthmadog —1A **22**

Rowley's House Museum, Shrewsbury —3B **26**

Royal Cambrian Academy, The, Conwy —3C **7**

Royal Forest of Dean Mining Museum, Clearwell —2C **61**

Royal Photographic Society, The, Bath —3D **67**

Royal Welsh Fusiliers Museum, Caernarfon —1D **13**

Ruthin Craft Centre Gallery —2C **17**

St Helens Museum & Art Gallery —1C **11**

St Helens Transport Museum —1C **11**

St John Medieval Museum, Hereford —1C **51**

Sally Lunn's House, Bath —3D **67**

Salt Museum, The, Northwich —3D **11**

Scolton Manor Museum —3C **43**

Sea Historic Gallery & Marine Life Aquarium, Pembroke (Penfro) —2C **53**

Segontium Roman Fort Museum, Caernarfon —1D **13**

Seiont II Maritime Museum, Caernarfon —1D **13**

Selvedge Farm Museum, Clarbeston Road —3D **43**

Seven Sisters Museum —2D **57**

Shambles Museum, The, Newent —3D **51**

Shropshire Regimental Museum, Shrewsbury —3B **26**

South Wales Borders Museum, Brecon (Aberhonddu) —3B **48**

South Wales Miners Museum, Cynonville —3D **57**

South Wales Police Museum, Bridgend (Pen-y-bont ar Ogwr) —2A **64**

Stapeley's Yesteryear Museum, Butt Green —2D **19**

Stone Science, Llanddyfnan —3D **5**

Sudley House, Mossley Hill —2A **10**

Swansea Maritime & Industrial Museum —3B **56**

Swansea Museum —3B **56**

Talyllyn Narrow Gauge Railway Museum, Tywyn —1A **28**

Tate Gallery Liverpool —2A **10**

Tenbury Museum, Tenbury Wells —2C **41**

Tenby Museum & Picture Gallery —2A **54**

Thornbury Museum —1D **67**

Tre'r-ddol Local Folk Museum —2B **28**

Turner House Gallery, Penarth —2C **65**

Turnpike Gallery, Leigh —1D **11**

University of Liverpool Art Gallery —1A **10**

University of Wales School of Art Museum & Gallery, Aberystwyth —3A **28**

Vale of Glamorgan Railway Visitor Centre, Barry Island (Ynys y Barri) —3C **65**

Valley Inheritance Museum, The, Pontypool (Pontypwl) —2D **59**

Victoria Art Gallery, Bath —3D **67**

Wales Aircraft Museum, Tredogan —3B **64**

Walker Art Gallery, Liverpool —1A **10**

Warrington Museum & Art Gallery —2D **11**

Water Folk Canal Centre Museum, Llanfrynach —3B **48**

Welsh Regiment Museum of The Royal Regiment of Wales, The, Cardiff (Caerdydd) —2C **65**

Welsh Folk Museum, St Fagans —2C **65**

Welsh Industrial & Maritime Museum, Cardiff (Caerdydd) —2C **65**

Welsh Slate Museum, Llanberis —1A **14**

Welsh Woollen Industry, Museum of the, Drefach —2C **45**

W.H.Smith Museum, Newtown (Y Drenewydd) —2C **31**

Williamson Art Gallery & Museum, Birkenhead —2A **10**

Wilson Museum of Narberth —1A **54**

Wonderful World of Welsh Wool, Llanwrtyd Wells —1D **47**

Woodspring Museum, Weston-super-Mare —3A **66**

Wrexham Maelor Heritage Centre, Wrexham (Wrecsam) —2A **18**

Wroxeter Roman City Museum —1C **33**

Ynysfach Iron Heritage Centre, Merthyr Tydfil —2B **58**

Y Tabernacl (The Museum of Modern Art, Wales), Machynlleth —1C **29**

National Park
Parc Cenedlaethol

See also Forest Park
Gweler hefyd Parc Coedwig
Brecon Beacons National Park —3B **48** / 1D **57** / 1A **58**

Pembrokeshire Coast National Park —2D **53** / 1B **52** / 2D **43**

Snowdonia National Park —2B **14** / 1C **23**

National Park Information Centre
Canolfan Wybodaeth y Parc Cenedlaethol

See also Forest Park and Tourist Information Centres
NOTE: Telephone Numbers are given in Italics
Gweler hefyd Parc Coedwig a Canolfan Groesco

Aberdovey (Aberdyfi) Information Centre —2B **28** 01654 767321

Abergavenny (Y Fenni) Information Centre —1A **60** 01873 853254

Betws-y-Coed Y Stablau Visitor Centre —2C **15** 01690 710426

Blaenau Ffestiniog Information Centre —3C **15** 01766 830360

Brecon (Aberhonddu) Information Centre —3B **48** 01874 623156

Broad Haven Information Centre —1B **52** 01437 781412

Craig-y-nos Information Centre —1D **57** 01639 730395

Dolgellau Information Centre —3C **23** 01341 422888

Harlech Information Centre —1A **22** 01766 780658

Haverfordwest (Hwlffordd) Information Centre —1C **53** 01437 760136

Llandovery (Llanymddyfri) Information Centre —2C **47** 01550 20693

Mountain Centre Visitor Centre, Libanus —3A **48** 01874 623366

Newport Information Centre (Pembrokeshire) —2D **43** 01239 820912

Pembroke (Penfro) Information Centre —2C **53** 01646 682148

St David's (Tyddewi) Information Centre —3A **42** 01437 720392

Saundersfoot Information Centre —2A **54** 01834 811411

Natural Attraction
Atyniad Naturiol

Aberdulais Falls —3C **57**

Aberedw Rocks —1B **48**

Aber Falls, Abergwyngregyn —1B **14**

Afon Arddu Waterfall, Llanberis —2A **14**

Afon Gamlan Cataracts, Ganllwyd —2C **23**

Afon Mellte & Afon Hepste Waterfalls, Pontneddfechan —1A **58**

Afon Pyrddin Waterfall, Pontneddfechan —2D **57**

Arthog Waterfalls —3B **22**

Avon Gorge, Bristol —2C **67**

Bala Lake (Llyn Tegid) —1A **24**

Bethania Waterfalls —2B **14**

Black Mountain, Upper Brynamman —1C **57**

Bleadon Hill —3A **66**

Blue Lagoon, Abereiddy —2A **42**

Brecon Beacons, Libanus —3B **48**

Brockley Combe —3B **66**

Brown Clee Hill, Hillside —3C **33**

Buck Stone, The, Staunton —1C **61**

Burrington Combe —3B **66**

Caldey Island —3A **54**

Cenarth Falls —1B **44**

Chew Valley Lake, Chew Stoke —3C **67**

Claerwen Reservoir, Elan Village —2D **37**

Conwy Falls, Betws-y-Coed —2D **15**

Devil's Bridge —1C **37**

Dinefwr Deer Park, Llandeilo —3B **46**

Dolgoch Falls —1B **28**

Elan Valley, Elan Village —2A **38**

Elegug Stacks, Merrion —3C **53**

Fairy Glen, Betws-y-Coed —2D **15**

Flat Holm —3D **65**

Forest of Dean, Parkend —2D **61**

Garw Fechan Woodland Park, Pontycymer —3D **57**

Gethin Woodland Park, Pentrebach —2B **58**

Gower (Gwyr), Swansea (Abertawe) —3D **55**

Great Orme, Llandudno —2C **7**

Grey Mare's Tail, The, Llanrwst —1C **15**

Hatch Mere, Hatchmere —3C **11**

Henrhyd Falls, Coelbren —1D **57**

Horseshoe Falls, Berwyn —3C **17**

Lake Vyrnwy (Llyn Efyrnwy),
Llanwddyn —2A **24**
Llwyn-on Reservoir, Llwyn-on-
Village —1B **58**
Llyn Alaw, Llanbabo —2C **5**
Llyn Brenig, Pentre-llyn-cymmer
—2A **16**
Llyn Clywedog, Llanidloes —3A **30**
Llyn Mair, Tan-y-bwlch —3B **14**
Llyn Trawsfynydd —1B **22**
Llyn-y-Fan Fach Escarpment,
Llanddeusant —3D **47**
Long Mynd, Church Stretton
—2B **32**
Machno Falls, Betws-y-Coed
—2D **15**
Melincourt Waterfall —2D **57**
Mere, The, Ellesmere —1B **26**
Moel Famau, Llanbedr-Dyffryn-
Clwyd —1C **17**
Mynach Falls, Devil's Bridge
(Pontarfynach) —1C **37**
Nedd Fechan Waterfall,
Pontneddfechan —2A **58**
Penpych Woodland Park,
Blaencwm —3A **58**
Pistyll Cain, Ganllwyd —2C **23**
Pistyll Rhaeadr, Tan-y-pistyll
—2B **24**
Ramsey Island —3A **42**
Rhaeadr Cynfal, Ffestiniog —3C **15**
Rhaeadr Ddu, Ganllwyd —2C **23**
Rhaeadr Mawddach, Ganllwyd
—2C **23**
Rhaeadr y Cwm, Ffestiniog —3C **15**
Rheidol Falls, Aberffrwd —1C **37**
Rodneys Pillar, Criggion —3D **25**
Shell Island (Mochras), Llanbedr
—2A **22**
Skokholm Island —2A **52**
Skomer Island —2A **52**
Snowdon, Llanberis —2B **14**
Stiperstones, The Bog —2A **32**
Sugar Loaf, Llwyn-du —1D **59**
Swallow Falls, Betws-y-Coed
—2C **15**
Symonds Yat —1C **61**
Talybont Reservoir, Aber Village
—1B **58**
Titterstone Clee Hill, Angelbank
—1C **41**
Water-break-its-neck Waterfall,
Llanfihangel-Nant-Melan —2C **39**
Wenlock Edge, Presthope —2C **33**
Wentwood Forest, Llanvair-Discoed
—3B **60**
Wrekin, The, Little Wenlock —1D **33**
Wyre Forest, Bewdley —1D **41**

**Nature Reserve/Bird Sanctuary
Gwarchodfa natur/
Warchodfa Adar**

*R.S.P.B., English Nature & Wildfowl
Trust only.*

Arthog Bog Bird Sanctuary —3B **22**
Avon Gorge Nature Reserve, Bristol
—2C **67**
Cadair Idris Nature Reserve,
Tal-y-llyn —3C **23**
Carngafallt Common
Nature Reserve, Elan Village
—2A **38**
Coed Garth Gell Bird Sanctuary,
Penmaenpool —3B **22**
Coedydd Aber Nature Reserve,
Abergwyngregyn —3B **6**
Coedydd Maentwrog (Llyn Mair)
Nature Reserve, Tan-y-bwlch
—3B **14**
Cors Caron Nature Reserve,
Tregaron —2B **36**
Craig-y-Cilau Nature Reserve,
Darren —1C **59**
Crymlyn Bog Nature Reserve,
Pentre-dwr —3B **56**
Cwm Clydach Bird Sanctuary,
Craig-cefn-parc —2B **56**
Cwm Idwal & Glydeiriau
Nature Reserve, Pont Pen-y-ben
glog —2B **14**
Cwm Wood Nature Reserve,
Elan Village —2A **38**
Dinas Bird Sanctuary, Ystradffin
—1C **47**
Dyffryn Wood Bird Sanctuary,
Rhayader (Rhaeadr Gwy) —2A **38**
Dyfi Nature Reserve, Ynyslas
—2B **28**
Gayton Sands Bird Sanctuary,
Neston —3D **9**
Gower Coast Nature Reserve,
Pitton —3D **55**
Gwenffrwd Bird Sanctuary,
Nant-y-Bai —1C **47**
Highbury Wood Nature Reserve,
Redbrook —2C **61**
Lake Vyrnwy Bird Sanctuary,
Llanwddyn —2A **24**
Llanelli Wildfowl & Wetlands Centre
—3A **56**
Morfa Dyffryn Nature Reserve,
Llanenddwyn —2A **22**
Nagshead Bird Sanctuary, Parkend
—2D **61**
Nant Irfon Nature Reserve,
Abergwesyn —3D **37**

Newborough Warren
Nature Reserve —1D **13**
Ogof Ffynon Ddu Nature Reserve,
Craig-y-nos —1D **57**
Oxwich Nature Reserve —1A **62**
Penhow Woodlands
Nature Reserve —1B **66**
Penmoelallt Forest Nature Reserve,
Llwyn-on Village —2A **58**
Point of Ayr Bird Sanctuary, Talacre
—2C **9**
Ramsey Island Nature Reserve
—3A **42**
Rhinog Nature Reserve,
Pentre Gwynfryn —2B **22**
Skomer Island Nature Reserve
—2A **52**
Slimbridge Wildfowl &
Wetlands Centre —2D **61**
Snowdon (Yr Wyddfa)
Nature Reserve, Bethania —2B **14**
South Stack Cliffs Bird Sanctuary,
Holyhead (Caergybi) —2B **4**
Stackpole & Bosherston Ponds
Nature Reserve, Bosherston
—3C **53**
Stanner Rocks Nature Reserve,
Walton —3D **39**
Stiperstones Nature Reserve, The
—2A **32**
Ty Canol Nature Reserve,
Felindre Farchog —2D **43**
Valley Lakes Bird Sanctuary,
Llanfihangel yn Nhowyn —3C **5**
Whiteford Nature Reserve,
Llanmadoc —3D **55**
Worms Head Nature Reserve,
Rhossili —3C **55**
Wyre Forest Nature Reserve,
Bewdley —1D **41**
Ynys-Hir Bird Sanctuary,
Eglwys Fach —2B **28**

**Place of Interest
*Man Diddorol***

Admiralty Arch, Holyhead
(Caergybi) —2B **4**
Alice in Wonderland Visitor Centre,
Llandudno —2C **7**
Anglesey Column,
Llanfair Pwllgwyngyll —3A **6**
Anglesey Model Village,
Newborough (Niwbwrch) —1D **13**
Animation World, Liverpool —2A **10**
Atcham Bridge —1C **33**
Avondale Glass, Kilgetty (Cilgeti)
—2A **54**

Babell Chapel, Cwmfelinfach —3C **59**

Bath Pump Room —3D **67**

Beatles Story, The, Liverpool —2A **10**

Bedford Park, Cefn Cribwr —1D **63**

Berwyn Chain Bridge —3C **17**

Bird World's Kids 'n' Family, Dwyran —1D **13**

Bodelwyddan 'Marble' Church —3B **8**

Bredwardine Bridge —1A **50**

Bristol Maritime Heritage Centre —2C **67**

Bristol Temple Church —2C **67**

Britannia Bridge, Llanfair Pwllgwyngyll —3A **6**

Bronyscawen Farm Chocolates, Llanboidy —3B **44**

Butlin's Starcoast World, Pwllheli —1D **21**

Cabot Tower, Bristol —2C **67**

Caernarfon Town Walls —1D **13**

Cains Brewery, Toxteth —2A **10**

Cantlop Bridge —1C **33**

Capel Lligwy, Moelfre —2D **5**

Cardiff Bay Visitor Centre, Cardiff (Caerdydd) —2C **65**

Carding Mill Valley Information Centre, Church Stretton —2B **32**

Carew Cross —2D **53**

Castle Park Arts Centre, Frodsham —3C **11**

Cefn Isaf Farm Trail, Pentre Gwynfryn —2B **22**

Celtica, Machynlleth —1C **29**

Cemmaes Windfarm —1D **29**

Centre for Alternative Technology, Pantperthog —1C **29**

Cheshire Workshops, Burwardsley —2C **19**

Chester Visitor Centre —1B **18**

Chirk Aqueduct —1D **25**

Clifton Suspension Bridge —2C **67**

Clifton Suspension Bridge Observatory —2C **67**

Clywedog Dam, Llanidloes —3A **30**

Clywedog Gorge Trail, Llanidloes —3A **30**

Conwy Suspension Bridge —3C **7**

Conwy Town Walls —3C **7**

Conwy Tubular Railway Bridge —3C **7**

Conwy Visitor Centre —3C **7**

Cosmeston Medieval Village —3C **65**

Country World, Gatesheath —1B **18**

Cwmcarn Forest Drive —3D **59**

Cwm Rheidol Hydro Electric Power Station Visitor Centre, Aberffrwd —1C **37**

Dan-yr-Ogof Dinosaur Park, Glyntawe —1D **57**

Dauphine's of Bristol —2D **67**

Dean Heritage Centre, Lower Soudley —1D **61**

Denbigh Town Walls —1B **16**

Derwen Churchyard Cross —2B **16**

Devil's Bridge Three Bridges —1C **37**

Dinorwig Discovery Centre, Llanberis —1A **14**

Dinorwig Power Station, Llanberis —2A **14**

Dinosaur Experience, Gumfreston —2D **53**

Dinosaur World, Colwyn Bay (Bae Colwyn) —3D **7**

Dryton Oak —1C **33**

Edvin Loach Saxon Church, Tedstone Wafer —3D **41**

Elan Valley Visitor Centre, Elan Village —2A **38**

Eliseg's Pillar, Llangollen —3D **17**

Ellin's Tower Information Centre, Holyhead (Caergybi) —2B **4**

Exploratory Hands-on Science Centre, Bristol —2C **67**

Ffestiniog Power Station Information Centre, Tanygrisiau —3B **14**

Ffestiniog Power Station, Tanygrisiau —3B **14**

Ffwrrwm Art & Craft Centre, Caerleon (Caerllion) —3A **60**

Fourteen Locks Canal Centre, Rogerstone —1D **65**

Gelert's Grave, Beddgelert —3A **14**

George III Jubilee Arch, Devil's Bridge (Pontarfynach) —1C **37**

Glamorgan Heritage Coast Centre, Southerndown —2D **63**

Glamorgan Nature Centre, Tondu —1D **63**

Glyncornel Environmental Centre, Llwynypia —3A **58**

Great Orme Cabin Lift, Llandudno —2C **7**

Green Wood Centre, The, Y Felinheli (Port Dinorwig) —1A **14**

Gregory Farm Rescue Centre, Brockweir —2C **61**

Grove Land Adventure World, Llangynin —1B **54**

Gunsmoke Cowboy Town, Seven Sisters —2D **57**

Gwydir Uchaf Chapel, Llanrwst —1C **15**

Harry Tuffin Animal Park, Church Stoke —2D **31**

Hawkstone Historic Park & Follies, Weston —2C **27**

Hen Gwrt (Old Court), Llantilio Crossenny —1A **60**

Heron's Brook Leisure Park, Narberth (Arberth) —1A **54**

Historic Warships at Birkenhead —1A **10**

Inigo Jones Tudor Slate Works, Groeslon —2D **13**

James Pringle Weavers, Llanfair Pwllgwyngyll —3A **6**

John Wesley's Chapel, Bristol —2C **67**

Jubilee Maze (Jubilee Park), Symonds Yat (West) —1C **61**

Jubilee Tower, Llanbedr-Dyffryn-Clwyd —1C **17**

Kaleidoscope Discovery Centre, Milford Haven (Aberdaugleddau) —2B **52**

Kempley St Mary's Church —3D **51**

Kilpeck Church —2B **50**

King Arthur's Labyrinth, Corris —1C **29**

King's Mill Visitor Centre, Wrexham (Wrecsam) —3A **18**

Knights Caverns, The, Rhyl —2B **8**

Kymin Naval Temple —1C **61**

Lake Vyrnwy Visitor Centre, Llanwddyn —3B **24**

Landsker Visitor Centre, Narberth (Arberth) —1A **54**

Langley Chapel, Ruckley —1C **33**

Ledbury Old Grammar School Heritage Centre —2D **51**

Lion Salt Works, Marston —3D **11**

Llandudno Pier —2C **7**

Llandyfeisant Church Interpretative Centre, Llandeilo —3B **46**

Llanelli Wildfowl & Wetlands Centre Visitor Centre —3A **56**

Llangar Old Parish Church, Corwen —3B **16**

Lloyd George Memorial, Llanystumdwy —1D **21**

Llyn Brenig Arcaeological Trail, Nantglyn —2A **16**

Llywelyn Cottage Information Centre, Beddgelert —3A **14**

Longdon on Tern Aqueduct —3D **27**

Lord Hill's Column, Shrewsbury —3C **27**

Maen Achwyfan Cross, Whitford (Chwitffordd) —3C **9**

Mary Jones Monument (Tyn-y-ddol), Llanfihangel-y-pennant —1B **28**

Mawddach Viaduct, Barmouth (Abermaw) —3B **22**

Meirion Mill, Minllyn —3D **23**

Menai Suspension Bridge, Menai Bridge (Porthaethwy) —3A **6**

Mere Visitor Centre, The, Ellesmere —1B **26**

Milford Marina, Milford Haven (Aberdaugleddau) —2C **53**

Minera Lead Mines Visitor Centre —2D **17**

Model House Craft & Design Centre, Llantrisant —1B **64**

Monnow Bridge, Monmouth (Trefynwy) —1C **61**

Nant Mill Visitor Centre, Coedpoeth —2D **17**

Newport Transporter Bridge —1A **66**

New Quay Bird & Wildlife Hospital, Cross Inn —3C **35**

New Quay Honey Farm, Cross Inn —3C **35**

Norwegian Church, Cardiff (Caerdydd) —2C **65**

Nostalgia World, Marton —2B **26**

Offa's Dyke Centre, Knighton (Tref-y-Clawdd) —1D **39**

Oldbury Power Station Visitor Centre, Oldbury-on-Severn —3D **61**

Oriel Llynfaes —3D **5**

Oswestry Heritage Centre —2D **25**

Overton Churchyard Yew Trees —3A **18**

Paxton's Tower, Llanarthney —1A **56**

Pembroke Power Station, Pwllcrochan —2C **53**

Penmaenpool Wildlife Information Centre —3B **22**

Penmon Cross —2B **6**

Penrhyddlan & Llidiartywaun Wind Farm, Pentre —3B **30**

Pontcysyllte Aqueduct, Trevor —3D **17**

Pont Minllyn —3D **23**

Pont-y-ty-pridd, Pontypridd —3B **58**

Portmeirion —1A **22**

Port Wall, Chepstow (Cas-gwent) —3C **61**

Powys Observatory, Knighton (Tref-y-Clawdd) —1A **40**

Pulteney Bridge, Bath —3D **67**

Puzzle Wood, Milkwall —2C **61**

Quarry Hospital Visitor Centre, Llanberis —1A **14**

Radford Farm & Shire Horse Centre —3D **67**

Rhossili Visitor Centre —3D **55**

Rhyl Skytower —2B **8**

'Rock of Ages', Burrington —3B **66**

Rotherwas Chapel, Lower Bullingham —2C **51**

Royal Welsh Showground, Llanelwedd —3B **38**

Rug Chapel, Corwen —3B **16**

Runston Chapel, Crick —3B **60**

St Beuno's Well, Clynnog-fawr —3D **13**

St Cybi's Well, Llangybi —3D **13**

St Govan's Chapel, Bosherston —3C **53**

St Gwenfaen's Well, Rhoscolyn —3B **4**

St Non's Chapel, St David's (Tyddewi) —3A **42**

St Seiriol's Well, Penmon —2B **6**

St Winefride's (Beaufort) Chapel & Well, Holywell (Treffynnon) —3C **9**

Seawatch, Moelfre —2A **6**

Severn Bridges —3C **61** / 1C **67**

Shrewsbury Quest, The —3B **26**

Shropshire & West Midland Agricultural Showground, Shrewsbury —3B **26**

Sir Bevil Grenville's Monument, Langridge —2D **67**

Snowdonia National Park Study Centre, Tan-y-bwlch —3B **14**

SS Great Britain, Bristol —2C **67**

Stuart Crystal, Chepstow (Cas-gwent) —3C **61**

Stuart Crystal Glassworks, Aberbargoed —3C **59**

Taff Gorge Caerphilly Countryside Service Visitor Centre, Tongwynlais —1C **65**

Tar Tunnel, The, Coalport —1D **33**

Tatton Park Old Hall, Knutsford —2D **11**

Techniquest Science Centre, Cardiff (Caerdydd) —2C **65**

Tintern Old Station Visitor Centre —2C **61**

Tortworth Chestnut —3D **61**

Trawsfynydd Power Station Visitor Centre —1B **22**

Trefrifawr Farm Trail, Penhelig —2B **28**

Trefriw Wells Spa —1C **15**

Ty-hyll (Ugly House), Betws-y-Coed —2C **15**

Tyndale Monument, North Nibley —3D **61**

Ucheldre Centre, Holyhead (Caergybi) —2B **4**

Underground Wartime Headquarters, Liverpool —1A **10**

Waterloo Bridge, Betws-y-Coed —2C **15**

Wellow Ford —3D **67**

Welsh Gold, Dolgellau —3C **23**

Welsh Royal Crystal Visitors Centre, Rhayader (Rhaeadr Gwy) —2A **38**

Welsh Whiskey, Llanfaes —3B **48**

Welsh Wildlife Centre Visitor Centre, The, Cardigan (Aberteifi) —1A **44**

Willsbridge Mill Visitor Centre —2D **67**

Wirral Country Park Visitor Centre, Thurstaston —2D **9**

Woodhey Chapel, Faddiley —2C **19**

Woodside Visitor Centre, Birkenhead —2A **10**

Wye Valley Visitor Centre, Symonds Yat (West) —1C **61**

Wylfa Power Station Visitor Centre, Tregele —1C **5**

Prehistoric Monument
Heneb Cyn-hanes

See also Hill Fort

Gweler hefyd Caer ar Fryn

Arthur's Stone, Dorstone —1A **50**

Barclodiad y Gawres Burial Chamber, Llanfaelog —3C **5**

Bodowyr Burial Chamber, Brynsiencyn —1D **13**

Bryn Celli Ddu Burial Chamber, Llanddaniel Fab —3A **6**

Caer Leb Earthwork, Brynsiencyn —1D **13**

Capel Garmon Burial Chamber —2D **15**

Carn Llechart Burial Chamber, Rhyd-y-fro —2B **56**

Carn Llechart Cairn Circle, Rhyd-y-fro —2B **56**

Carreg Coetan Arthur Burial Chamber, Newport —2D **43**

Castell Bryn Gwyn Earthwork, Brynsiencyn —1D **13**

Cefn Coch Stone Circle
  (`Druids Circle'), Penmaenmawr
                              —3C **7**
Din Dryfol Burial Chamber, Bethel
                              —3C **5**
Din Lligwy Settlement
  (Capel Lligwy Hut Group),
                  Moelfre —2D **5**
Dyffryn Ardudwy Burial Chamber
                              —2A **22**
Hangstone Davey, Broadway
                              —1B **52**
Harold's Stones, Trelleck —2B **60**
Holyhead Mountain Hut Group,
        Holyhead (Caergybi) —2B **4**
Llech Idris Standing Stone,
              Bronaber —1C **23**
Lligwy Burial Chamber, Moelfre
                              —2A **6**
Maen Ceti (Arthur's Stone)
  Burial Chamber, Reynoldston
                              —3D **55**
Maen-y-bardd Burial Chambers,
              Rowen —3C **7**
Mitchell's Fold Stone Circle,
        Priest Weston —2A **32**
Offa's Dyke, Craignant —1D **25**
Offa's Dyke, Knighton
        (Tref-y-Clawdd) —1D **39**
Offa's Dyke, Tintern —2C **61**
Parc Le Breos Burial Chamber
  (Giant's Grave), Parkmill —1A **62**
Penmaen Burial Chamber —1A **62**
Penrhos Feilw Standing Stones,
        Holyhead (Caergybi) —2B **4**
Pentre Ifan Burial Chamber,
        Felindre Farchog —2D **43**
Porth Dafarch Hut Circles,
        Holyhead (Caergybi) —2B **4**
Presaddfed Burial Chambers,
              Bodedern —2C **5**
St Lythans Burial Chamber —2C **65**
Samson's Jack Standing Stone,
              Oldwalls —3D **55**
Stanton Drew Cove —3C **67**
Stanton Drew Stone Circles —3C **67**
Stoney Littleton Long Barrow,
              Wellow —3D **67**
Three Leaps, The, Pentraeth
                              —3A **6**
Tinkinswood Burial Chamber,
        St Nicholas —2B **64**
Trefignath Burial Chamber,
        Holyhead (Caergybi) —2B **4**
Ty Mawr Standing Stone, Holyhead
        (Caergybi) —2B **4**
Ty Newydd Burial Chamber,
        Llanfaelog —3C **5**

Railway
Rheilffordd

Preserved, Steam, Narrow Gauge
Wedi'i gwarchod ,Stêm,Reilffordd
Gul
Aberystwyth Cliff Railway —3A **28**
Avon Valley Railway, Willsbridge
                              —2D **67**
Bala Lake Railway, Llanuwchllyn
                              —1D **23**
Birkenhead Tramway —2A **10**
Brecon Mountain Railway, Pontsticill
                              —1B **58**
Bridgnorth Castle Hill Railway
                              —2D **33**
Bristol Harbour Railway —2C **67**
Cat Funicular Railway, The,
              Pantperthog —1C **29**
Corris Railway —1C **29**
Dean Forest Railway, Lydney
                              —2D **61**
Eirias Park Railway, Colwyn Bay
        (Bae Colwyn) —3D **7**
Fairbourne & Barmouth Steam
        Railway, Fairbourne —3B **22**
Ffestiniog Railway, Porthmadog
                              —1A **22**
Great Orme Tramway, Llandudno
                              —2C **7**
Gwili Railway, Bronwydd Arms
                              —3D **45**
Halton Miniature Railway —2C **11**
Llanberis Lake Railway —1A **14**
Llangollen Railway —3C **17**
Mydlewood Railway, Marton
                              —2B **26**
Pontypool & Blaenavon Railway,
              Blaenavon —2D **59**
Rhyl Miniature Railway —2A **8**
Saundersfoot Steam Railway,
              Stepaside —2A **54**
Severn Valley Railway, Bridgnorth
                              —2D **33**
Snowdon Mountain Railway,
              Llanberis —2A **14**
Swansea Vale Railway, Llansamlet
                              —3B **56**
Talyllyn Railway, Tywyn —1A **28**
Teifi Valley Railway, Henllan
                              —1C **45**
Telford Steam Railway, Horsehay
                              —1D **33**
Vale of Rheidol Railway,
        Aberystwyth —3A **28**
Welsh Highland Railway,
        Porthmadog —1A **22**
Welshpool & Llanfair Light Railway,
        Llanfair Caereinion —1C **31**

Roman Remains
Olion Rhufeinig

Blackpool Bridge Roman Road,
        Upper Soudley —2D **61**
Brecon Gaer Roman Fort
  (Y Gaer/Cicucium), Aberyscir
                              —3B **48**
Caer Gybi Roman Fortlet, Holyhead
        (Caergybi) —2B **4**
Canovium Roman Fort,
        Ty'n-y-groes —3C **7**
Carmarthen Roman Amphitheatre
                              —3D **45**
Castell Collen, Llandrindod Wells
                              —2B **38**
Chester Roman Amphitheatre
                              —1B **18**
Chester Roman Garden —1B **18**
Cold Knap Roman Building, Barry
        (Barri) —3B **64**
Deva Roman Experience, Chester
                              —1B **18**
Isca (Caerleon) Fortress Baths,
        Caerleon (Caerllion) —3A **60**
Isca (Caerleon) Roman
  Amphitheatre, Caerleon (Caerllion)
                              —3A **60**
Isca (Caerleon) Roman Fortress,
        Caerleon (Caerllion) —3A **60**
Roman Steps, Pentre Gwynfryn
                              —1B **22**
Segontium Roman Fort, Caernarfon
                              —1D **13**
Tomen-y-mur Roman Amphitheatre,
        Gellilydan —1C **23**
Venta Silurum Roman Town
        (Caerwent) —3B **60**
Viroconium Roman Town, Wroxeter
                              —1C **33**

Theme Park
Parc Thema

Gullivers World, Warrington —1C **11**
Oakwood, Canaston Bridge
                              —1D **53**
Pleasure Island Theme Park,
        Otterspool, Liverpool —2A **10**

Tourist Information Centre
Canolfan Groeso

OPEN ALL YEAR

NOTE: Telephone Numbers are
given in Italics
Aberaeron —2D **35** *01545 570602*

Abergavenny (Y Fenni) —1A **60**
01873 857588
Aberystwyth —3A **28**
01970 612125
Bala —1A **24** *01678 521021*
Bath —3D **67** *01225 462831*
Betws-y-Coed —2C **15**
01690 710426
Birkenhead —2A **10**
0151 647 6780
Bishop's Castle —3A **32**
01588 638467
Brecon (Aberhonddu) —3B **48**
01874 622485
Bridgnorth —2D **33** *01746 763358*
Bristol —2C **67** *0117 9260767*
Bristol Airport, Lulsgate Bottom
—3C **67** *01275 474444*
Bromyard —3D **41**
01885 482038 / 482341
Builth Wells (Llanfair-ym-Muallt)
—3B **38** *01982 553307*
Caerleon (Caerllion) —3A **60**
01633 422656
Caernarfon —1D **13** *01286 672232*
Caerphilly (Caerffili) —1C **65**
01222 880011
Cardiff (Caerdydd) —2C **65**
01222 227281
Cardigan (Aberteifi) —1A **44**
01239 613230
Carmarthen (Caerfyrddin) —3D **45**
01267 231557
Chepstow (Cas-gwent) —3C **61**
01291 623772
Chester (Railway Station) —1B **18**
01244 322220
Chester (Town Hall) —1B **18**
01244 317962
Chester Visitor Centre —1B **18**
01244 351609 / 318916
Cinderford —1D **61** *01594 822581*
Coleford —1C **61** *01594 836307*
Colwyn Bay (Bae Colwyn) —3D **7**
01492 530478
Conwy —3C **7** *01492 592248*
Cwmcarn —3D **59** *01495 272001*
Dolgellau —3C **23** *01341 422888*
Eardisland —3B **40** *01544 388226*
Ewloe (Ewlo) Services —1D **17**
01244 541597
Fishguard Harbour (Abergwaun
  Porthladd), Goodwick (Wdig)
  —2C **43** *01348 872037*
Fishguard Town (Tref Abergwaun)
  —2C **43** *01348 873484*
Haverfordwest (Hwlffordd)
  —1C **53** *01437 763110*

Hay-on-Wye (Y Gelli Gandryll)
  —1D **49** *01497 820144*
Hereford —2C **51** *01432 268430*
Holyhead (Caergybi) —2B **4**
01407 762622
Ironbridge —1D **33** *01952 432166*
Kington —3D **39** *01544 230778*
Knighton (Tref-y-Clawdd) —1D **39**
01547 528753
Knutsford —3D **11**
01565 632611 / 632210
Lake Vyrnwy (Llyn Efyrnwy),
  Llanwddyn —3B **24**
01691 870346
Ledbury —2D **51** *01531 636147*
Leominster —3B **40** *01568 616460*
Liverpool —1A **10** *0151 709 3631*
Liverpool (Albert Dock) —2A **10**
0151 708 8854
Llandrindod Wells —2B **38**
01597 822600
Llandudno —2C **7** *01492 876413*
Llanelli —2A **56** *01554 772020*
Llanfair Pwllgwyngyll —3A **6**
01248 713177
Llangollen —3D **17** *01978 860828*
Llanidloes —3A **30** *01686 412605*
Llanwrtyd Wells —1D **47**
01591 610666
Ludlow —1C **41** *01584 875053*
Machynlleth —1C **29**
01654 702401
Magor (Magwyr) Services —1B **66**
01633 881122
Market Drayton —1D **27**
01630 652139
Merthyr Tydfil —2B **58**
01685 379884
Mold (Yr Wyddgrug) —1D **17**
01352 759331
Nantwich —2D **19**
01270 610983 / 610880
Narberth (Arberth) —1A **54**
01834 860061
Newent —3D **51** *01531 822145*
Newport (Casnewydd)(Newport)
  —1A **66** *01633 842962*
Newport (Shropshire) —3D **27**
01952 814109
Newtown (Y Drenewydd) —2C **31**
01686 625580
Oswestry Mile End
  (Croesoswallt Mile End) —2A **26**
01691 662488
Oswestry Town (Croesoswallt Tref)
  —2D **25** *01691 662753*
Pembroke (Penfro) —2C **53**
01646 622388

Pont Abraham Services,
  Pontardulais —2A **56**
01792 883838
Pontneddfechan —2A **58**
01639 721795
Pontypridd —3B **58** *01443 409512*
Porthcawl —2D **63** *01656 786639*
Porthmadog —1A **22**
01766 512981
Pwllheli —1C **21** *01758 613000*
Queenswood, Hope under Dinmore
  —3C **41** *01568 797842*
Rhayader (Rhaeadr Gwy) —2A **38**
01597 810591
Rhyl —2B **8** *01745 355068*
Ross-on-Wye —3D **51**
01989 562768
Runcorn —2C **11** *01928 576776*
Ruthin (Rhuthun) —2C **17**
01824 703992
Sarn Park Services —1A **64**
01656 654906
Shrewsbury —3B **26** *01743 350761*
Swansea (Abertawe) —3B **56**
01792 468321
Telford —1D **33** *01952 291370*
Tenbury Wells —2C **41**
01584 810136
Tenby (Dinbych-y-Pysgod) —2A **54**
01834 842402
Thornbury —1D **67** *01454 281638*
Tregaron —3B **36** *01974 298144*
Warrington —2D **11**
01925 442180 / 444400
Welshpool (Trallwng) —1D **31**
01938 552043
Weston-super-Mare —3A **66**
01934 626838
Whitchurch —3C **19** *01948 664577*
Widnes —2C **11** *0151 424 2061*
Wrexham (Wrecsam) —2A **18**
01978 292015

OPEN SUMMER SEASON ONLY

Abercraf, Glyntawe —1D **57**
01639 730284
Aberdovey (Aberdyfi) —2B **28**
01654 767321
Bangor Services, Llandegai —1A **14**
01248 352786
Barmouth (Abermaw) —3B **22**
01341 280787
Barry Island (Ynys y Barri) —3C **65**
01446 747171
Blaenau Ffestiniog —3C **15**
01766 830360
Borth —2B **28** *01970 871174*

Church Stretton —2B **32**
01694 723133
Corris —1C **29** *01654 761244*
Crickhowell (Crughywel) —1D **59**
01873 812105
Elan Valley (Cwm Elan),
Elan Village —2A **38**
01597 810898
Ellesmere —1B **26** *01691 622981*
Harlech —1A **22** *01766 780658*
Kilgetty (Cilgeti) —2A **54**
01834 814161
Llanberis —1A **14** *01286 870765*
Llandarcy —3C **57** *01792 813030*
Llandovery (Llanymddyfri) —2C **47**
01550 720693
Milford Haven (Aberdaugleddau)
—2C **53** *01646 690866*
Monmouth (Trefynwy) —1C **61**
01600 713899
Much Wenlock —2D **33**
01952 727679
Mumbles (Mwmbwls), Oystermouth
—1B **62** *01792 361302*
Newcastle Emlyn (Castell Newydd
Emlyn) —1C **45** *01239 711333*
New Quay (Ceinewydd) —2C **35**
01545 560865
Pembroke Dock (Doc Penfro)
—2C **53** *01646 622246*
Penarth —2C **65** *01222 708849*
Prestatyn —2B **8** *01745 889092*
Presteigne (Llanandras) —2A **40**

01544 260650
Rhos-on-Sea (Llandrillo yn Rhos)
—2D **7** *01492 548778*
St David's (Tyddewi) —3A **42**
01437 720392
Tywyn —1A **28** *01654 710070*

Vineyard
Gwinllan

Brecon Court Vineyard, Llansoy
—2B **60**
Broadfield Gardens & Vineyards,
Bowley —3C **41**
Cwm Deri Vineyard, Martletwy
—1D **53**
Gwinllan Ffynnon Las Vineyard,
Aberaeron —2D **35**
Llanerch Vineyard, Clawdd-coch
—2B **64**
Three Choirs Vineyards,
Botloe's Green —3D **51**
Wroxeter Roman Vineyard —1C **33**

Wildlife Park
Parc Bywyd Gwyllt

See also Aviary/Bird Garden,
Farm Park, Zoo
Gweler hefyd Adarfa/Gardd Adar,
Parc Fferm, Sw
Aberaeron Wildlife & Leisure Park
—2D **35**

Manor House Wildlife &
Leisure Park, St Florence —2D **53**
Penscynor Wildlife Park, Cilfrew
—3C **57**
Stepaside Bird & Animal Park
—2A **54**

Windmill
Melin wynt

Llynnon Towermill, Llanddeusant
—2C **5**

Zoo/Safari Park
Sw/Barc Saffari

See also Bird Garden, Farm Park,
Wildlife Park
Gweler hefyd Gardd Adar,
Parc Fferm, Parc Bywyd Gwyllt
Borth Animalarium —3B **28**
Bristol Zoo, Clifton —2C **67**
Chester Zoo, Upton Heath —3B **10**
Knowsley Safari Park, Prescot
—1B **10**
Welsh Mountain Zoo, Colwyn Bay
(Bae Colwyn) —3D **7**